PRINTED IN U.S.A.   G.S.

INTRODUCTION

THE importance of this volume will be recognized by all students of North American affairs. Although everyone knows that the United States and Canada have acted upon each other like powerful magnets, to draw those who, true to the adventurous spirit of the New World, followed where opportunity beckoned, yet only recently have attempts been made to obtain detailed studies, based upon comprehensive measurements of this great interplay between the North American peoples. This volume, however, is only one of three in this series which deals with the various aspects of Canadian-American migration. The volume by the late Professor Marcus Lee Hansen, entitled *The Mingling of the Canadian and American Peoples*, told the story as reflected in the annals of history. This remarkable book has already made its place as a fascinating and authoritative interpretation of the causes of migration and the factors which determined its direction, bringing into the well-known narrative of the westward movement of the American people the counterplay of movements across the Canadian-American border. A parallel volume to the present one deals with the Canadian-born in the United States. The author, Dr. Leon E. Truesdell, the Chief Statistician for Population of the Bureau of the Census at Washington, in *The Canadian Born in the United States*, offers for the first time an authoritative picture of the movement and settlement of Canadians in the United States.

The present volume deals with the migrations of Americans to Canada and their settlement there. The authors are Dr. R. H. Coats, who made the Dominion Bureau of Statistics at Ottawa a model which has been imitated by other countries, and the late Mr. M. C. Maclean, his Chief of the Social Analysis Branch, who coupled profound insight with his mathematical powers.

The fact that ninety per cent of the Canadians who have gone to the United States since 1880 migrated because of lack of economic opportunity in Canada and that most of them settled in blocks not far within the frontiers of the United States does not differentiate them in any fundamental way from other migrants of the same period. What marked them off from the European immigrant was the fact that they fundamentally belonged to the same racial stock as those among whom they settled and therefore never presented any serious problems of social and political readjustment.

It is significant, in the light of the problems of today, that there was little attempt by legislation to block the migrations to and fro until comparatively recent years. For instance, during the last quarter of the nineteenth century, at the very time when the young Dominion prepared to defend its economic independence by the national tariff policy of Sir John A. Macdonald, the young men who left Ontario to pioneer in Michigan, Iowa, or Kansas were conscious of one primary need—that of seeking homes for themselves in the open fields or in the rising cities of the Middle West. So definitely did they mingle with their fellow settlers in their new homeland that, except for the French Canadians in New England, they left almost no record that would mark them out as belonging to any other stock than that dominant in the United States.

Fortunately, alongside the records and documentary sources which the historian uses, there has developed a mass of impersonal data in the census offices of both Canada and the United States from which the statistician can draw conclusions not only as to the extent and nature of the movements of population but also as to the laws which seem to emerge from the long perspectives in which the facts of the common life acquire their full meaning. Statistics have been termed "the science of insignificant things," but this only means that when they fall within the reach of its measurement, however unimportant they may seem in themselves, they then acquire significance as an index of human attitudes and desires. It is in this setting that the statistical study of the mingling of Canadian and American peoples is now at last presented in two authoritative surveys, the content of which cannot lightly be challenged because they are presented in the absolute terms of mathematics.

It seems certain that the reader of any of these three volumes will be surprised by the number of substantial migrations across the border in both directions which have been taking place more or less continuously since the last quarter of the seventeenth century, for the American and Canadian populations as a whole have seldom been aware of the regional effects of these movements. Professor Hansen has woven them into the pattern of North American development; the statisticians, concentrating on recent times, have analysed their effects upon the American and Canadian societies of today. Only the student of these elusive data can fully appreciate the long and arduous task which has confronted the authors of these studies and the mastery of detail which has permitted them to reach beyond the immediate problems of local and temporary nature to the synthesis in which the movement as a whole is so simply and so adequately stated. It is to be hoped that the results of this major effort at clarification in Canadian-American history will not remain the exclusive possession of a few technical specialists but will correct the perspectives and enlarge the vision of the citizens of both countries.

JAMES T. SHOTWELL

FOREWORD

THE basic materials for this study of the American-born in Canada were planned and to a considerable extent assembled by the late M. C. Maclean, Chief of the Branch on Social Analysis of the Dominion Bureau of Statistics. They will be found in Part II, Chapters I to X. The general approach and many of the implications of Part I, which is by way of interpretation and summary, were also subjects of discussion and agreement between us—my first association with the study being that of director and editor. Of the interpretative matter (Part I), however, only partial and unfinished transcripts were preserved at Maclean's death—untimely as well in an acute personal sense—and these have now been so completely made over in the pages which follow that responsibility, particularly for their organization and emphasis, must be primarily mine. That their final presentation has been without benefit of the clarity of thought which Maclean brought to all that he undertook of such work is a loss which only his former colleague can fully appreciate and deplore.

R. H. COATS

DOMINION BUREAU OF STATISTICS, CANADA.
AUGUST 31, 1942.

CONTENTS

PART I

THE DISTRIBUTION OF THE AMERICAN-BORN AND ITS SIGNIFICANCE

PART II
STATISTICAL ANALYSIS OF THE AMERICAN-BORN IN CANADA

TABLES

PART I

DIGRESSION ON THE CANADIAN-BORN POPULATION OF THE UNITED STATES

ADDENDUM

DAY-TO-DAY MOVEMENTS ACROSS THE BORDER

PART II

CHAPTER V

CHAPTER VI

CHAPTER VII

CHAPTER VIII

MAPS AND CHARTS

PART I

THE DISTRIBUTION OF THE AMERICAN-BORN
AND ITS SIGNIFICANCE

THE AMERICAN-BORN IN CANADA

THE DISTRIBUTION OF THE AMERICAN-BORN AND ITS SIGNIFICANCE

INTRODUCTORY

AN earlier volume of this series well exemplifies the Historian's characteristic approach upon the many-stranded theme of the mingling of the Canadian and the American peoples.* But plainly another technique, that of the Statistician—not necessarily unknown to History—should be invoked, at least upon the more recent years. Population is the broadest single interest of Statistics. For the present purpose the materials are abundant, and they go back the better part of a century—indeed it is their plethora that embarrasses. A study like the present must be sharply selective, both of current details and in the backward view: it can but seize upon main, for the most part contemporary, significances, at the same time making accessible enough of the source materials to permit of independent judgment and to prompt further inquiries at the fountain-head. Throughout, the present argument is in pure numbers and inductive.

The Census is of course (to vary the metaphor) the great quarry. It dates for Canada from 1851.† In it such facts as the age, sex, conjugal condition, birthplace, citizenship, occupation, race, language, religion, of every person in the country are covered at ten-year intervals (in the case of birthplaces, our obvious starting point, those of the parents are included as well). When these are not only summed but cross-classified to bring out their interplay, we have the picture whole as nowhere else. What part are immigrants? from what countries did these come and in what years? what manner of people are they, judged by social canons such as education, obedience to law, and the like?—are questions abundantly answerable. Vital statistics and immigration records add to the accounting, but these are the

---

*Hansen and Brebner, *The Mingling of the Canadian and American Peoples.*

†There were of course many Canadian censuses previous to 1851 (the first was in 1666), but they are either too early for the present purpose, or they do not lend themselves readily to analysis and comparison in detail with the United States Census (established in 1790). For an account of Canadian censuses and other population records from the beginning—a prolific family—with a restatement of totals, see *Seventh Census of Canada, 1931*, I (Ottawa, 1936), 133-53; this extends and completes a survey first attempted in the *Census of Canada, 1870-71*, IV (Ottawa, 1876).

day-books rather than the stock-sheet of the matter. In the Census, as in a settling basin, is seen the mergence of all those currents and cross-currents whose spectacle as passing show too often engenders legend and illusion. Though the Canadian flow into the United States is subject to separate and comprehensive treatment in a later volume, some reference to it is necessary in these pages, if only to explain certain features in the present analysis and to bring out by contrast certain interpretations that have been placed upon them.

THE PRESENT SITUATION—METHOD OF ANALYSIS

Let us begin with the existing situation—the broad figures of the 1931 Census. In it the population of the Dominion is given as 10,376,786, of which 8,069,261, or 77.8 p.c., were born in Canada, and the rest, 2,307,525, or 22.2 p.c., in other countries. To the latter the largest single contributor was England, with 723,864 (7.0 p.c.), but the United States stood second, with 344,574 (3.3 p.c.), Scotland being third, with 279,765 (2.7 p.c.). The total born in the British Isles was 1,138,942 (11.0 p.c.); in other British territories, 45,888* (0.4 p.c.); and in other foreign countries, chiefly of Continental Europe, 778,121 (7.5 p.c.). Thus, of all the foreign-born of Canada (i.e., all born outside the British Commonwealth, numbering 1,122,695 in 1931, or 10.8 p.c.), the American-born made up 30.7 p.c. No other foreign country had half so many. At the beginning of the century, before the great immigration, the American-born made up 45.9 p.c.

These figures even as preliminary are impressive. But it is "behaviour" as well as mass effect that we must explore.† Here, perforce, a word on method: What criterion shall we apply to these 344,574 American-born in Canada, as a whole and in their various aspects and characteristics, in order to interpret what their presence means in the country to which they have come?

It is essential, as just remarked, to observe and analyse them by age, sex, conjugal condition, racial origin, and all the other rubrics of the Census —and this has been done *seriatim* in the main body of this study. But clearly the overlying criterion of a phenomenon like immigration is *distribution*, the evenness or unevenness of their scatter or spread—by which is meant their degree of conformity to the average behaviour, whether of number or characteristic, of the population among whom they have settled. Clearly the even diffusion of any extraneous element within a given body is different altogether from its presence otherwise. The distribution test brings out at

---

*Including 731 born at sea.

†As shown in Part II, Chapter II, if to the above figure are added those born in Canada having one or both parents American, a total of about 800,000 is obtained as representing our American "stock."

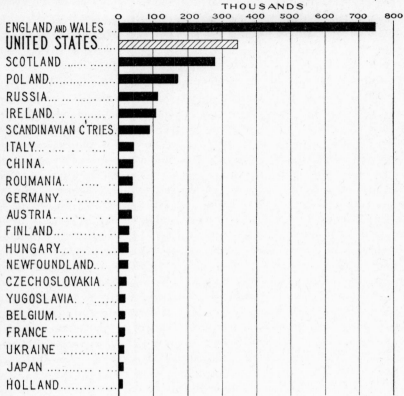

POPULATION OF CANADA
BORN IN
SELECTED FOREIGN COUNTRIES, 1931
THOUSANDS

once many of the salient features and results of an immigration movement; as we shall see, it may even permit an induction as to activation or cause. It is, in fact, of the essence of "mingling."

Distribution in this sense obviously has an immediate broad significance in three applications. These are: (1) the distribution of the immigrants by areas; (2) their distribution by population groups—say, in each 25,000 of the receiving country; and (3) their distribution by occupations. The first will connote in a measure the political impact; the second (basically at least) the social; and the third the economic. The three of course must be conjoined in considerable degree; we cannot assess the significance of the American-born in, say, the District of Patricia (in northern Ontario) without at the same time taking into account the general population of the region and its economic structure.

But before presenting the facts in the case on the above plan, certain general considerations that determine the movements and characteristics of a migrating population should be briefly discussed, as they explain something of the method that has been adopted in marshalling the data which follow. The subject is many-sided and so lacking in conventional approach that it must be made clear from the outset what it is that calls for elucidation.

When we observe and try to measure and interpret the distribution of a given people, we begin with the concept of *propensity*, that is, the *qualities* that account for their distribution—in which are included such characteristics as the presence or absence of gregariousness, the ability or lack of ability to make a living under varying circumstances, the possession or non-possession of enterprise and the spirit of adventure. But these are usually overlaid and complicated statistically by two external forces which we may term respectively the *capacity* to spread and the *necessity* to spread.

By capacity in this use is meant the degree of spread that arises out of, or that may be attributed to, the size of the population in question. It is obvious that the American-born, numbering 344,574 in Canada, are capable of spreading much more widely than, say, the Bulgarian-born, with only 1,467. But on the most cursory view, capacity in this sense, though it must be held in mind, does not in itself explain the distribution of the foreign-born. For example, the Bulgarian-born just mentioned, though less than one two-hundredth part of the American-born in numbers are distributed over something better than two-fifths the number of Canadian counties. Again, the Swiss-born and the Icelandic-born are about equal in numbers (around 6,000), but the former are found in 169 of the 222 counties of Canada and the latter in only 87. Again, of those born in Belgium and Yugoslavia, there are enough of either (about 17,000) to afford an average of, say, 77 in each Canadian county, but the Yugoslavs have twice this average or more in 26 counties, while the Belgians have twice the average or more in only 21 counties. Differences like these recur throughout the population record, so that evidently something beyond capacity in the sense of numbers determines the difference in spread.

Thus we arrive at the concept of the *necessity* to spread, which though a function of size, is the opposite of *capacity*. In the latter the tendency depicted is of a people spreading as much as it can, in the former as holding together as much as it can. The French Canadian of Quebec offers an illustration. Originally settled on small contiguous strips of land, he is found overflowing in census after census, first to neighbouring areas, later (as these filled up) over Canada and the adjoining United States. Though of gregarious instincts, the French-Canadian group is one of the most widely spread in Canada, even discounting its size. Equally gregarious, the Ukrainians, originally in colonies upon the land, are today expanding (the near-by lands repleted) into the cities and new northern areas, an illustration of the necessity to spread begotten of size. The Icelandic-born, on the other hand, afford probably the best example of a people whose small numbers have relieved it of the necessity to spread. Length of residence in the country is of course another important determinant of migration, but it is so correlated with size as to be difficult to measure separately.

The general propensity to spread, then, is a quality which should be measured only after correction for the above-mentioned determinants. From whatever combination of causes, the Scottish race (a term which includes ancestry as well as birth) stands first for wide and even distribution throughout the Dominion; nearly always in minorities, equally invariably the Scottish are found with neighbours of like derivation, a characteristic which holds not only for counties and census districts, but goes down to over five thousand Canadian municipalities. We shall have occasion to use the figures of the Scottish race as a standard or "control" hereinafter.

DISTRIBUTION OF THE AMERICAN-BORN, BY AREAS

Beginning, then, the actual measurement of the American-born in Canada by the first of the above-mentioned criteria, namely their distribution geographically or by areas, an arresting situation is revealed. There are 222 counties or other census districts in Canada, and not one of these but contains persons who were born in the United States. The American-born are spread more widely, that is, they are found in more parts of Canada, than are the native-born of any other country except England and Canada itself—the exact opposite, for example, of the Japanese, who are not represented at all in 147 of the 222 divisions above mentioned. Even such "unlikely" regions as the Abitibi District of Quebec, the northermost parts of Manitoba and Saskatchewan, and the Northwest Territories are well represented by American-born. The smallest absolute number is 31 in the County of Deux Montagnes, Quebec; the largest is 22,638 on Montreal Island. Relatively to other populations, the highest percentages are west of Manitoba where the maximum in any one division (in a section of southern Alberta—the Yukon also ranks very high) is 18.7 p.c. of the total population, the lowest being 0.2 p.c. (in the County of Saguenay, Que.). Thus, although the American-born are found everywhere in Canada, in no county or similar area are they more than a third of what would constitute a majority.

The details may be pursued in the tables of Part II, Chapter II. Easy to grasp is the map-frontispiece to the present volume, which depicts the

American-born in each county and census division throughout Canada by differentiations according to the degree of concentration in each, i.e., their proportion to total population. More readily than in a table the map enables the infiltration to be examined across the country and its import seized both by localities and by combinations of localities. The drawing is based upon the fact that in 1931 the American-born made up 3.3 p.c. of the population of Canada; if, therefore, they were spread evenly over the country, every county or census division would have 3.3 p.c. The map differentiates multiples or fractions of this percentage.

POPULATION OF CANADA BORN IN THE UNITED STATES
BY PROVINCES , 1931

THOUSANDS

	0	10	20	30	40	50	60	70	80

ALBERTA.............
SASKATCHEWAN........
ONTARIO.............
QUEBEC.............
BRITISH COLUMBIA..
MANITOBA...........
NEW BRUNSWICK....
NOVA SCOTIA........
PRINCE EDWARD Is....
YUKON..............
NORTHWEST TERRITORIES.

Especially interesting is it to compare the American-born with other immigrants in regard not only to breadth but evenness of distribution. If the American-born were apportioned evenly county by county across Canada, each would have 1,552—and in the same way a figure may be obtained for the native-born of every other country. By comparing the variations of the native-born immigrants from each country from its average, and eliminating the influence of size already adverted to, the following list of indexes* in descending order of evenness (ascending order of unevenness) is obtained:—

*The indexes are obtained by subtracting the numbers in each of the columns 3 to 7 of Table XI (p. 70) from the corresponding figures of total population at the top, squaring, adding the squares, and extracting the square root. The method gives intelligible results and at the same time tends to eliminate the influence of size since the heavy dependence of column 7 upon smallness is counter-balanced by the dependence of the other columns, particularly column 3, upon largeness, although in the case of the very small populations the effect produced is likely to be erratic.

Rank	Birthplace	Index	Rank	Birthplace	Index
1.	Scotland	100	15.	China	139
2.	Ireland	101	16.	Roumania / Sweden	140
3.	England	106			
4.	Wales	107	18.	Norway / Russia	144
5.	Denmark	112			
6.	France	114	20.	Hungary	146
7.	Holland	115	21.	Italy	155
8.	Switzerland	116	22.	Finland	156
9.	*United States*	*118*	23.	Lithuania	162
10.	Belgium / Germany	124	24.	Greece	164
			25.	Yugoslavia	172
12.	Austria	125	26.	Bulgaria	216
13.	Poland	129	27.	Iceland	228
14.	Czechoslovakia	132	28.	Japan	247

Comment upon these figures might range far. Here it is enough to emphasize that not only are the American-born the most widely distributed geographically of the native-born of any foreign country, but they also rank high among the foreign-born for evenness of distribution by areas, only those born in Denmark, France, Holland, and Switzerland taking precedence in this regard. Each of these latter countries has a very small native-born population in Canada, which may introduce an element of unreality into the comparison (see foot-note). There is reason then for the statement that the American-born is the highest of the foreign-born populations in wideness of distribution, in distribution by counties, and also in distribution by municipalities.

DISTRIBUTION OF THE AMERICAN-BORN RELATIVELY TO POPULATION

Our second measurement concerns the distribution of the American-born relatively to population. The first was by geographical units, the second brings the population content of these units into the forefront: the first reckoned the chances of American-born being found in a specific area, the second will show their chances of being found in a specific population group. For the latter, we marshal them according to their percentage of the total population in each unit. To assign meaning to these percentages we use a "control" in the manner previously suggested: in other words we judge them not by ideal considerations but by the highest real standard that can be found of cognate character. In the present case we shall employ two such controls—the distribution of the Scottish and German stocks respectively— the first as affording the highest criterion we know of all-round evenness, the second for the reason that German racials have been present in Canada from the earliest times (the majority are Canadian-born) and have had, therefore, the fullest opportunity to spread; (the Germans are also fairly comparable in point of size with the American-born—473,544 compared with 344,574).*

As already noted, the American-born make up 3.3 p.c. of the total population of Canada. The 222 counties of Canada are, of course, unequal in population, so that an equal *number* of American-born in each would not indicate evenness from the standpoint now under consideration. If, however, we find the same *percentage* (3.3 p.c.) in each, we may safely assume a like proportion in any similar grouping and thus argue complete evenness of distribution. *Pro tanto*, the closer we approach 3.3 p.c. of American-born in any group, the more even the distribution, a trustworthy measure of the latter being the difference between the 3.3 p.c. and the actual proportion. The county is perhaps over-large as a unit for this method, but it is the smallest practicable.

The exhibit brought together on this principle† again discloses an exceedingly even distribution of the American-born—less, it is true, than the high standard set by the Scottish race, but greatly superior to that of the German race, which for reasons already stated we might have expected to be very even. Comparing in detail the spread of the American-born with that of the Scottish race, there is apparent a greater tendency in the latter to remain close to the average; a few counties in Nova Scotia and Prince Edward Island have very high proportions, and a few others in Quebec very low, but on the whole less difference from the average is maintained than in the case of the American-born. In the matter of concentration, the American-born are well graduated, whereas concentrations of the Scottish race, where they occur, have all the appearance, statistically speaking, of the freakish and accidental. In other words, while we can predict the number of Scottish better than the number of American-born in a population group, the prediction for the Scottish will occasionally fall wide of the mark, whereas that for the United States, though not so close as a general rule, will never be beyond moderate distance.

Comparing the American-born with the German race in Canada, some interesting differences stand out. Notwithstanding that the German stock has been present in Canada, particularly in parts of Nova Scotia and Ontario, almost as long as the British races, the American-born are much the more evenly spread. Although German racials make less than 5 p.c. of the population of Canada, they form a slight majority of the population (50.3) in one county, and approximately half the population (49.6) in another. The effect

*The Canadian Census asks, in addition to birthplace, the "racial origin" of each individual, by which is meant the original habitat of the family prior to emigration to this continent (see also foot-note†, p. 18). The Scottish race is selected as being still more evenly spread than the Scottish-born—a fact which is generally true of racial as compared with birthplace statistics.

†Part II, Chapter II, Tables XIV and XV.

is still more marked when municipalities rather than counties are taken. Yet the Germans rank second only to the Scandinavians from continental Europe for evenness of distribution by racial origin.

Perhaps the clearest summing-up may be made as follows: In 105 counties the Scottish exceed their average for Canada (13 p.c. of the population) by sufficient to extend the average to 165 counties; in 63 counties the American-born exceed their average (3.3 p.c.) by enough to extend it to 156 counties; while in the 62 counties where those of German race reach their average or more (4.5 p.c.) there are enough to give that average to 168 counties. In other words, the Scottish concentrate in 105 counties to an extent that may be measured as 1.6; the American-born concentrate in 62 counties to the extent of 2.5; while those of German stock concentrate in 65 counties to the extent of 2.7. Expressing these figures in index numbers, with the Scottish as base (representing the minimum of unevenness), we obtain: Scottish origin, 100; American-born, 156; German origin, 176.*

The indexes listed below measure the evenness of distribution of the several races in Canada, with the American-born interjected. These will assist in the general interpretation of the American-born figures, but they particularly anticipate a reason for their evenness to be developed later on, namely, that the American-born represent a variety of racial strains. The measure in this case is based upon data for 5,049 municipalities or census divisions, correction being made for size by removing any existing correlation.

Rank	Race	Index	Rank	Race	Index
1.	Scottish	100	12.	Russian	289
2.	English	104	13.	Czechoslovakian	292
3.	French	105	14.	Polish	308
4.	Irish	105	15.	Roumanian	339
5.	Welsh	147	16.	Hungarian	404
6.	*American-born*	*156*	17.	Chinese	487
7.	Scandinavian	174	18.	Ukrainian	540
8.	German	176	19.	Finnish	617
9.	Dutch	189	20.	Italian	809
10.	Austrian, n.o.s.	221	21.	Indian	846
11.	Belgian	261	22.	Hebrew	896

A possible criticism of these data may be forestalled—that they do not differentiate between rural and urban. They do not, for instance, reveal that the considerable spread of the Chinese† and the very small spread of the Hebrews are largely urban phenomena, while the concentration of the Ukrainians is rural. The map-frontispiece, however, makes clear that the distribution of the American-born is not one-sided, but is both rural and

---

*Another measure is, of course, the standard deviation as a percentage of the mean. For the three members in the comparison this is: Scottish origin, 0.94 (an index of 100); American-born, 1.14 (an index of 121); German origin, 1.66 (an index of 176).

†Except in British Columbia which strongly influences the index in the table.

urban and otherwise independent of physical conditions—though climate alone, with its social and economic implications, has a range of variation in Canada that is exceeded in few other countries. Thus their largest concentrations are in places so widely different in type as the Yukon, which is sub-Arctic, and the County of Kent which lies in southernmost Ontario; as the dry belt of Alberta, and the moist lands of Vancouver Island; as the French-speaking environs of Montreal, and York County which surrounds Toronto in the heart of English-speaking Ontario (the two last-named have almost equal percentages of American-born, as have likewise such extremes as the Fond du Lac district of Lake Athabaska in Saskatchewan and King's County in Prince Edward Island). The American-born in a word are represented whether the group-locale is cold or sunny, arid or well-watered, English or French-speaking, rural or urban, east or west.

DISTRIBUTION OF THE AMERICAN-BORN, BY OCCUPATIONS

We come now to our third criterion, an economic one, that of occupation. Here again, relatively speaking, the figures are of an extraordinary evenness. The percentage which the American-born constitutes of the total occupied in Canada is 4.3 in the case of males, 3.4 in the case of females. Now, if we run through the various crafts and callings—industries, trades, and professions—of the Canadian Census, we find these general percentages approached in greater degree by the American-born than are the corresponding percentages by the immigrants from any other country. Variations, of course, there are. High percentages are found in groups in which the American-born appear as owners and managers; these, however, are mostly in the specialized occupations, and the numbers affected are small. Again, as would be expected, the presence of 46,904 American-born male farm owners (there are also 1,268 females) increases the percentage for that class, bringing it to 7.5 for males. On the other hand, the numbers of American-born are low in occupations like clerical and miscellaneous manufacturing, loggers, public employment, and common labour. But the point is, these highs and lows are nowhere to be considered excessive, and they deviate from their mean far less than is observed for the other foreign-born in Canada. To particularize a little:—

Seventy-one occupational groups, all told, are differentiated in the statistics on which this analysis is based; of these, 30 are below the general percentage of 4.3 for males, and 41 are above. If we eliminate "owners and managers" down to the farming category (and it involves but 2,500 individuals), the classes above the average are reduced to 29, and a very even division above and below is obtained. In these, no class departs from

the average further than 7.5 p.c. on the high side, or 1.1 p.c. on the low.*
In other words, the great mass of the American-born do not segregate
themselves in groups that stand out relatively to the rest of the population. This points at once, as already said, to the invalidity of stressing any
one occupational characteristic among the American-born as immigrants
—as that they figure overwhelmingly or even mainly as agriculturists, a
common impression. That large numbers of well-to-do United States farmers have taken advantage of low-priced lands in the West to become
Canadians is of course true. It is a fact, likewise, that few unskilled labourers
have emigrated to Canada from the highly industrialized United States.
But such generalizations should be reviewed in light of the fact that it is
not the specialization of the American-born that is striking in such statistics,
but their fidelity to the average. The number of agriculturists is large, but
so too is the number of agriculturists in the rest of the population both of
Canada and the United States (the decade 1921-31 incidentally saw a decline
in the relative standing of American-born agriculturists in Canada, especially
in the farm-labourer class), and the peopling of the "last best West" was
of course not predominantly a United States movement. No more does
common labour show a sweeping departure from the average—and common
labourers are at the bottom, as agriculturists are at the top, of the scale.

The predominance of United States "owners and managers" which, more
than agriculturists, might be singled out as the point of chief United States
impact, must not be misinterpreted. It is partly due, as we shall presently
see, to the fact that the American-born have been longer in Canada than
other immigrants and are older than the Canadian-born. The predominance
does not necessarily assess comparative qualities or qualifications (this
point is enlarged upon in Part II, Chapter x).

In the professions, in which 4.1 p.c. of the gainfully occupied American-
born males and 22.6 p.c. of the American-born females are engaged (a higher
proportion than among the Canadian-born), the spread, while not so even
as in non-professional occupations, is more even than for the British-born,
especially among females. Some concentration of the American-born is
evident under the heading of religion (the entry into religious brotherhoods
of American-born children of French-Canadian emigrés).

---

* Or, if we adopt a compilation that differentiates by specific crafts rather than by industries
and status, the range is from 1.3 to 7.6, around a mean of 4.5. "Farmers and stockraisers"
and "farm labourers" which represent the bulk of the gainfully occupied in agriculture and
account for 65,835 American-born, register 6.0 p.c.—not far from the mean. There are 14
occupations above 7.6 p.c., but again they are highly specialized and few in aggregate numbers
(5,530), "purchasing agents and buyers" (959) and "owners and managers of metal manu-
factories" (815) being the two largest. Others include Pullman porters (trained personnel from
the United States) and "oil drillers" in Alberta (Texan miners brought in on the opening of
the Turner Valley).

Perhaps the best single demonstration of the immediate thesis is the following: If we select the 25 occupations in which the American-born are most highly represented, and make selections on the same principle for those born in the British Isles and on the continent of Europe respectively, we will find that the American-born males constitute only 94.8 p.c. of their total, while the British-born constitute 95.27 p.c. of theirs, and the Continental European-born 98.0 p.c. of theirs. That the American-born should be more evenly distributed by occupations than the British-born, whom we would expect to find taking part in every phase of the country's activity, and still more evenly distributed than all Continental Europeans taken together, notwithstanding the latter's greater multiplicity of social and occupational characteristics, may be regarded as particularly significant. Any single country of birth—France, Germany, Roumania—will show much higher concentrations than the United States.

Causal Factors in the Distribution of the American-Born

The foregoing has made abundantly clear the outstanding characteristic of the American-born in Canada, namely, their very even distribution, whether the measure be by areas, by population groups or by occupations. Apparent exceptions will on examination prove striking for their closeness to, rather than for their distance from, the averages which represent absolute evenness. Thus agriculturists are less than one and one-half the average, and if deducted from general industry leave the remainder little below. Again, domestic servants, whom we might expect to find as low as agriculturists are high, are close to the average. In a word, no class is strikingly high nor strikingly low—none more than twice the average—those far enough away to mark them as "typically" American being so few in numbers that they may be set aside. The fact remains of first-class importance in itself, quite apart from anything it may reveal as to activating cause or causes.

But does it throw light upon the latter? It may be remarked at once that, axiomatically, the underlying significance of conformity to an average in such a case is the absence of any single or special cause of major magnitude. Perfect conformity indeed would suggest that the determining causes are numerous and, therefore, individually unimportant, though collectively the most important: weighty and widely publicized factors there may be, but they are few and tend to offset one another and therefore do not act as determinants. On the latter point and to repeat somewhat: there is a very large element of agriculturists among the American-born in Canada, also a large proportion whom some would regard as "typically" American, also a large number who came in "boom" years, also many who for special reasons drifted to particular regions. None of these, however, notwithstanding that special motives and reactions might pre-eminently be predicated of a large, wealthy, and highly industrialized country like the United States *vis à vis* an undeveloped one of varied resources upon its border, may be said to have determined the present-day spread of the American-born in Canada—for it would not be difficult to find, corresponding to each, an equally striking one of opposite tendency.

Our interpretation at this point introduces two concepts which must be kept in mind in assessing immigrant behaviour. One, which for lack of a more satisfactory term we may designate "generic," includes the operation of general forces, such as a racial tendency (e.g., gregariousness), also of some pervasive special force—say, the economic condition of the country to which the migrant moves, or of the country from which he moves, or of the time at which he moves. Under the term "individualistic" or "specific," on the other hand, we may distinguish the operation of a number of minor and approximately equal forces, or of larger but compensating forces in combination—the point being that they emanate from personal characteristics and vary from person to person. On these definitions, non-conformity to an average would indicate the preponderance of generic or general, while conformity points to specific or individualistic forces at work. The Scottish race, for example, is on the whole individualistic, as distinguished from certain others in whom the preponderating springs of action are plainly racial predilection, fecundity, occupational preference, climatic adaptability, or the like. Discrimination must nevertheless be invoked in such analysis, for opposites may mean the same thing. For instance the fact that the Hebrews are found in large proportions in a very few localities (77 p.c. in five cities) argues what we have agreed to call generic motivation, but so quite as definitely does a small number of Chinese in a large number of places, for it is here only the reflection of restricted occupational status: both phenomena are due to circumstances quite removed from individualistic considerations.

With the above by way of preliminary we may proceed to the more detailed discussion of a number of factors obviously of a causal nature in the present set-up of the American-born in Canada. Such are: (1) length of residence in the country and of the period during which settlement has taken place; (2) the "racial" element in the United States inflow; (3) the movement to Canada of children born to Canadians resident in the United States; and (4) sundry causes, including similarity in language and social customs, proximity, the tourist trade, etc.

Length of Time of the American-Born in Canada—Process of Settlement

If a people are found settled evenly in a country in approximately equal numbers over a considerable period of time, it argues against special or intermittent motive, such as the nationalistic one, the exploitation of a single field of enterprise, or such like—which would spell fluctuations and concentrations. The time element involved may be measured in two ways: (1) by the number of American-born found in Canada from census to census back as far as possible; (2) by the length of residence in the country declared by the American-born in the latest census (the Canadian Census records the year of immigration in the case of everyone not born in Canada). As we shall see by both measurements, the American-born have been in Canada in well-sustained numbers over many decades, overlapping several economic cycles—in varying proportions it is true but representing in the ebb and flow a remarkably consistent relation to the current trend.

(1) Applying the first method, there were about one-seventh as many American-born in Canada in 1841 (49,000) as in 1931 (344,574) ninety years later. The total, however, had its ebbs as well as flows in the meantime. Between 1861 and 1871 it decreased, as in the case of other immigrant peoples: thus, while the immigrant population of Canada as a whole declined by 62,000 in that decade, the decline in American-born was 5,000. The other decrease took place between 1921 and 1931, the major part (as we surmise from the Quinquennial Census of the Prairie Provinces, 1926) between 1921 and 1926.

All the other decades of the interval recorded increases. The period of greatest growth was 1901-11, when the American-born rose by 175,781: allowing for deaths, this postulates a permanent inflow of about 189,000. The question is, was the phenomenon peculiar to the American-born? The answer is in the negative. The American-born flowed into the Prairie Provinces to the net extent of 146,514 in that decade. But meanwhile natives from the other provinces of Canada swelled the same population by 182,769; in other words, more persons moved into the prairies from the rest of Canada with under five million population to draw upon than from the United States with over one hundred million. The British Isles contributed 190,666, Continental Europe 160,338. It was a period of general migration, not of American-born migration in particular. Again, the numbers are striking mainly because concentrated in point of time: spread over twenty years, they would have been in no sense abnormal. The inflow in the opening year of the decade was, in fact, so rapid as to compel the conclusion that either the earlier arrivals did not stay or the later ones were unable to find footing. (The Census, of course, records, not the numbers who moved in, but the numbers who stayed.) Moreover, the subsequent movement from

POPULATION BORN OUTSIDE OF CANADA

1851 – 1931

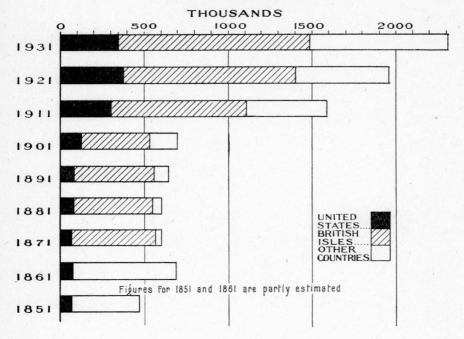

THOUSANDS

UNITED STATES....
BRITISH ISLES.....
OTHER COUNTRIES.

Figures for 1851 and 1861 are partly estimated

the United States to Canada has also been large; as we shall see, it has resulted in a larger portion of our present American-born than the earlier rush, although the total of American-born has not recently (1921-31) been maintained.

Further, after an exceptionally heavy immigration movement a certain time must elapse to permit of its distribution over the country. A notable feature of the Census of 1911 is a congestion of population at what might be considered immigration clearing centres. Between 1911 and 1921 these disgorged their excess either over or out of the country. This process must be discounted in measuring results of the heavy United States immigration of 1901-11, at the close of which two of the Prairie Provinces were as heavily represented in American-born as all the rest of Canada put together. Since 1911, the American-born have been rapidly evening up, as between provinces, some leaving the prairies (and Canada also) and others moving into the older provinces.

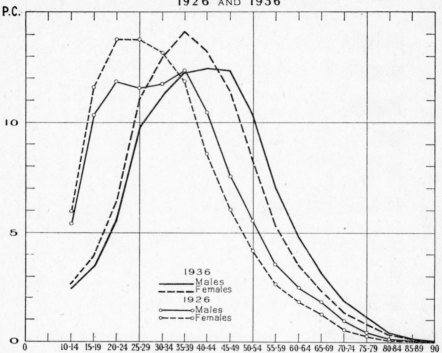

PERCENTAGE DISTRIBUTION OF AMERICAN - BORN
IN THE
PRAIRIE PROVINCES BY QUINQUENNIAL AGE GROUPS AND SEX
1926 AND 1936

A comparison of the years 1891, before the period of heavy immigration, 1911 or immediately after, and 1931 when twenty years had worked out their effect on distribution, makes still clearer the manner in which the American-born have spread over Canada. They were well distributed in 1891, not so well distributed at the peak of immigration in 1911, and again well distributed in 1931. Obviously, length of time in the country has been of importance in the distribution of the American-born.

(2) The second means of measuring the sojourn of an immigrant population—the more direct one—is by noting their years of arrival as recorded in the 1931 Census. The first point to emerge is that, out of the 344,574 American-born resident in Canada in that year, only 102,825, or about 30 p.c., were survivors of those arriving in 1901-11, while 46,347 had arrived before that period, and 195,402 since. Now those arriving before

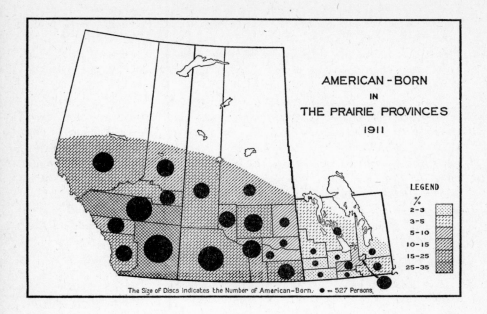

AMERICAN - BORN
IN
THE PRAIRIE PROVINCES
1911

LEGEND
%
2-3
3-5
5-10
10-15
15-25
25-35

The Size of Discs indicates the Number of American-Born. ● = 527 Persons.

1901 must have been at least 30 years old in 1931—probably much older—judging by the age distribution of immigrant arrivals in general. It follows, therefore, that the 46,347 above-mentioned were survivors of, say, 100,000 who had made a permanent home in Canada, while those arriving in 1901-11 were, on the same basis, survivors of nearly 130,000, and those arriving since 1911 of an original 225,000. Recalling that during 1901-11 the American-born (in the Census also) increased by 176,000, it will be seen that a large proportion of the 1901-11 arrivals must have remained in Canada, but that the dependence of the 1931 population upon these arrivals and their spread was comparatively small—less than one-third; certainly not enough to warrant the conclusion that the 1931 American-born population of Canada was the residue of an agricultural movement which took place twenty years earlier. Those American-born who have come in since 1911 are larger in numbers than all the others combined, notwithstanding an increasing tendency on the part of such immigration to be temporary in character compared with the growth of the immigrant stock in general. It is also apparent that, on the whole, the American-born have been a longer time in Canada than the Scottish-born (whom we again select as still more evenly spread), an average 20.0 years comparing with an average of 17.6

years.* It is clear, therefore, that though length of residence in Canada is important, it is by no means the only explanation for evenness of spread, since the 1901-11 American-born are confined largely to the Prairie Provinces and the pre-1901 American-born made up less than one-seventh of the 1931 total. It is the recent arrivals that are making the distribution still more even.

The reason for the latter conclusion is suggested when we examine years of arrival by provinces. Of 57,819 American-born arrived since 1926, only about 22,100 were found in the four western provinces, while about 17,000 were found in Quebec and the Maritimes. As Quebec and the Maritimes have only 66,802 American-born, the arrivals between 1926 and 1931 made up 25 p.c. of that number. There is a strong presumption that this consisted of American-born children of Canadian parents, a movement which will be discussed in a moment; in other words a part cause of the United States movement into Canada was a previous movement from Canada to the United States.

Racial Composition of the American-Born

The racial composition of the American-born makes for evenness of distribution in Canada—and in an interesting way. The Canadian Census asks a specific question which the United States Census does not, namely, racial origin, i.e., (in addition to colour and birthplace of parents) the original habitat of the family prior to settlement on this continent. Thus, we can break up our American-born in terms of the cultural sources from which they derive, and see what the latter implies as affecting distribution (birthplace and birthplace of parents admittedly imply much, but this goes further back).† For example, if our American-born were found to be largely of British origin, especially Scottish, we might expect to see them evenly distributed, the British showing "scatter" in the highest degree; whereas

*In further illustration of the time influence, the average length of residence of the American-born by provinces is:—

	Years
Prince Edward Island	15.5
Nova Scotia	17.6
New Brunswick	18.5
Quebec	20.6
Ontario	19.1
Manitoba	17.9
Saskatchewan	20.0
Alberta	20.2
British Columbia	20.9
Yukon	25.6

That the three westernmost provinces show a longer period than the eastern indicates that United States immigration to the latter is, on the whole, more recent than the 1901-11 immigration to the western—in spite of the fact that there was a large element of American-born already settled in the East before 1901. Recent immigration, not length of residence alone, is influential in the observed spread in the East.

†The Canadian Census does not accept the reply "American" or "United States" as a definition of origin in the case of the American-born.

if they were of Italian, Ukrainian, or Hebrew origin, we should be prepared for the opposite. But, equally, evenness may be the result if the incomers are not of one racial strain but of several, and if they tend in that case to break up on arrival into racial constituents each gravitating towards its kind. This is an interesting illustration of evenness resulting at second hand from a factor which at first hand makes for unevenness—and this is the characteristic behaviour of the American-born immigrants to Canada. They are of many racial strains, and each seeks out its own all over the Dominion.

Thus we are at once struck by the fact that 55,630 of the American-born are French in origin, and that 31,780 of these (about 27 p.c.) are in Quebec, where they constitute over 64 p.c. of the entire American-born (49,406) of that province (a doubling in the last twenty years) due largely to the fact that many of them are descendants of French-Canadian emigrants to the United States (of which more anon). So, likewise, in New Brunswick, where those of French origin make up about one-third of the American-born, whereas the proportion of French origin in Canada as a whole is about one-sixth. But in lesser degree, and in a more subtle way, the behaviour of the other races corresponds. Thus, Prince Edward Island and Nova Scotia have more than their proportion of the Scottish American-born; New Brunswick more of the English; British Columbia more of the "other British"; and the Prairie Provinces more of the "other than British" races. Of the Hebrews, over three-fourths are in Ontario and Quebec. Nearly all the Japanese American-born are in British Columbia. We can also observe for each race its characteristic of evenness or the opposite in operation; the Scottish American-born, for example, are spread much as are other Scottish-born.

An interesting foot-note to the above is the following: In the decade 1921-31, the American-born in Canada decreased from 374,024 to 344,574, or by 29,450. The decrease was in the British and Scandinavian strains, for the French, German, Italian, and Eastern European showed increases. (The French and German increased about 5,000 each; the Czechoslovak, Polish, and Italian slightly; while the Lithuanian, Ukrainian, and Roumanian doubled. On the other hand, the British, Scandinavian, Dutch, and other European stocks decreased drastically: the three main British races and Scandinavians together lost about 33,000.) Obviously, a trend of this sort is of opposite effect to what we have been contemplating, viz., the even distribution of the American-born as a by-product of variety in racial strains. If it continues, the American-born will be less evenly distributed in the future than at present but this will still be due to the factor of persisting racial tendencies.

The materials brought together for this section are therefore of more than narrow interest. They envisage the "melting-pot." When we find the American-born, province by province, approximating in proportions of specific racial strains to the corresponding proportions in the population as a whole, we may more than suspect race gravitation, notwithstanding that immersion in the aforesaid 'pot' may be unto the third and fourth generation. The subject is worthy of fuller analysis than is possible here; the interested reader should pursue it into that factual detail which is the corrective of loose thinking.*

Immigration of American-Born Children of Canadian-Born Parents

Another factor which, as prefigured, we must isolate in this analysis is the tendency of children born of Canadian parents in the United States to return to the original family habitat. The Census throws this into relief in its data on the nativity of parents. We discover that of our 344,574 American-born in 1931, approximately one-fifth (66,953) have both parents Canadian-born; 110,128 have at least one parent Canadian-born; and 144,970 or over 42 p.c., have one parent either Canadian or other-British. (See frontispiece map.) Little more than half, at most, can have both parents American-born. Significantly, more than half of those having both parents Canadian are in Quebec and the Maritimes, where only 16,462, or about a quarter of the total American-born, have both parents born outside of Canada. This, then, explains why so many American-born are found in Quebec and the Maritimes where other immigrant populations are small, though pre-1901 immigration was almost entirely to Eastern Canada. It also counterweighs the West and thus explains in part the even distribution of the American-born since 1911 and why it has come to pass that no county in Canada is without them.†

The birthplaces of parents have not been compiled by individual countries since 1891, but only broadly as "Canadian," "British," and "foreign." It is interesting that in 1891 there were about 31,000 or 38 p.c. more persons of American-born parentage in Canada than there were American-born. But there were over three times as many persons of Scottish and Irish-born parentage as there were of the Scottish and Irish-born in Canada, and over twice as many in the case of the English—in fact the Newfoundland-born alone showed a smaller ratio in this respect than the American-born. The United States and Newfoundland have, in common, a history of heavy previous immigration, and their low ratios reflect the fact that many of their emigrants to Canada had parents born in Europe. The figures for 1891 follow:—

---

*See also pp. 38-40 for the repercussion of racial origin on naturalization.

†Ontario and New Brunswick have had a large share of the United States inflow from an early period, whereas Quebec had its most striking accretion in the latest twenty years (1911-31) when its American-born increased by two-thirds. This return to Canada of the children of Quebec-born parents also accounts for the fact that in all the eastern provinces the American-born increased between 1921 and 1931, while in the newer provinces (with fewer potential parents in the United States) they decreased.

Country	Place of Birth	Place of Birth of Father	Place of Birth of Mother	(2)÷(1)
	(1)	(2)	(3)	(4)
Canada	4,185,877	3,090,543	3,326,354	74
Newfoundland	9,336	10,208	11,841	109
England	219,688	524,506	428,229	239
Scotland	107,584	368,510	312,786	343
Ireland	149,184	552,057	487,766	370
United States	80,915	111,627	111,165	138
Germany	27,752	82,955	71,952	299
Scandinavia	7,827	11,747	10,219	150
France	5,381	11,860	8,693	220
Russia	9,222	16,291	16,028	177
Italy	2,795	3,943	3,264	141

Sundry Causes

There remain a considerable number of causes for the movement of American-born to Canada whose statistical measurement would lead us far afield but whose cumulative effect is powerful.

Similarity in Language and Social Customs.—This is often cited as promoting the population interchange between Canada and the United States. The language implied is English and the tradition British. But, as we have seen, race is a factor in the attraction of population—and race spells variety in language (especially in mother tongue), as in religion, social habits, and cultures generally. That the United States requires its native-born of whatever race to learn English has a meaning for Canada too in the assimilation of such as pass through that crucible. But English speech assists only in the admixture of the English-speaking. French also must be brought into the picture, seeing that it is an official language in Canada and that 1,108,039 persons or 13.56 p.c. of the population (47.69 p.c. in the case of Quebec) speak French alone. Now of the French-Canadian born who to the number of 360,724 were living in the United States in 1930, only 31,701 or 8.8 p.c. were unable to speak English. However, of their children born in the United States and numbering 596,926, all but 3,068 or 0.5 p.c. could speak English, (so that of the entire French-Canadian stock of 957,650 in the United States only 34,769 or 3.6 p.c. were of non-English speech).* Nevertheless it would be safe to assume that the great majority of these spoke French also as "mother-tongue"† (for of 55,630 American-born of French origin in Canada, 47,267 declared French to be their mother-tongue in 1931), and that in so far as language is concerned the "pull" that brought so many of them to Canada in recent years—overwhelmingly to French-speaking Canada—was the French language, though their all but equal command of English is of great interest.

*These statistics are for population 10 years of age and over.
†For definition see p. 120.

Proximity.—Proximity makes for evenness of distribution, as is well illustrated in the map-frontispiece. Immediate proximity, however, does not appear essential; its absence as an influence is more striking than its presence. (On the other hand, proximity affects all-powerfully the *locale* of the Canadian-born in the United States.) The *tourist trade* by familiarizing Americans with all parts of Canada—itself promoted by general proximity— has doubtless helped to extend United States penetration beyond border regions. And of course there are variants in plenty. The Yukon has a large legacy of American-born from the gold rush at the beginning of the century. The Northwest Territories and the District of Patricia have populations of Indian trappers, many of whom came in from the United States. Certain isolated regions have small industries peculiar to the United States, though elsewhere United States population has not followed American capital (the American-born of Oshawa and Ford City—now East Windsor—are relatively few). So slight a matter as the growth of Canadian interest in baseball may account for American-born population in specific cases. In brief, the American-born are settled on the border in some sections, but not so settled in others.

Comparative Densities.—These are another powerful factor which it would take much space to measure. The map-frontispiece again reveals how the newer and less densely settled areas of Canada have been receiving American-born, as indeed they have been receiving other immigrants, including many from the more saturated parts of Canada. In 1921-26 there was a pronounced movement northward in the Prairie Provinces; the American-born shared in this and *pro tanto* diminished their concentration in the southern and older sections, where most of the movement originated.

DIGRESSION ON THE CANADIAN-BORN POPULATION OF THE UNITED STATES

The discussion must at this point digress for a moment on the Canadian-born population of the United States, though this is subject-proper of a later volume of the present series. If the United States has been the main foreign contributor to Canadian population—second only to the British Isles—vastly greater, not only relatively but even absolutely, and at periods altogether different in kind, has been the movement the other way— a fact our statistical feet have just stumbled upon. Only by envisaging that tremendously important factor in Canadian development can the receipt back of the descendants of these emigrants, and on the scale and in the manner just described, be understood. Only, too, by observing the distribution of these Canadians over the country of their adoption, can we appreciate (mainly by contrast) the springs which have actuated much of the present distribution of the American-born in Canada. The truth is, the historic Canadian "exodus" is the largest and most significant single episode, certainly to a Canadian, scarcely less to an American, in the whole history of Canadian-American population relations.*

From the United States Census over the past eighty years, it appears that as early as 1850 their Canadian-born numbered 147,711, which by 1931 had increased to the large figure of 1,286,389, or 3.7 times the number of the American-born in Canada. As Canada's population is less than one-eleventh that of the United States, our relative contribution has been over forty times greater. It has ranged, according to revised estimates, from a net 117,000 in the fifties, to 335,000 and 297,000 in the eighties and nineties, respectively, dropping to 143,000 in the first and to 41,000 in the second decade of the century, but rising again to 274,000 in the latest census. Though the United States contribution to Canada has never been more

*The data on this phase were obtained by courtesy of the United States Census Bureau, but the definitive treatment must of course be sought in the volume by Dr. Truesdell which is to follow.

CANADIAN-BORN POPULATION IN THE UNITED STATES
COMPARED WITH
AMERICAN-BORN IN CANADA
1850-51 to 1930-31

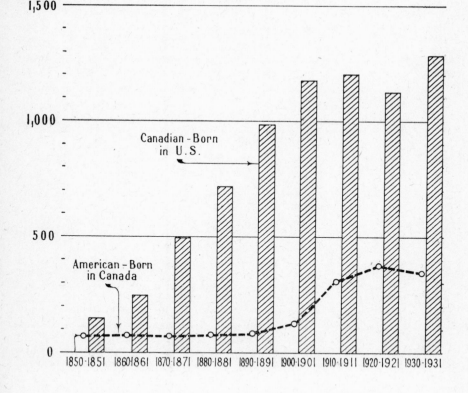

than negligible to that great country—189,000 in the decade of greatest movement—in the eighties, for every thousand that Canada added to the native-born at home, there were sent 717 to the Canadian-born of the United States! Even in the nineteen-twenties, there were added 223 to the Canadians of the United States for every additional 1,000 in the census at home (*exodus redivivus*), in spite of 300,000 "returned Canadians" in the immigration figures of 1926-31 (Table 1). Today Canadians make

TABLE 1

Proportions of Population Moving from the United States to Canada and from Canada to the United States, with Estimated Net Increases, Adjusted for Deaths: 1851-1931

Census Year	Canadian-Born in the United States			American-Born in Canada		
	Number	Percentage of Total Canadian Population	Percentage[1] of Total United States Population	Number	Percentage[1] of Total United States Population	Percentage of Total Canadian Population
1851	147,711	6.06	0.64	63,000[2]	0.27	2.59
1861	249,970	7.74	0.79	70,000[2]	0.22	2.17
1871	493,464	13.38	1.28	64,613	0.17	1.75
1881	717,157	16.58	1.43	77,753	0.16	1.80
1891	980,938	20.30	1.56	80,915	0.13	1.67
1901	1,179,922	21.97	1.55	127,899	0.17	2.38
1911	1,204,637	16.72	1.31	303,680	0.33	4.21
1921	1,124,925	12.80	1.06	374,022	0.35	4.26
1931	1,286,389	12.40	1.05	344,574	0.28	3.32

	Net Increase in Decade		Estimated New Population—Allowing for Deaths	
	Canadian-Born in the United States	American-Born in Canada	Canadian-Born in the United States[3]	American-Born in Canada
1851	......	......	......	......
1861	102,259	7,000	126,000	13,000
1871	243,494	−5,387	283,000	3,000
1881	223,693	13,140	303,000	20,000
1891	263,781	3,162	378,000	11,000
1901	198,984	46,984	356,000	55,000
1911	24,715	175,781	214,000	189,000
1921	−79,712	70,342	113,000	101,000
1931	161,464	−29,448	341,000	8,000

[1] Based on the United States Census, which is taken one year before the Canadian Census; the data are therefore for the decades 1850 to 1930, respectively. The final columns do not allow for emigration. [2] Estimated. [3] By courtesy of U.S. Census Bureau which writes: "The mortality in each decade of the population resident in the country at the beginning of the decade was estimated to be 16 percent in the case of the Canadian-born in the United States and 10 percent in the case of the United States born in Canada. Survival rates for the estimate of the mortality of the Canadian-born in the United States were derived by taking the mean of the age-specific survival rates for the United States Original Registration States from the life table for 1909 to 1911 and those from the life table for 1919 to 1921 for the Registration States of 1920. These survival rates were then applied to the enumerated number of Canadian-born in the United States in 1910 to obtain the mortality rate of 16 percent for the decade 1910 to 1919. This rate was assumed to apply to each decade. The estimate of the mortality rate of the American-born in Canada was similarly derived by applying the age-specific survival rates for the Canadian population for 1921 to 1930 to the age distribution of American-born in Canada in 1931. It should be noted that these rates are only approximations to the true rates and are necessarily subject to wide ranges of possible error in the earlier decades."

up more than 9 p.c. of the entire foreign-born of the United States. In the final event about 12.4 p.c. of all Canadian-born people are today living in the United States (it was 21.97 p.c. in 1901), whereas of the American-born, less than one-third of 1 p.c. are in Canada. Including all of Canadian stock, perhaps a quarter are south of the border, while less than one-fourth of 1 p.c. of the United States stock are north. To such disparity has the movement proceeded.*

Neither the Canadian nor the United States Census shows the country of birth of the immigrant population by year of arrival, except in broad groups of which the earliest is "before 1900-01." Only 13.5 p.c. of the American-born in Canada fall into this category; assigning these a mean year of 1885, the average length of residence of all the American-born works out at 20.0 years. In the case of the Canadian-born in the United States, however, 39.5 p.c. date from before 1900, making the estimate by the same method more tenuous. But by a calculation based on other census data allowing for the survival of the increases in each decade (which works out closely for the American-born in Canada) we arrive at a confirmatory figure of 27 years. Thus the present Canadian-born population of the United States has lived more than a third again as long in their adopted country as have the American-born in Canada.

But it is the forces creating such differences that stand out for inquiry. To uncover these let us pursue the inquiry as before and see what light the distribution criteria shed. For violent contrast we are already prepared. As we are primarily concerned with the return to Canada of the children of these emigrants, let us for strategic purposes examine the year 1910, which follows hard upon the exodus and clearly pictures its results (the Canadian-born were almost as numerous in the United States in 1910 as they are today). Table 2 herewith supplies the data.

By areas, then, in 1930 the Canadians are widely scattered in the United States, but the scatter is apparent rather than real. Three States contain half the Canadian-born, eleven States contain nearly 80 p.c. The largest representation is, of course, in New England, with 518,865, and the second largest in the North-Central States with 360,426, the Middle Atlantic States follow with 182,430, and the three Pacific States are next with 167,892. Massachusetts is the largest "Canadian" State, with 289,496, Michigan is second with 203,783, while New York stands third with 149,148. Out of the million and a quarter Canadian-born, eleven States have less than 1,000 each, while another fourteen States have less than 5,000 each.

When we come, secondly, to the analysis by population groups, the crux of the matter emerges. The Canadian-born in the United States, unlike the American-born in Canada, segregate in *blocs*—that is, they *bloc* wherever they settle in anything approaching large numbers. Now, a conclusion like this requires examination in fullest detail; the investigation, therefore, was carried down to county areas and the wards of cities, a mass of data that can be grasped only in scatter diagrams and tables of class intervals. The broad results may be summarized as follows:—

*The result may be further epitomized thus: Canada has received one-thirtieth of its present population from the United States, whereas the latter has received but one one-hundredth from Canada. *Per contra*, Canada has lost one-eighth to the United States, but the latter less than one three-hundred-and-fiftieth to Canada.

In nearly 3,000 counties thus examined a fair degree of spread was found (though only 768 counties had more than 100 each)—much better proportionally to Canada's population than the similar scatter of the American-born in Canada. But when we consider these scattered Canadians as a proportion of the total Canadian-born in the United States, they shrink almost to insignificance—say, 5 p.c. Most of the Canadian-born in the United States are found in a comparatively small number of places where they form considerable percentages of the totals. These *blocs* occur, generally speaking, in the easily accessible regions—Ontarians in New York and Michigan, Easterners in New England.

But let us go on to the cities. Undoubtedly, the tendency of the Canadian emigrant is citywards. It is often said that the exodus is but the lure of the "white lights," powerful in Canada itself and increasingly so the larger the city (therefore most powerful across the boundary); but this is not the case. Canadians do not emigrate predominantly to the largest cities in the United States, and there is evidence to show that where they do so emigrate the predominant attraction is not the cities but the presence of earlier Canadian emigrants in these cities—this holds at least since 1880, when the Canadians began to *bloc*. From observations over a number of decades of just where and how the Canadian aggregations in the United States have grown, it may be ventured that the strength of the latter influence to the former is as three to one. In this connection a study of the distribution of Canadians by United States city wards (embracing the 107 United States cities of more than 50,000 population in 1910, and representing an aggregate population of 24,000,000 of whom 446,000 were Canadians) reveals that the Canadians did not spread evenly. Though they were found in 1,391 out of a total of 1,412 wards—again a great scatter—the mass was congregated in wards where it formed relatively large percentages. There were only 116 wards with more than 1,000 Canadians, but there were more in these 116 than in all the remaining 1,296. Canadian cities have no such phenomenon *qua* American-born.

In the case of counties as in cities it again appears that the Canadians are not unevenly distributed but tend to settle in the middle-sized ones, and for the same reasons as in the smaller wards of the cities. Half of the Canadians in the United States (not in the larger cities) are in United States population groups between 20,000 and 80,000, i.e., they are neither in the largest centres nor in the most thinly settled districts—another contrast to the American-born in Canada who are found in large numbers along the frontiers of settlement. This obtains today no less than in 1910 though there have been both up and down trends since.

Coming to occupations, however—the third measuring rod for distribution—rather strikingly, a very even distribution is found: the Canadians follow the same distribution as the rest of the United States population. Out of 84 selected occupational classes in the United States Census, more than 50 show the Canadians deviating less than 1 p.c. from their average in all occupations. Any segregation that is in evidence, therefore, is due, it would appear, to social influences—to customs and characteristics that persist amongst them—not to their occupation or employment. There are variations, of course, occupationally, but Canadians have obviously invaded all the industries. The ones chiefly avoided have been farming and contingent occupations needing capital.

The purpose of this rapid and *per se* inadequate survey, is not direct but indirect—to throw light upon the feature of causation. It is still popular to regard the immigrant as essentially an adventurer, seeking far horizons from urge of spirit—in more matter-of-fact language, not so much fleeing a low standard of living as pursuing a higher. That this is so in many cases the present analysis undoubtedly bears out: when he scatters in the new country he wears that stamp. Thus, we may set down the American in Canada as broadly pertaining to this category. Likewise, we can read the individualist in the enormous scatter which characterizes 65,000 of the Canadians in the United States, a scatter which is much greater relatively than that of the American-born over Canada—that is, much larger proportionately to the despatching country. But the fact remains that this dispersed and wandering element is only a fraction and a small one—slightly over 5 p.c.— of the Canadian movement as a whole. When the residue is scrutinized, we encounter the earmarks—apart from an element of, say, 30 p.c. that represent the "pull" of cities and like miscellaneous attractions—not of an individualistic but of a mass movement, a movement which must find its explanation in the economic circumstances not of the receiving but of the sending country, a third of it representing what is left of an overflow which began sporadically but culminated in rural Ontario and Quebec several decades ago, and which halted in spots just over the border, where a new home was made under circumstances as like the old one as possible—in a word an attempt to "move" without "migrating."* Once set up, these became nuclei for subsequent overflows, essentially of a social nature: Canadians have kept on going to the places whither Canadians had preceded; 62 p.c. of Canadians in the United States are in this latter category. These have not emigrated to the parts of the United States which were expanding most rapidly: they have not been straws sucked into a vortex. The same may be said of the children of Canadians in the United States: they have moved about less than the Americans.†

*A useful distinction set up by P. K. Whelpton in his *Needed Population Research* (Lancaster, Pa., 1938), p. 123. The movement from Canada to the United States may be roughly divided into three periods: (1) prior to 1860, when conditions bearing on emigration were extremely varied; (2) 1860-80, when the overflow was from the densely settled rural parts of Quebec and Ontario; (3) after 1880, when the exodus became general. The emigrants of the first period were distributed widely and evenly in the United States. Those of the second went to border States, to be followed by those of the third with an increasing tendency to invade the cities (more particularly certain wards of certain cities). There is little or no correlation since 1870 between the numbers of Canadian emigrants to destinations in the United States and the movement of other people to these destinations, a more trustworthy test than interpretation by isolated historical or economic events. As to the Canadian "stock" in the United States, they are to be found on the whole living in the same areas as the Canadian-born—only a negligible proportion show evidence of having moved with the tide of "continental" migrations. The Canadian participants in the early continental movements described by Professor Hansen left few local descendants.

†A large proportion of the European emigrants to the United States of the present century have been decidedly not of the "adventurer" type—at any rate they have dispersed but little from their port of landing.

To *bloc* is not ordinarily desired in an immigrant. But it may be repeated that the Canadian, as an individual, spreads not less in the United States but more, for, as already pointed out, the 65,000 widely scattered Canadians in the United States are a much larger proportion of the Canadian, than are the 345,000 American-born in Canada of the United States people. In 1850, in the face of transportation difficulties, Canadians were to be found almost everywhere in the United States, in the true pioneering spirit and without depletion of the Canadian counties. It is not an inherent tendency but a *vis a tergo*—a population movement, not an individualistic movement —that accounts for the later situation just outlined. Had the American-born come to Canada in equal proportion, one in five, of mathematical necessity they would have acted similarly.* In point of fact the Canadians in the United States throw in their lot freely with the Republic, which for a century and more has welcomed such infiltration and even yet makes exception in its favour. They intermarry freely; their conjugal status is not abnormal, though marriage is not so common as in Canada; their sex is preponderatingly female; they naturalize though not to the same extent as the British, Germans, and Scandinavians. We have of course two official languages in Canada, and the United States Census records French-Canadian settlers "with a difference." But the French language in the United States ranks low beside others that are equally non-official in that country, and the French outside Quebec cannot be called a *bloc* race either in Canada or the United States. At the same time the French Canadian has undoubtedly taken root less deeply in the United States than has his English-speaking compatriot. He is less prone to naturalize, though longer in the country. His masculinity is greater and he tends less to own a home (the English-speaking Canadian in the United States exceeds the American himself in the latter respect). Yet he comes strongly under the influence of his United States surroundings, as other statistics reveal.

The occupational data in particular show assimilability on the part of Canadians, who went primarily to the United States as wage-earners. Apparently many took on new occupations after their transfer and have changed occupations several times. Many were young people who had no fixed occupation when they left (declared occupations on their immigration are of little meaning). In fact, there is absolutely no evidence of occupation being specially affected either way: as between Canada and the United States the interchange on an occupational basis has been without apparent system. We have lent merchants and clerical workers, and borrowed insurance and real estate vendors; lent labourers and borrowed hod carriers; lent housekeepers and cooks, and borrowed servants; lent lawyers and borrowed clergymen. Of course, the longer residence of the Canadian-born in the United States has given them more time to fit into the local scheme.

An interesting question is the extent to which the return of American-born of Canadian stock betokens a family as opposed to an individual

---

*The *blocing* of Canadians in the United States is not, of course, sole evidence of the *vis a tergo* referred to. The argument runs:—given the two types of immigrants mentioned, A, a small adventurous body; and B, an overflow of population; how will these respectively behave in the new country? Available evidence shows that the former scatter widely, whilst B proceeds to the most easily accessible habitat and keeps together. The B type represents perhaps nine-tenths of the Canadian-born in the United States.

movement. A case study of the Canadian Census, wherein the Canadian-born parents of American-born offspring could be easily segregated, would lay this bare. Meanwhile the census tabulations do not separate the ordinary family of American stock from the Canadian-stock family. But it is at least significant that 7.8 p.c. of the American-born are under 10 years of age (and therefore presumably living with parents), while only 2.1 p.c. of the British-born are in that category, and only 4.3 p.c. of the Continental European-born.* Noteworthy, too, is the fact that in the eastern provinces the proportion of American-born under 10 years of age is higher than that of the Canadian-born from the neighbouring provinces. In Nova Scotia, for example, of 7,901 born in New Brunswick only 683 were under 10 years, but of 7,222 American-born the number was 1,666. Ontario and Quebec, however, show less positive results, and the western provinces reverse the story, their American-born being like other immigrants in this regard. There is a difference in our American-born East and West, of which this is not the only instance.

The point in this digression as a whole need not be laboured. From an overflow of such kind and proportions as the Canadian *exodus* of the last quarter of the nineteenth century repercussion is inevitable. Such repercussion has taken the form of an element *sui generis* among the American-born of the present Canadian population.

*The actual figures of population by birthplace, with the number less than 10 years of age and ratios, 1931, are:—

Birthplace	Total	Ages 0-9 Total	Ages 0-9 Percent
Canada	8,069,261	2,123,065	26.3
British Isles	1,138,942	24,271	2.1
British Possessions	45,888[1]	1,493	3.3
Europe	714,462	30,857	4.3
Asia	60,608	388	0.6
United States	344,574	26,807	7.8

[1]Includes 731 born at sea.

TABLE 2

Canadian-Born Living in the United States, by Mother Tongue (French and Other), Classified by Geographical Divisions and States of Residence: Census Years 1850-1930

NOTE.—Data supplied by courtesy of the United States Bureau of the Census. Those for 1900 and earlier include persons born in Newfoundland. Figures under designation "French" represent white persons of French mother tongue, omitting the few non-white French. Classification as "French" and "Other" not available for years prior to 1890.

Division and State	1930 Total	1930 French	1930 Other	1920 Total	1920 French	1920 Other
All Divisions	1,286,389	370,852	915,537	1,124,925	307,786	817,139
New England	518,865	264,261	254,604	476,256	240,385	235,871
Maine	73,995	36,947	37,048	74,420	35,580	38,840
New Hampshire	50,992	37,682	13,310	52,312	38,277	14,035
Vermont	27,194	17,320	9,874	24,885	14,181	10,704
Massachusetts	289,496	115,241	174,255	263,478	108,691	154,787
Rhode Island	39,325	31,501	7,824	36,482	28,887	7,595
Connecticut	37,863	25,570	12,293	24,679	14,769	9,910

TABLE 2—continued

*Canadian-Born Living in the United States, by Mother Tongue (French and
Other), Classified by Geographical Divisions and States of Residence:
Census Years 1850-1930*

Division and State	1930 Total	1930 French	1930 Other	1920 Total	1920 French	1920 Other
All Divisions	1,286,389	370,852	915,537	1,124,925	307,786	817,139
Middle Atlantic	182,430	33,336	149,094	138,300	17,045	121,255
New York	149,148	28,955	120,193	112,804	15,560	97,244
New Jersey	16,665	2,470	14,195	10,396	772	9,624
Pennsylvania	16,617	1,911	14,706	15,100	713	14,387
East North Central	296,996	42,308	254,688	253,892	29,267	224,625
Ohio	27,345	2,606	24,739	24,670	1,277	23,393
Indiana	6,267	682	5,585	5,147	406	4,741
Illinois	43,988	6,189	37,799	38,773	4,032	34,741
Michigan	203,783	28,539	175,244	165,902	18,635	147,267
Wisconsin	15,613	4,292	11,321	19,400	4,917	14,483
West North Central	63,430	10,531	52,899	80,705	10,459	70,246
Minnesota	27,216	6,484	20,732	33,862	6,796	27,066
Iowa	6,353	608	5,745	8,944	401	8,543
Missouri	5,460	588	4,872	6,562	299	6,263
North Dakota	12,509	1,354	11,155	15,743	1,533	14,210
South Dakota	3,414	492	2,922	4,462	508	3,954
Nebraska	4,410	436	3,974	5,780	351	5,429
Kansas	4,068	569	3,499	5,352	571	4,781
South Atlantic	17,663	2,055	15,608	13,041	813	12,228
Delaware	479	61	418	453	23	430
Maryland	2,307	291	2,016	1,894	117	1,777
District of Columbia	1,729	223	1,506	1,726	147	1,579
Virginia	1,647	157	1,490	1,947	106	1,841
West Virginia	980	118	862	981	54	927
North Carolina	948	80	868	663	15	648
South Carolina	280	31	249	271	24	247
Georgia	1,104	109	995	965	50	915
Florida	8,189	985	7,204	4,141	277	3,864
East South Central	3,167	347	2,820	3,201	179	3,022
Kentucky	934	96	838	903	50	853
Tennessee	949	92	857	988	47	941
Alabama	919	117	802	904	52	852
Mississippi	365	42	323	406	30	376
West South Central	8,433	994	7,439	8,768	590	8,178
Arkansas	715	77	638	893	58	835
Louisiana	1,009	222	787	1,186	157	1,029
Oklahoma	2,146	243	1,903	2,489	126	2,363
Texas	4,563	452	4,111	4,200	249	3,951

Table 2—continued

Canadian-Born Living in the United States, by Mother Tongue (French and Other), Classified by Geographical Divisions and States of Residence: Census Years 1850-1930

Division and State		1930			1920	
	Total	French	Other	Total	French	Other
All Divisions	1,286,389	370,852	915,537	1,124,925	307,786	817,139
Mountain	27,513	3,678	23,835	34,097	3,482	30,615
Montana	11,193	1,966	9,227	14,700	2,211	12,489
Idaho	4,529	571	3,958	4,961	476	4,485
Wyoming	1,144	118	1,026	1,440	92	1,348
Colorado	5,845	572	5,273	7,642	418	7,224
New Mexico	618	62	556	738	42	696
Arizona	2,037	158	1,879	1,964	90	1,874
Utah	1,192	97	1,095	1,471	45	1,426
Nevada	955	134	821	1,181	108	1,073
Pacific	167,892	13,342	154,550	116,665	5,566	111,099
Washington	48,269	4,340	43,929	43,179	2,581	40,598
Oregon	17,946	1,345	16,601	13,800	679	13,121
California	101,677	7,657	94,020	59,686	2,306	57,380

Division and State		1910			1900	
	Total	French	Other	Total	French	Other
All Divisions	1,204,637	385,083	819,554	1,179,922	394,461	785,461
New England	526,239	278,156	248,083	511,190	275,377	235,813
Maine	76,223	35,013	41,210	67,077	30,895	36,182
New Hampshire	57,878	40,865	17,013	58,967	44,416	14,551
Vermont	26,058	14,643	11,415	25,655	14,982	10,673
Massachusetts	297,369	134,659	162,710	293,169	134,387	158,782
Rhode Island	41,954	34,087	7,867	39,277	31,530	7,747
Connecticut	26,757	18,889	7,868	27,045	19,167	7,878
Middle Atlantic	148,369	27,012	121,357	139,427	29,705	109,722
New York	123,551	24,563	98,988	117,535	27,150	90,385
New Jersey	9,135	1,203	7,932	7,132	1,105	6,027
Pennsylvania	15,683	1,246	14,437	14,760	1,450	13,310
East North Central	273,140	46,614	226,526	297,645	55,420	242,225
Ohio	23,692	2,310	21,382	22,767	2,870	19,897
Indiana	5,838	789	5,049	5,934	947	4,987
Illinois	45,751	7,440	38,311	50,595	9,102	41,493
Michigan	172,863	28,083	144,780	184,398	32,422	151,976
Wisconsin	24,996	7,992	17,004	33,951	10,079	23,872

Table 2—continued

Canadian-Born Living in the United States, by Mother Tongue (French and Other), Classified by Geographical Divisions and States of Residence: Census Years 1850-1930

Division and State	1910			1900		
	Total	French	Other	Total	French	Other
All Divisions	1,204,637	385,083	819,554	1,179,922	394,461	785,461
West North Central	102,849	17,920	84,929	124,678	21,366	103,312
Minnesota	41,121	11,062	30,059	47,578	12,047	35,531
Iowa	11,619	944	10,675	15,687	1,515	14,172
Missouri	8,069	779	7,290	8,616	1,049	7,567
North Dakota	21,507	2,376	19,131	28,166	3,105	25,061
South Dakota	6,010	998	5,012	7,044	1,135	5,909
Nebraska	7,335	674	6,661	9,049	1,035	8,014
Kansas	7,188	1,087	6,101	8,538	1,480	7,058
South Atlantic	8,681	763	7,918	6,920	627	6,293
Delaware	504	63	441	298	41	257
Maryland	1,430	110	1,320	1,230	87	1,143
District of Columbia	1,161	109	1,052	906	93	813
Virginia	1,360	104	1,256	1,130	103	1,027
West Virginia	872	88	784	711	71	640
North Carolina	543	29	514	480	36	444
South Carolina	282	39	243	204	30	174
Georgia	801	70	731	759	79	680
Florida	1,728	151	1,577	1,202	87	1,115
East South Central	3,509	331	3,178	3,379	412	2,967
Kentucky	1,070	98	972	1,208	134	1,074
Tennessee	1,156	91	1,065	1,045	119	926
Alabama	833	96	737	706	89	617
Mississippi	450	46	404	420	70	350
West South Central	8,670	1,045	7,625	6,883	1,027	5,856
Arkansas	1,074	119	955	1,093	159	934
Louisiana	1,191	250	941	1,034	247	787
Oklahoma	2,871	320	2,551	1,807	224	1,583
Texas	3,534	356	3,178	2,949	397	2,552
Mountain	36,612	5,276	31,336	32,190	5,356	26,834
Montana	13,842	2,874	10,968	13,826	3,266	10,560
Idaho	5,371	796	4,575	2,923	395	2,528
Wyoming	1,431	143	1,288	1,248	150	1,098
Colorado	9,581	789	8,792	9,797	959	8,838
New Mexico	1,023	111	912	764	84	680
Arizona	1,827	177	1,650	1,269	152	1,117
Utah	1,690	114	1,576	1,331	128	1,203
Nevada	1,847	272	1,575	1,032	222	810
Pacific	96,568	7,966	88,602	57,610	5,171	52,439
Washington	39,482	3,711	35,771	20,284	1,892	18,392
Oregon	12,409	1,146	11,263	7,508	872	6,636
California	44,677	3,109	41,568	29,818	2,407	27,411

Table 2—continued

Canadian-Born Living in the United States, by Mother Tongue (French and Other), Classified by Geographical Divisions and States of Residence: Census Years 1850-1930

Division and State	Total	1890 French	Other	1880	1870	1860	1850
All Divisions	980,938	302,496	678,442	717,157	493,464	249,970	147,711
New England	380,167	205,761	174,406	242,928	159,445	70,828	49,008
Maine	52,076	23,882	28,194	37,114	26,788	17,540	14,181
New Hampshire	46,321	34,107	12,214	27,142	12,955	4,468	2,501
Vermont	25,004	13,650	11,354	24,620	28,544	15,776	14,470
Massachusetts	207,601	96,286	111,315	119,302	70,055	27,069	15,862
Rhode Island	27,934	22,591	5,343	18,306	10,242	2,830	1,024
Connecticut	21,231	15,245	5,986	16,444	10,861	3,145	970
Middle Atlantic	110,062	23,593	86,469	100,094	91,538	59,901	50,281
New York	93,193	22,597	70,596	84,182	79,042	55,273	47,200
New Jersey	4,698	395	4,303	3,536	2,474	1,144	581
Pennsylvania	12,171	601	11,570	12,376	10,022	3,484	2,500
East North Central	275,573	46,789	228,784	233,589	165,559	85,008	40,742
Ohio	16,515	1,291	15,224	16,146	12,988	7,082	5,880
Indiana	4,954	360	4,594	5,569	4,765	3,166	1,878
Illinois	39,525	5,944	33,581	34,043	32,550	20,132	10,699
Michigan	181,416	30,446	150,970	148,866	89,590	36,482	14,008
Wisconsin	33,163	8,748	24,415	28,965	25,666	18,146	8,277
West North Central	126,087	18,924	107,163	91,249	51,918	22,032	4,226
Minnesota	43,580	10,910	32,670	29,631	16,698	8,023	1,417
Iowa	17,465	886	16,579	21,097	17,907	8,313	1,756
Missouri	8,525	559	7,966	8,685	8,448	2,814	1,053
North Dakota	23,045	3,009	20,036 }	10,678	906	1,458[1]	......
South Dakota	9,493	1,061	8,432 }				
Nebraska	12,105	838	11,267	8,622	2,635	438[1]	......
Kansas	11,874	1,661	10,213	12,536	5,324	986	......
South Atlantic	5,412	284	5,128	3,926	2,249	1,209	795
Delaware	309	14	295	246	112	39	21
Maryland	1,020	68	952	988	644	333	215
District of Columbia	655	32	623	452	290	59	32
Virginia	780	19	761	585	327	389	235
West Virginia	374	25	349	295	207	......	......
North Carolina	355	16	339	425	171	48	30
South Carolina	159	12	147	141	77	86	57
Georgia	609	47	562	348	247	178	108
Florida	1,151	51	1,100	446	174	77	97

[1] In 1860 Dakota Territory included most of the area of the present State of Montana and about half the present State of Wyoming. Most of the other half of Wyoming was included in Nebraska Territory.

Table 2—concluded

Canadian-Born Living in the United States, by Mother Tongue (French and Other), Classified by Geographical Divisions and States of Residence: Census Years 1850-1930

Division and State	Total	1890 French	Other	1880	1870	1860	1850
All Divisions	980,938	302,496	678,442	717,157	493,464	249,970	147,711
East South Central	3,158	124	3,034	2,195	2,227	1,428	479
Kentucky	1,173	50	1,123	1,070	1,082	618	275
Tennessee	1,020	25	995	545	587	387	76
Alabama	620	35	585	271	183	239	49
Mississippi	345	14	331	309	375	184	79
West South Central	4,995	270	4,725	3,985	1,653	1,442	677
Arkansas	947	36	911	787	342	154	41
Louisiana	762	95	667	726	714	830	499
Oklahoma	420	11	409	......	......	......	......
Texas	2,866	128	2,738	2,472	597	458	137
Mountain	25,584	3,361	22,223	14,426	5,907	1,615	376
Montana	9,040	2,213	6,827	2,481	1,172	1	......
Idaho	1,791	124	1,667	584	334	2	......
Wyoming	1,314	96	1,218	542	329	1	......
Colorado	9,142	575	8,567	5,785	753	684	......
New Mexico	681	25	656	280	125⎫	76	38
Arizona	732	27	705	571	142⎭		
Utah	1,222	38	1,184	1,036	687	647	338
Nevada	1,662	263	1,399	3,147	2,365	208	......
Pacific	49,900	3,390	46,510	24,765	12,968	6,507	1,127
Washington	17,412	1,607	15,805	2,857	1,121	407[2]	......
Oregon	6,460	431	6,029	3,019	1,187	663	293
California	26,028	1,352	24,676	18,889	10,660	5,437	834

[1] In 1860 Dakota Territory included most of the area of the present State of Montana and about half the present State of Wyoming.   Most of the other half of Wyoming was included in Nebraska Territory.
[2] In 1860 the present State of Idaho was included in Washington Territory.

Summary of Influences Affecting Distribution

To resume the main discussion:—

In perspective, we have now examined the leading conceptions that have been emphasized at one time or another regarding the United States penetration of Canada. It has been found, in face of the commonly overlooked evenness of penetration, that such emphasis may be undue or misleading if the object is to view conditions steadily and whole.* Free lands, invest-

*E.g., Goldwin Smith, in his *Reminiscences*, p. 417, writing in 1903, says: "As I write, settlers from the United States are pouring into the North-West Territories, which they were sure to do when Minnesota and Dakota land became dear. The North-West will be American." Goldwin Smith saw only the comparatively small beginnings of the tide, which flowed increasingly for a decade, yet in 1931 only 7 p.c. of the prairie population was American-born.

ment openings, opportunities for employment, race predilection, with many other attracting forces have operated, but none stands out in the broad result. We have examined some few of these at length, only to find that it is a misnomer to designate them as "main" causes—rather is each a combination of several causes often vaguely differentiated and sometimes overlooked. Thus, length of time in the country makes for evenness of spread, but so likewise does the fact that the immigrants have come in at different times. Race is influential, not in the way usually accepted, but from the fact that there have been several races involved; one very important phase of this has its root in the previous emigration of Canadians to the United States. Again, if the movement of 1901-11 accounted for the American-born, the West would be their characteristic habitat, whereas they are found throughout the Dominion (as many, nearly, in the Maritimes as in Manitoba; in Ontario as in Saskatchewan, and many more in Quebec and British Columbia than in Alberta) including region and population groups where even the most ubiquitous of other immigrants have not penetrated. *In fine*, the reasons are so numerous and interlocking as to baffle complete enumeration, let alone

PERCENTAGE DISTRIBUTION OF TOTAL POPULATION, AMERICAN -BORN AND "OTHER IMMIGRANT POPULATION" BY QUINQUENNIAL AGE GROUPS
1931

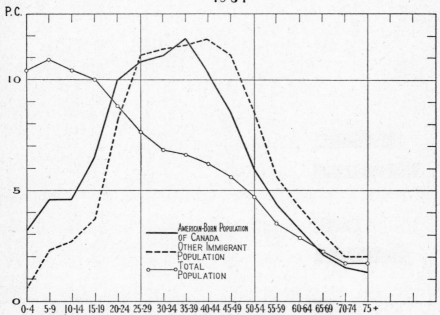

analysis, the whole bearing out the interpretation that evenness of spread connotes many causes and negatives any simple explanation.

With like clarity also we have derived in considerable degree the motivation of the American-born in Canada. They have not come as a "population" moving to another country (as did, say, the United Empire Loyalists, or several of our modern immigrant stocks), for on balance they have not come at any particular time, to any one part, in any one occupation class, as any one race (though they have added to the proportions of our German and Scandinavian stocks), or as adherents to any one religion (rather have they added a considerable number of sects). From dynamic facts like these, their ordinary attributes, from which so many of the major as well as the more subtle influences of an immigration movement spring, might be assumed normal and helpful—as indeed they turn out to be. By sex, the males and females of the American-born are nearly equal—they do not show the excessive masculinity of Continental European stocks, though males are somewhat in excess west of the Lakes as are females in Ontario and the eastern provinces.* The proportion of married comes nearer to

*The figures of masculinity (number of males per 1,000 females) by birthplace, for Canada, 1931, are:—

Canada	1,021
British Isles	1,143
British possessions	1,085
Continental Europe	1,586
Asia	6,187
United States	1,034

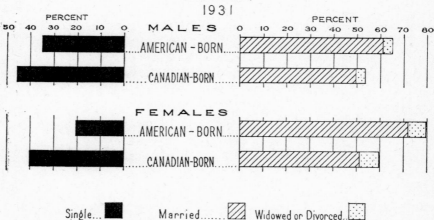

CONJUGAL CONDITION OF AMERICAN - BORN
15 YEARS OF AGE AND OVER
IN
CANADA
1931

that of native Canadians than to any others, both being small. Their age content is such that they have materially assisted in moderating the abnormality caused by other immigration, with its long train of undesirable repercussions. (See charts, pp. 35 and 36.) In language, the mother tongue of 82 p.c. is one or other of the official languages of Canada (though they have buttressed the English speech). The percentage of illiterate American-born is smaller than that for any other country of birth except the Empire countries; this however reflects age and race, the latter being a determinant also of religion.* The American-born, it may be added, is more law-abiding than the average Canadian: In 1931 there were 304 convictions for indictable offences for each 100,000 of the population in general, but only 287 for the American-born, though the latter had a higher rate than the general population for robbery, horse and cattle stealing, false pretences and fraud, forgery, and carrying unlawful weapons.†

Significance of the Distribution of the American-Born

It goes without saying that the even distribution of an immigrant people affords the maximum opportunity for a free intermingling of the two populations and for the freest possible interchange of ideas and cultures on almost every plane. Great as are the penetrating powers of a common press, a common literature, and an overlapping radio, they probably do not transcend continuous daily personal contacts—though as yet we may not test such judgments with exactness. The even distribution, however, of the American-born over Canada spells, on the face of it, that they are at one and the same time disseminating their influence widely and themselves becoming Canadianized.

Above all, since immigrating people are much fewer in numbers than the population of their adopted country, the tendency to settle widely and evenly argues absence of political motive, for the more they spread the more permanently they place themselves in minorities and the less do they sway political decisions by weight of numbers. The average population of a county in Canada is 47,000; conceivably the American-born might by concentration command a majority in 14 out of the 222 counties. Instead, they have settled in all 222 counties, with the result that their largest

---

*Illiteracy, or the inability to read and write, it may be pointed out, is the hall-mark of definite anti-social attributes: illiterates in Canada have larger families but send fewer children to school; have more children illiterate over a certain age; send more of their wives and children to work and at lower pay; work for lower pay themselves; and show more illegitimacy.

†The general crime rate increased to 405 in 1939, but that for American-born residents remained unchanged. Details regarding the various offences, cross-classified by race, sex, age, etc., are available on an annual basis since 1876 in the Dominion Bureau of Statistics.

proportion in any one county is less than 19 p.c. (Total American-born are only 332 in each 10,000 of population.) If such minorities influence opinion it must be by personal qualities alone. As a class, we should expect the American-born in Canada to be influenced rather than to exert influence. The United States farmer who settles among thirty others of a nationality different from his own is not seeking to imbue these with American views of government, morals or religion—though if he can farm or trade to better result than his neighbours, or otherwise exploit his personality, he will achieve a following.

So much *a priori*,—and the penetration of Canada as previously mentioned has features that are as yet incapable of direct statistical appraisal, a remark which applies particularly in any attempt to analyse its results and significance. On two points, however, that touch respectively the political and the social aspect in the foregoing, at least a measure of statistical treatment is possible. It has been seen that the even distribution of the American-born over Canada, on the face of it, facilitates their Canadianization. On the political side of this process certain statistics as to the naturalization of the American-born in Canada, i.e., their readiness to exchange their United States citizenship for that of Canada, have point, while in the wider social field the statistics showing the extent to which the American-born have intermarried with Canadians and thus forsaken national ties in the creation of a new family life are equally conclusive. Particularly must we examine both these tendencies in the light of the racial elements composing the American-born which tend to negative a wholly unbiased intermingling with Canadians: racially, as we have seen, the American-born split up. If, therefore, we find that the fact of United States birth in a series of racial strains increases the extent to which these races become naturalized and intermarry, clearly the American-born are accelerating race infusion and the unification of citizenship in Canada. With the presentation of the evidence under these two headings in turn the present study may draw to a close.

NATURALIZATION OF THE AMERICAN-BORN

If there is any evidence of nationalist impulse in the American-born in Canada, it lies in the fact that most of them came originally of Canadian or British stock. This is true more particularly of the recent arrivals—and the earlier ones have not remained. But, as just said, we are here concerned with a different phase of the subject. It may be defined in concrete in the question: Does a person of foreign origin, when born in the United States, become naturalized more readily in Canada than one of the same racial origin born elsewhere? The data on this point are highly significant.* Not only have 72.4 p.c. of the American-born been naturalized as compared with only

*See Table LVII, p. 136, which shows the percentage naturalized of each race in Canada differentiated as: (1) American-born, and (2) born elsewhere. Allowance must be made for certain factors (for example, length of time in the country) that may explain a certain degree of variation in the figures. Correction for these is impossible (the figures of racial origin by year of immigration to Canada are available, also those of countries of birth by year of immigration, but the American-born by races have not been compiled by years of immigration); by indirect evidence, they are not of first importance.

NATURALIZATION OF FOREIGN-BORN IN CANADA
FOR SELECTED COUNTRIES, 1931
The widths of the bars are adjusted to represent relative numbers

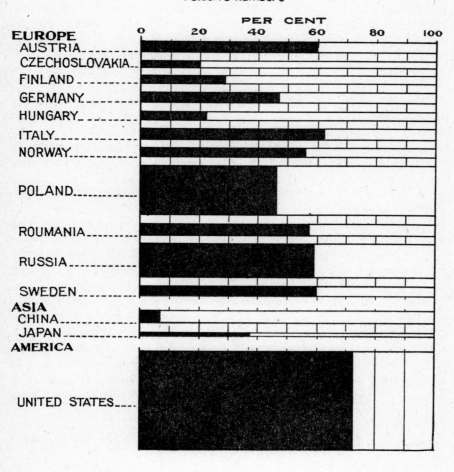

45.9 p.c. of the total foreign-born, but the great majority of the races represented among the former show higher percentage naturalized. The only exceptions are in the case of Hebrews, Icelanders, Italians, Japanese, and a few others of small proportions, and even for these, excluding the Icelanders, the percentages are only slightly lower. Perhaps the outstanding examples are afforded by those of French and German descent, of which the numbers of American-born and of those born elsewhere outside of Canada are considerable. But a comparison of the Norwegian and Swedish statistics is of special interest: the Norwegian population of Canada shows a greater proportion naturalized than the Swedish, but it is clear that this is because of the greater proportion of American-born among the former, for the Swedish-born elsewhere show a higher proportion than the Norwegian-born elsewhere. Other examples could be cited to illustrate the fact that the proportion of American-born definitely influences the percentages naturalized of the various races in Canada. Part of this must be due to the fact that the American-born among them spread more freely.

INTERMARRIAGE

The more even the distribution of a foreign-born people, the greater the opportunity for intermarriage with the population of the adopted country. Marriages are sometimes negotiated by correspondence, even by radio, but propinquity still provides the maximum of opportunity. Again, where single males predominate in an immigration movement, the necessity for their marriage with the native stock is apparent.

In 1931, of 3,829 American-born grooms in Canada, only 807 or 21 p.c. married American-born brides, while 2,458 married Canadian-born and other British-born, the remainder choosing, or being chosen by, women from a considerable variety of countries. Of 2,946 American-born brides on the Canadian register, only 807 or about 27 p.c. married American-born, the remainder marrying as follows: 1,377, or 47 p.c., Canadian-born; 368, or 12 p.c., born in other British territory; 394, or 13 p.c., born elsewhere.

This would seem to argue almost complete indifference on the part of the American-born in Canada as to the country of birth of their mates. Proximity indeed appears the leading factor. Though not strictly relevant, a tabulation of the number of American-born in each province marrying brides born in that province, born in the United States, born elsewhere in Canada, and born in other countries may be cited. Those marrying brides born in the province where the marriage took place are about half the total number.

The small percentage of intermarriage among the American-born in Canada is emphasized if comparison is made with the figures for other foreign-born. Length of time in Canada of course plays a part, but the showing in certain cases is remarkable in view of the numbers of the same race in Canada who are Canadian-born or American-born. For example, 65.7 p.c. of the Polish-born married brides who were also born in Poland, though the majority of the females of Polish race in Canada were born in Canada or the United States. But in spite of the fact that our American-born males in general might have found American-born females of the same race in Canada, only 21 p.c. of them so married.

Thus *a posteriori* we demonstrate the pervasiveness, the individualistic character, and the general assimilability or tendency to fusion of the American-born in Canada. This is perhaps no new discovery: the value of the treatment lies in its *aperçu* of the subject whole; its test of assumptions based on a partial and therefore blurred and facile outlook (a "continental" movement, an "agrarian" movement or the like); and its enlargement of the causal concept. Certain familiar generalizations have been shown not as foundationless, but as resulting from over-emphasis and distortion of single features. Clearly, an immigrant movement that includes all races, ages, and occupations of its country of origin, and is found throughout its country of adoption in whatever occupations and relations offer, cannot be explained in narrow terms. If such explanations are put forward, it is essential to measure them and view them in due proportion and setting, otherwise they obscure appraisal of what remains one of the most important problems in Canadian national development.

A final conclusion would not seem iconoclastic. The evenness of spread portrayed, and the multiplicity of its causes, ensure *en reverse* a permanent United States-derived population in Canada—one at least that is not removable by single cause. It is true that the American-born decreased between 1921 and 1931, but this is an exception which proves the rule, for 40 p.c. of the decrease took place in a class whose attraction was a special one—a certain type of agriculture—and as a result even the American farmer of the West is declining as a class among the American-born of Canada today. The moral appears to be that the manner of settlement is all-important. If the inward movement is influenced primarily by individual familiarity with what the country offers, as happens with the great majority of immigrants from the United States, rather than by short-run financial appeal, the increase will not be *en masse*, but is more likely to be permanent and assimilable. To this conclusion at least the example of the American-born in Canada over the past half-century points. High-pressure salesman-ship and other intensive methods of peopling the country have not in broad perspective accounted for them, and they remain among the best assets added to our population by immigration.

ADDENDUM
DAY-TO-DAY MOVEMENTS ACROSS THE BORDER

This study has not drawn upon migration records, the meaning of which for permanent population is a problem, statistical and other, of the first order, woefully pregnant of misunderstanding (to remain so till we can speak of the birth rate with something of our science regarding the death rate).* But an appropriate addendum remains—to appraise that day-to-day human intercourse across the Canada-United States border which adds so large a "floating" quota to the comparatively static figures we have been considering. (Immigration has little to do with it—indeed less than 1 p.c. of it is immigrant.) How many, and of what classes, are these travellers and "trippers" over the three-thousand-mile-long frontier? What is the significance of the movement, that is, what obstacle, if any, does the political boundary offer to it? In other words, are the people on one side as free to go to a place on the other side (distances being equal) as to one on their own—say, to visit a relative or exchange work-days with a friend? Again, is the border country a "neutral zone," and is the homogeneity of Americans and Canadians in inverse proportion to their distance therefrom? What effects have ease or difficulty in crossing upon social relations in general and the exchange of permanent population in particular? The following will attempt a quantitative answer to some of these questions on which considerable vagueness has prevailed both as to the facts and their meaning.

The available data are rather intractable, but they can be broken down in some degree (see Statements A and B). As just remarked, the vast majority of the crossings are of a purely temporary nature. We take the more or less typical year of 1931, as coinciding with the Census.

First, almost 13 million United States motorists entered Canada on tourist permits—8.6 million on 1-day permits, almost 4.5 million on 60-day permits (but who stayed on the average only about 6 days), and 2,232 on 6-month permits (whose average length of stay was about 85 days). In addition, entrants by rail or steamer numbered over 1 million, while crossings by pedestrians, motorists other than those on tourist permits, travellers by air, bus, ferry, etc., numbered over 2.5 million.

Canadian entries into the United States of a temporary nature meanwhile numbered over 1.6 million motorists on tourist permits, nearly 350,000 travellers by rail or steamer, and over 5 million pedestrians, motorists other than on tourist permits, travellers by air, bus, ferry, etc.

The official records do not permit us to distinguish "persons" from "crossings" in these figures—the same individual may cross a number of times a year, in extreme cases 365 times or even more. The only definite

---

*The main features of the immigration movement, however, from the United States to Canada are summarized for the fiscal years 1908-31 in Statements D to G (pp. 50-52).

information on persons as distinguished from crossings is the fact that daily passes were issued to 8,625 residents of Canada, mostly workmen, who crossed daily to an aggregate of over 2.6 million times, and to 1,301 residents of the United States of the same class whose aggregate was 400,000. In addition, there were over 900,000 crossings by 8,800 Canadian residents, and over 2 million crossings by 21,000 United States residents holding intermittent boundary passes, both of which classes crossed the border not more than three times a week on an average. These figures must be added to the crossings already enumerated.

Summing up, about 19.5 million persons entered Canada from the United States in one capacity or another in this particular year, while almost 11 million Canadians of similar categories crossed the border into the United States. Thus, there were over 30 million crossings in the course of the year over this unique international boundary already so favourite a theme for oratory on another though not inherently loftier plane. Again, we note the disparity that perennially appears in such figures: the United States, with twelve times the population, originates less than double the crossings. In other words, the Canadian pays a visit to the United States six or seven times as often as does the American to Canada.

Let us pursue the theme in another and equally compelling way with the question: How many Americans might one count on finding within the Canadian gates on a typical day in this typical year? The calculation, which obviously rests on the length of stay of the visitors (obtained from the official reports on motor crossings above described, and for other classes from a sample questionnaire), is as follows:—

		Days
Immigrants	$(15,195 \times 365)$	5,546,175
Motorists on—		
1-day permits	$(8,598,730 \times 1)$	8,598,730
60-day permits	$(4,409,259 \times 6)$	26,455,554
6-month permits	$(2,232 \times 85)$	189,720
Rail and steamer travellers	$(1,177,429 \times 10)$	11,774,290
Holders of United States Border Passes—		
Active	$(1,301 \times 312)$	405,912
Intermittent	$(21,186 \times 104)$	2,203,344
Pedestrians, travellers by aeroplane, ferry, etc.	$(2,545,427 \times 1.5)$	3,818,140
Total		58,991,865

Thus in 1931-32 the average floating population from the United States per day the year round was approximately 162,000, a figure which, considering that the movement in 1931 was on a descending scale, is low. It is an impressive showing. This army of almost a sixth of a million from the United States, which every day is found in the Dominion, is larger than any Canadian city except Montreal, Toronto, Winnipeg, and Vancouver. It is over one and three-quarter times the population of Prince Edward Island and nearly 40 p.c. of the population of the Province of New Brunswick which sends ten members to the House of Commons and ten to the Senate of Canada.

Moreover, the influence of a floating population, made up preponderatingly of adults and the more active types of individuals, is greater than that of an equal static population. Its size should be compared not with the total of the latter but with that part of it which is in the active period of life—say from 20 to 60 years of age—the number of which in Canada in 1931 was 5,182,000. Thus, the United States floating population ranks as 1 to every 32 persons in the static population. This has drawbacks as well as advantages, but that it effects an immeasurable contact with the *mores* of the Republic is beyond question. Include the 344,574 permanent American-born, and one might say that every tenth person the ordinary active Canadian is apt to meet in the daily round is or has come from the United States. Certainly the average Canadian is as familiar with an American as with a Canadian of another province. The influence is ubiquitous; it renews itself daily; it embraces all classes.

Meanwhile a Canadian army, smaller indeed but in its way as remarkable, is daily familiarizing Canada to the United States people on their own soil. A calculation on a similar basis as the above reveals that the number of Canadians in the United States on an average day in the same year was approximately 84,000. The details follow:—

		Days
Emigrants	(14,541×365)	5,307,465
Motorists on tourist permits	(1,610,565×6)	9,663,390
Rail and steamer travellers	(346,629×12)	4,159,548
Holders of United States Border Passes—		
Active	(8,625×312)	2,691,000
Intermittent	(8,784×104)	913,536
Pedestrians, travellers by ferry, aeroplane, etc.	(5,226,183×1.5)	7,839,274
Total		30,574,213

This is a small force over against the 120 millions of the United States, and compared with twice that number of United States visitors operating upon Canada's 10 millions, but again the Canadian impact is shown as proportionally six or seven times that of the United States, from the standpoint of the originating population. The large border cities on the United States side are in part the lure; moreover the Canadian has four times as many compatriots to attract him; further, the centre of the Canadian population is much nearer the border.

Social Intercourse

On the point of the social intercourse which this discussion betokens, we may recur to an aspect of intermarriage which must suffice for single reference. We obtain this by noting, province by province, the number of males marrying American-born brides compared with those marrying brides born in other provinces, and collating the figures with the correspondingly-born resident female population (Statement C, p. 49). For example, in Nova Scotia, the number of American-born females (single 15 years of age or older, widowed and divorced) was 1,051 in 1931, compared with 1,381 born in New Brunswick (the province of greatest intermarriage), a ratio of 0.76. But in the marriages of the five-year period 1929-33 there were 259 American-born brides and only 199 New Brunswick-born, a ratio of 1.30. In other words, 24.6 p.c. of the American-born females in Nova Scotia married Nova Scotian males but only 14.4 p.c. of the resident New Brunswick females. New Brunswick males show a similar if less pronounced preference for United States over Nova Scotian brides, reflected in percentages of 33.0 and 22.0, respectively. Likewise, as between the contiguous provinces of Ontario and Quebec, marked United States preferences are shown. In the West, however, interprovincial marriages between children of foreign-born parentage reverse the trend—again the race motif. The general conclusion is that United States birthplace imposes no curb on marriage.

Thus, while ministers and consuls maintain formal relations between the two countries as elsewhere, an army of 250,000 private individuals continuously engages in those daily social and business contacts that are the warp and woof of mutual understanding. The scale is without parallel elsewhere. It is, of course, a far cry from political and economic fusion, as the shrinkage in border passages of Canadian workmen under the depression shows.* But to the question for what does the boundary count in the ordinary personal intercourse of the two peoples, the present discussion will be at least a contribution towards an objective answer, and an indication of how a fuller one may be obtained.

APPENDIX TO THE ADDENDUM

(1) SUMMARY STATISTICS OF MOVEMENTS ACROSS THE BORDER

There are considerable difficulties in the way of an exact calculation of the day-to-day movements across the Canada-United States border, as an enumeration of the available data will show. The main source is, of course,

---

*The number on daily passes according to United States immigration reports, fell from 10,070 in 1931 to 4,193 in 1932, to 3,404 in 1933 and to 2,642 in 1934.

The rhetoric upon the whole subject of the boundary is, of course, immense and familiar: a late variant is by Johannes Stoye, *The British Empire; its Structure and its Problems* (London, [1936]), p. 314: "The impulse for the Anglo-American rapprochement will be provided by the frontier between Canada and the U.S.A., which is three thousand miles long, and is a straight line that might have been drawn with a ruler and is justified by no tradition, by no geographical exigencies, by no economic advantages and therefore by nothing at all. An amalgamation of the two countries is out of the question. But an abandonment of the present rivalry is becoming a pressing necessity. It will take the form of a political collaboration of a higher order such as has never yet existed anywhere in the world, and it will be founded on the idea of English co-operation, which we have seen to be the foundation of the British Empire and will likewise serve an Anglo-Saxon Empire as support and foot-stool."

the immigration records of the two countries. An "immigrant" is a person who intends to settle permanently in the country of destination, but the records also include citizens returning after residence for some time in the other country, also students and diplomats. The numbers of these are reasonably well known. In addition, however, the immigration and customs authorities record the periodical "crossings" of workmen, tourists, border dwellers visiting back and forth, etc. As previously stated, these records, for the most part, do not distinguish "persons," e.g., one person crossing the border daily for a year is recorded as 365 crossings.

Many of the data of the respective Immigration Departments can be used to check one another. Thus, Canada records the number of "persons returning," i.e. Canadians who have crossed the border in the year and come back, while the United States Department refers to the southward crossing of these as "aliens crossing." Canada records "tourists" coming in; the United States refers to these on their return as "citizens returning." There are a few supplementary materials such as the annual reports of the two countries dealing with the tourist trade as an element in the balance of international payments—also the official reports on international bridge, ferry, and tunnel operations, which draw on independent sources. Allowing for possible errors and omissions, the various data corroborate one another sufficiently to enable a fairly accurate calculation of border crossings. For purposes of reference the available data are assembled in Statements A and B.

Statement A presents the known details of total crossings over the Canada-United States border. Owing to the difficulty of patrolling so extended a boundary, there are undoubtedly some additional crossings, but the immigration and customs services are vigilant, and it may be assumed that the unrecorded crossings are so few that, for practical purposes, they may be disregarded.

Statement B shows the movement of persons who may be presumed to be living near the border. With the material at present available, it is impossible to delimit the movements of particular classes of border crossers to persons living within rigidly defined areas. It is a matter of official record, however, that almost 80 p.c. of motorists entering Canada on 60-day permits come from the States bordering on Canada, and, as the majority of one-day motorists and of various other classes such as pedestrians, ferry travellers, etc., undoubtedly come from areas close to the border, it is safe to say that more than 80 p.c. of the "over the border" movement of Americans is drawn from the States bordering on Canada or from 36 p.c. of the United States population. As a matter of fact, it is probably drawn from a much more restricted area and population.

Statistical data concerning the distance of penetration into the country visited are also incomplete. It is apparent that certain classes, such as one-day motorists, pedestrians, ferry travellers, etc., which account for a substantial proportion of the total in either direction, cannot penetrate very far. Certain other classes, such as the holders of active or intermittent passes, definitely live close to the border and visit adjacent points for short periods of time. The same is true of large numbers of other persons who cross to attend theatres in border cities, visit relatives or friends, attend schools, shop, etc.

It is clear that pre-war restraints on crossing, including not only legal but considerations over the entire range of personal predilection, were small, if they existed at all. There is no evidence that the Canadian borderer does not consider the American as his neighbour in much the same light as a Canadian situated at the same distance. The record, in fact, indicates attraction rather than restriction.

A—*Total Movements Across the Canada-United States Border: Calendar Year 1931*

Item	CANADA	Maritime Provinces	Quebec	Ontario	Prairie Provinces	British Columbia[1]
FROM UNITED STATES TO CANADA						
ALL CROSSINGS	19,377,880	2,156,977	2,114,144	13,998,531	399,107	709,121
Immigrants to Canada	15,195	1,369	3,288	7,120	2,212	1,206
Returned Canadians[2]	20,352	4,138	4,532	7,680	915	3,087
Motorists Entering Canada on Tourist Permit—For one day	8,598,730	602,690	611,925	7,086,068	190,912	107,135
Not exceeding 60 days	4,409,259	181,986	1,202,244	2,571,285	74,004	379,740
Not exceeding 6 months	2,232	216	1,251	594	48	123
Travellers by rail or steamer	1,177,429	70,646	153,066	706,457	47,097	200,163
Crossings by persons holding United States identification cards—[3] Active	405,912	....	....	405,912	....	....
Intermittent	2,203,344	....	....	2,203,344	....	....
Other crossings[4]	2,545,427	1,295,932	137,838	1,010,071	83,919	17,667
FROM CANADA TO UNITED STATES						
ALL CROSSINGS	10,802,454	1,786,579	733,478	7,433,658	209,781	638,958
Emigrants from Canada	14,541	1,422	4,031	4,810	3,305	973
Motorists entering United States on tourist permit	1,610,565	28,311	397,728	702,231	76,299	405,996
Travellers by rail or steamer	346,629	51,995	76,258	155,983	13,865	48,528
Crossings by persons holding United States identification cards—[3] Active	2,691,000	....	....	2,691,000	....	....
Intermittent	913,536	....	....	913,536	....	....
Other crossings[4]	5,226,183	1,704,851	255,461	2,966,098	116,312	183,461

[1]Includes Yukon. [2]Persons who had settled in the United States but returned to Canada to take up permanent residence. [3]Active crossings are by those who cross the border daily or at least 4 times a week on an average; intermittent crossings are by those who cross the border not more than 3 times a week on an average. [4]Include pedestrians, travellers by ferry, aeroplane, local motorists, etc.

B—*Crossings Over the Canada-United States Border by Persons Presumed to be Living Near the Border: Calendar Year 1931*

Item	CANADA	Maritime Provinces	Quebec	Ontario	Prairie Provinces	British Columbia
			FROM UNITED STATES TO CANADA			
United States Border Population (Border Township)	4,074,000	63,000	111,000	3,681,000	140,000	79,000
ALL CROSSINGS	13,753,413	1,898,622	749,763	10,705,395	274,831	124,802
Motorists on one-day tourist permit	8,598,730	602,690	611,925	7,086,068	190,912	107,135
Persons Holding United States Identification Cards—[1]						
Active—						
Number of persons	1,301	....	....	1,301	....	....
Estimated crossings	405,912	....	....	405,912	....	....
Intermittent—						
Number of persons	21,186	....	....	21,186	....	....
Estimated crossings	2,203,344	....	....	2,203,344	....	....
Other crossings [2]	2,545,427	1,295,932	137,838	1,010,071	83,919	17,667
			FROM CANADA TO UNITED STATES			
Canadian Border Population (Border Townships)	552,110	29,413	39,340	348,741	31,864	102,752
ALL CROSSINGS	8,830,719	1,704,851	255,461	6,570,634	116,312	183,461
Persons Holding United States Identification Cards—[1]						
Active—						
Number of persons	8,625	....	....	8,625	....	....
Estimated crossings	2,691,000	....	....	2,691,000	....	....
Intermittent—						
Number of persons	8,784	....	....	8,784	....	....
Estimated crossings	913,536	....	....	913,536	....	....
Other crossings [2]	5,226,183	1,704,851	255,461	2,966,098	116,312	183,461

[1] Active crossers are those who cross the border daily or at least 4 times a week on an average—the number of crossings shown was estimated by allowing 6 crossings per person per week; intermittent crossers are those who cross the border not more than 3 times a week on an average. The number of crossings shown was estimated by allowing two crossings per person per week. [2] Include pedestrians, travellers by ferry, aeroplane, local motorists, etc.

C—*Canadian-Born Males Marrying American-Born Brides Compared with those Marrying Brides Born in Other Provinces: 1929-33*

NOTE.—The figures in italics are those of largest intermarriage.

Province of Birth and Residence of Groom Marrying Out of Province	Number of Grooms	Birthplace of Bride other than Province of Groom						
		United States	Prince Edward Island	Nova Scotia	New Brunswick	Quebec	Ontario	Manitoba
CANADA[1]	28,249	5,059	183	775	656	2,121	2,131	1,413
Prince Edward Island	145	58	......	*31*	9	9	6	4
Nova Scotia	1,283	259	64	......	*199*	52	33	8
New Brunswick	1,218	357	67	*299*	......	208	25	8
Quebec	4,096	1,160	14	103	244	......	*982*	45
Ontario	12,401	1,728	12	218	154	*1,600*	......	503
Manitoba	2,496	249	1	16	11	80	352	......
Saskatchewan	2,312	477	11	18	8	64	327	*468*
Alberta	2,174	554	6	42	14	70	195	152
British Columbia	2,124	217	8	48	17	38	211	225

	Birthplace of Bride other than Province of Groom—concluded			Eligible Female Population, Census 1931[2]		Ratio of American-Born Brides to American-Born Eligibles	Ratio of Neighbouring Province-Born Brides to Neighbouring Province-Born Eligibles
	Saskatchewan	Alberta	British Columbia	Born in United States	Born in Neighbouring Province with largest number of Brides		
CANADA[1]	1,249	621	264	41,632	42,433	......	......
Prince Edward Island	5	2	1	182	187	31.9	16.6
Nova Scotia	6	15	13	1,051	1,381	24.6	14.4
New Brunswick	6	9	5	1,083	1,358	33.0	22.0
Quebec	25	6	9	7,838	9,739	14.8	10.1
Ontario	373	178	101	10,191	15,170	17.0	10.5
Manitoba	*401*	64	27	2,281	2,735	10.9	14.7
Saskatchewan	......	74	27	7,354	5,365	6.5	8.7
Alberta	*231*	......	81	7,586	2,623	7.3	8.8
British Columbia	202	*273*	......	4,066	3,875	5.3	7.0

[1]Exclusive of Yukon and Northwest Territories.   [2]Single, 15 years of age or over, widowed and divorced.

(2) SUMMARY STATISTICS OF IMMIGRATION FROM THE UNITED STATES TO CANADA, 1908-31

The first three Statements, D to F, show figures of immigration from the United States to Canada, analysed from three different standpoints, namely, by main national groups, by provinces of declared destination, and by declared occupations. The Statements cover the fiscal years ended March 31, 1908 to 1931, inclusive. Figures showing United States citizens, British nationals, and others are available from 1904 to 1907 on a different fiscal-year basis, but prior to 1904 only the total immigration from the United States is available. A fourth Statement is added showing the number of

Canadian citizens returned to Canada from the United States during the fiscal years ended March 31, 1925 to 1931, inclusive; no earlier record of this movement is available.

D—*Immigration from the United States to Canada, Years Ended March 31, 1908-31*

Year Ended March 31—	Numbers				Percentages of Totals		
	Total	United States Citizens	British Nationals	Others	United States Citizens	British Nationals	Others
1908..............	53,152	31,411	2,674	19,067	59.2	5.0	35.8
1909..............	54,294	33,474	2,894	17,926	61.7	5.3	33.0
1910..............	91,048	65,190	3,662	22,196	71.7	4.0	24.3
1911..............	104,884	77,353	5,007	22,524	73.8	4.8	21.4
1912..............	114,326	91,840	6,236	16,250	80.4	5.4	14.2
1913..............	119,418	92,061	7,398	19,959	77.1	6.2	16.7
1914..............	89,892	74,745	6,374	8,773	83.2	7.1	9.7
1915..............	41,768	34.745	3,541	3,482	83.2	8.5	8.3
1916..............	25,853	21,370	2,796	1,687	82.7	10.8	6.5
1917..............	51,143	42,261	3,324	5,558	82.6	6.5	10.9
1918..............	58,185	47,818	3,444	6,923	82.2	5.9	11.9
1919..............	31,955	28,280	1,725	1,950	88.5	5.4	6.1
1920..............	40,728	36,628	2,250	1,850	89.9	5.6	4.5
1921..............	38,310	33,891	2,768	1,651	88.5	7.2	4.3
1922..............	21,670	18,782	1,825	1,063	86.7	8.4	4.9
1923..............	16,566	14,095	1,641	830	85.1	9.9	5.0
1924..............	17,211	14,928	1,478	805	86.8	8.6	4.6
1925..............	15,818	13,171	1,794	853	83.4	11.2	5.4
1926..............	18,778	15,442	2,251	1,085	82.2	12.0	5.8
1927..............	21,025	17,820	2,239	966	84.8	10.6	4.6
1928..............	25,007	21,260	2,696	1,051	85.0	10.8	4.2
1929..............	30,560	26,539	3,061	960	86.9	10.0	3.1
1930..............	30,727	26,751	3,121	855	87.1	10.2	2.7
1931..............	24,280	20,723	2,938	619	85.4	12.1	2.5

E—*Immigration from the United States to Canada, by Provinces of Declared Destination, Years Ended March 31, 1908-31*

Year Ended March 31—	Total[1]	Maritime Provinces	Quebec	Ontario	Prairie Provinces	British Columbia
	No.	No.	No.	No.	No.	No.
1908..............	53,152	48	666	739	43,610	7,907
1909..............	54,294	304	1,880	2,082	38,356	11,644
1910..............	91,048	1,381	5,591	8,409	58,906	16,599
1911..............	104,884	1,710	5,993	10,978	59,919	26,234
1912..............	114,326	1,694	7,534	18,085	65,845	21,167

[1]Includes other immigrants, mostly to Yukon.

E—*Immigration from the United States to Canada, by Provinces of Declared Destination, Years Ended March 31, 1908-31—concluded*

Year Ended March 31—	Total[1]	Maritime Provinces	Quebec	Ontario	Prairie Provinces	British Columbia
	No.	No.	No.	No.	No.	No.
1913	119,418	2,199	8,570	20,503	61,212	26,875
1914	89,892	1,421	7,981	16,791	51,066	12,603
1915	41,768	1,023	4,851	9,171	23,750	2,973
1916	25,853	828	2,778	8,137	12,834	1,273
1917	51,143	797	5,251	18,613	23,161	3,024
1918	58,185	781	3,147	18,576	32,182	3,274
1919	31,955	617	2,109	6,846	20,068	2,219
1920	40,728	688	2,627	9,468	24,557	3,258
1921	38,310	718	3,379	10,713	19,804	3,601
1922	21,670	470	1,683	6,306	11,549	1,570
1923	16,566	308	1,465	4,476	8,751	1,456
1924	17,211	412	2,027	5,337	7,608	1,794
1925	15,818	299	2,096	4,853	6,589	1,953
1926	18,778	375	2,499	5,202	8,543	2,107
1927	21,025	387	2,907	5,835	9,539	2,316
1928	25,007	389	3,834	9,062	9,237	2,465
1929	30,560	761	4,585	12,464	10,130	2,591
1930	30,727	1,214	5,109	13,041	8,520	2,770
1931	24,280	1,495	4,719	11,322	4,980	1,754

[1]Includes other immigrants, mostly to Yukon.

F—*Immigration from the United States to Canada, by Declared Occupations, Years Ended March 31, 1908-31*

Year Ended March 31—	Total	Farming	Labour	Mechanics	Trading	Mining	Female Domestics	Other
	No.	No.	No.	No.	No.	No.	No.	No.
1908	53,152	43,905	4,619	2,133	1,189	953	57	296
1909	54,294	39,444	6,694	3,944	1,779	1,035	160	1,238
1910	91,048	58,364	13,412	8,381	4,475	2,293	595	3,528
1911	104,884	58,967	21,288	9,919	3,479	2,645	1,057	7,529
1912	114,326	54,793	36,342	8,692	2,750	2,483	1,096	8,170
1913	119,418	41,826	35,488	19,815	4,501	1,822	1,733	14,233
1914	89,892	34,726	14,438	16,290	4,507	1,707	1,725	16,499
1915	41,768	19,092	3,733	8,372	1,583	461	954	7,573
1916	25,853	10,272	2,024	5,965	893	224	619	5,856
1917	51,143	19,100	6,914	12,612	2,145	765	858	8,749

F—*Immigration from the United States to Canada, by Declared Occupations,
Years Ended March 31, 1908-31—concluded*

Year Ended March 31—	Total	Farming	Labour	Mechanics	Trading	Mining	Female Domestics	Other
	No.	No.	No.	No.	No.	No.	No.	No.
1918	58,185	24,850	10,997	8,280	2,308	640	1,008	10,102
1919	31,955	15,734	2,195	4,235	1,497	332	804	7,158
1920	40,728	20,344	2,297	7,241	1,437	382	693	8,334
1921	38,310	15,862	4,590	6,659	2,487	487	713	7,512
1922	21,670	10,934	1,172	2,147	1,414	145	530	5,328
1923	16,566	9,027	648	1,422	867	200	472	3,930
1924	17,211	7,421	1,753	1,778	1,887	248	441	3,733
1925	15,818	6,712	1,307	1,774	1,641	202	363	3,819
1926	18,778	7,953	1,675	1,904	1,474	149	506	5,117
1927	21,025	8,127	1,752	2,475	1,526	168	538	6,439
1928	25,007	8,361	2,323	3,260	2,430	185	516	7,932
1929	30,560	9,040	2,844	5,290	3,461	255	626	9,044
1930	30,727	7,169	2,973	5,517	3,861	186	634	10,387
1931	24,280	5,864	1,079	3,084	3,022	58	636	10,537

G—*Canadian Citizens Returned to Canada from the United States, Years
Ended March 31, 1925-31*

Year Ended March 31—	Numbers				Percentages of Totals		
	Total	Canadian-Born	British-Born Outside Canada	Canadian Naturalized	Canadian-Born	British-Born Outside Canada	Canadian Naturalized
1925	43,775	36,473	4,487	2,815	83.3	10.3	6.4
1926	47,221	40,246	4,102	2,873	85.2	8.7	6.1
1927	56,957	49,255	5,326	2,376	86.5	9.4	4.1
1928	39,887	35,137	3,280	1,470	88.1	8.2	3.7
1929	33,798	30,008	2,795	995	88.8	8.3	2.9
1930	29,830	26,959	2,030	841	90.4	6.8	2.8
1931	30,209	26,811	2,111	1,287	88.7	7.0	4.3

PART II

STATISTICAL ANALYSIS OF THE AMERICAN-BORN IN CANADA

CHAPTER I

BASIC STATISTICS OF THE AMERICAN-BORN POPULATION OF CANADA—PERIOD OF IMMIGRATION—THE AMERICAN STOCK IN CANADA

THE broad statistics of the American-born population of Canada are presented in Table I, based on: the Dominion decennial censuses since 1871 (quinquennial for the Prairie Provinces since 1906); censuses of Upper and Lower Canada, Nova Scotia, New Brunswick, and Prince Edward Island taken in 1851 and in 1861; and various still earlier enumerations that included birthplace.*

In 1841, a round century ago, the American-born in Canada were estimated at 49,000, of whom 32,809 were in Ontario and the remainder mainly in Nova Scotia, New Brunswick and the Eastern Townships of Quebec. Ten years later, the figure had risen to 63,000, with little relative change in distribution. Between 1861 and 1871 the number dropped from 70,000 to 65,000 in a movement common to all the foreign-born population of Canada. From 1871 to 1911, however, succeeding decades showed increases; from 1901 to 1911 the number more than doubled as a result, chiefly but not entirely, of the movement to the Prairie Provinces, the eastern provinces increasing about 16 p.c., or about the same as the general natural increase. For the decade 1911-21 the increases were not as pronounced, the rise being from 303,680 to 374,022, but it was not until 1921-31 that the figures showed a net decline, 344,574 being the total for the 1931 survey of the Dominion. There is evidence that this decline was due to a heavy outward movement from the West during 1921-26, partly counterbalanced by an inflow during 1926-31 into Eastern Canada. The latter movement has continued, and represents in large part the 'return' of the children of Canadian-born parents in the United States.

*For an account of these early enumerations, see Volume I of the 1931 Census of Canada, pp. 133-53, which extends and completes the data on the subject first brought together in Volume IV of the Census of 1871.

TABLE I

American-Born Population of Canada: 1817-1931

Year	CANADA	Prince Edward Island	Nova Scotia	New Brunswick	Quebec	Ontario
	No.	No.	No.	No.	No.	No.
1817			262			
1841-2	49,000[1]	150[2]				32,809
1844					11,946	
1848		540[2]				32,579
1851-2	63,000[1]				12,482	43,732
1861	70,000[1]	330[2]	1,950	3,050[2]	13,648	50,758
1870						
1871	65,000[1]	350[2]	2,239	4,088	14,714	43,406
1881	77,753	609	3,004	5,108	19,415	45,454
1891	80,915	582	3,238	4,278	18,524	42,702
1901	127,899	764	4,394	5,477	28,405	44,175
1906						
1911	303,680	829	4,802	5,766	29,843	55,676
1916						
1921	374,022	1,215	7,016	8,268	42,122	70,729
1926						
1931	344,574	1,380	7,222	8,794	49,406	72,525

Year	Manitoba	Saskatchewan	Alberta	British Columbia	Yukon	Northwest Territories
	No.	No.	No.	No.	No.	No.
1817						
1841-2		5[3]				
1844		10[3]				
1848						
1851-2						
1861						
1870	166					
1871						
1881	1,752	116		2,295		
1891	3,063	710	1,251	6,567		
1901	6,922	2,705	11,172	17,164	6,707	14
1906	12,023	35,464	43,251			
1911	16,328	69,628	81,357	37,548	1,891	12
1916	18,274	87,907	91,674			
1921	21,644	87,617	99,879	34,926	557	46
1926	18,077	75,479	78,167			
1931	17,903	73,008	78,959	34,706	526	145

[1] Estimated but believed to be within 2,000. [2] Estimates based on the total number of foreign-born and on the proportion American-born of the total foreign-born at the nearest census. [3] Approximate.

Period of Immigration

It is interesting to marshal the census data by period of immigration of American-born in Canada. Space restricts this to the latest census. Table II gives the figures for 1931 classified by sex and by rural and urban composition, while Tables III and IV give percentage figures as an aid to interpretation.

In comparing American-born with the total immigrant population of 1931, it will be observed that the former have been longer in the country; over 43 p.c. of the American-born came in prior to 1911 compared with 38 p.c. of the total immigrant population. The influence of the War of 1914-18 is plainly indicated in the figures for the decade 1911-21; 12.44 p.c. of the American-born arrived in 1916-20, and only 8.50 p.c. of the total immigrants. The drop in immigration after 1921, however, was more accentuated among the American-born; from 1926-31, the percentage for the latter was 15.38, which when studied in conjunction with the data on ages and nativity (see pp. 62 and 64) permits the deduction that recent immigration from the United States has consisted largely of the children of Canadian-born parents. Further evidence of this is seen in the fact that a larger proportion of these American-born immigrants settled in the eastern provinces; in Prince Edward Island, for example, the percentage who arrived in 1926-30 was 33.53, compared with a percentage of 8.10 for Saskatchewan.*

*Other phenomena associated with period of immigration, especially as regards differential immigration, are discussed in Chapter III.

Table II

American-Born, Rural and Urban, by Sex, Classified by Period of Immigration, Canada: 1931

Note.—Figures exclude repatriated Canadians.

Province and Period of Immigration	Total			Rural			Urban		
	Both Sexes	Male	Female	Both Sexes	Male	Female	Both Sexes	Male	Female
	No.	No.	No.	No.	No.	No.	No.	No.	No.
Canada [1]	344,574	175,140	169,434	179,036	98,991	80,045	165,538	76,149	89,389
1931 (5 mos.)	5,115	2,598	2,517	2,470	1,319	1,151	2,645	1,279	1,366
1926-30	52,704	26,455	26,249	23,893	12,537	11,356	28,811	13,918	14,893
1921-25	28,787	13,906	14,881	14,091	7,282	6,809	14,696	6,624	8,072
1916-20	42,634	20,768	21,866	24,242	12,539	11,703	18,392	8,229	10,163
1911-15	64,294	32,907	31,387	35,827	20,007	15,820	28,467	12,900	15,567
1901-10	102,825	55,037	47,788	59,163	34,792	24,371	43,662	20,245	23,417
Before 1901	46,347	22,614	23,733	18,620	10,156	8,464	27,727	12,458	15,269

[1]Totals include immigrants for whom year of immigration was not reported.

TABLE II—continued

American-Born, Rural and Urban, by Sex, Classified by Period of Immigration, Canada: 1931

NOTE:—Figures exclude repatriated Canadians.

Province and Period of Immigration	Total			Rural			Urban		
	Both Sexes	Male	Female	Both Sexes	Male	Female	Both Sexes	Male	Female
	No.	No.	No.	No.	No.	No.	No.	No.	No.
Prince Edward Island[1]..	1,380	680	700	999	498	501	381	182	199
1931 (5 mos.)...............	29	10	19	25	9	16	4	1	3
1926-30.........................	453	232	221	335	173	162	118	59	59
1921-25.........................	149	73	76	109	54	55	40	19	21
1916-20.........................	189	96	93	148	79	69	41	17	24
1911-15.........................	169	78	91	120	55	65	49	23	26
1901-10.........................	167	78	89	117	51	66	50	27	23
Before 1901..................	195	104	91	129	73	56	66	31	35
Nova Scotia[1]..................	7,222	3,355	3,867	3,862	1,859	2,003	3,360	1,496	1,864
1931 (5 mos.)...............	249	133	116	170	96	74	79	37	42
1926-30.........................	2,069	975	1,094	1,220	571	649	849	404	445
1921-25.........................	712	350	362	411	219	192	301	131	170
1916-20.........................	767	331	436	446	216	230	321	115	206
1911-15.........................	833	363	470	388	170	218	445	193	252
1901-10.........................	1,140	515	625	493	227	266	647	288	359
Before 1901..................	1,383	664	719	702	351	351	681	313	368
New Brunswick[1]...........	8,794	4,037	4,757	5,615	2,633	2,982	3,179	1,404	1,775
1931 (5 mos.)...............	237	124	113	142	67	75	95	57	38
1926-30.........................	2,246	1,099	1,147	1,530	754	776	716	345	371
1921-25.........................	948	436	512	594	284	310	354	152	202
1916-20.........................	1,053	439	614	667	291	376	386	148	238
1911-15.........................	1,070	496	574	662	301	361	408	195	213
1901-10.........................	1,450	607	843	927	408	519	523	199	324
Before 1901..................	1,747	820	927	1,074	524	550	673	296	377
Quebec[1].........................	49,406	23,247	26,159	11,588	5,881	5,707	37,818	17,366	20,452
1931 (5 mos.)...............	1,075	507	568	272	140	132	803	367	436
1926-30.........................	10,552	5,175	5,377	2,611	1,349	1,262	7,941	3,826	4,115
1921-25.........................	4,876	2,268	2,608	1,155	572	583	3,721	1,696	2,025
1916-20.........................	4,651	2,129	2,522	1,018	472	546	3,633	1,657	1,976
1911-15.........................	6,694	3,119	3,575	1,356	716	640	5,338	2,403	2,935
1901-10.........................	10,124	4,696	5,428	2,174	1,067	1,107	7,950	3,629	4,321
Before 1901..................	11,178	5,233	5,945	2,946	1,525	1,421	8,232	3,708	4,524
Ontario[1]..........................	72,525	34,017	38,508	21,462	10,749	10,713	51,063	23,268	27,795
1931 (5 mos.)...............	2,017	1,033	984	896	480	416	1,121	553	568
1926-30.........................	16,697	8,199	8,498	5,022	2,588	2,434	11,675	5,611	6,064
1921-25.........................	7,828	3,682	4,146	2,247	1,110	1,137	5,581	2,572	3,009
1916-20.........................	8,363	3,887	4,476	2,387	1,162	1,225	5,976	2,725	3,251
1911-15.........................	10,214	4,830	5,384	2,851	1,451	1,400	7,363	3,379	3,984
1901-10.........................	12,480	5,717	6,763	3,502	1,724	1,778	8,978	3,993	4,985
Before 1901..................	14,388	6,436	7,952	4,434	2,180	2,254	9,954	4,256	5,698

[1]Totals include immigrants for whom year of immigration was not reported.

TABLE II—continued

American-Born, Rural and Urban, by Sex, Classified by Period of Immigration, Canada: 1931

NOTE:—Figures exclude repatriated Canadians.

Province and Period of Immigration	Total			Rural			Urban		
	Both Sexes	Male	Female	Both Sexes	Male	Female	Both Sexes	Male	Female
	No.	No.	No.	No.	No.	No.	No.	No.	No.
Manitoba[1]	17,903	9,027	8,876	9,483	5,148	4,335	8,420	3,879	4,541
1931 (5 mos.)	182	96	86	78	40	38	104	56	48
1926-30	2,264	1,192	1,072	1,106	610	496	1,158	582	576
1921-25	1,511	743	768	881	454	427	630	289	341
1916-20	2,832	1,425	1,407	1,779	920	859	1,053	505	548
1911-15	3,155	1,571	1,584	1,456	801	655	1,699	770	929
1901-10	5,001	2,504	2,497	2,613	1,453	1,160	2,388	1,051	1,337
Before 1901	2,860	1,468	1,392	1,526	857	669	1,334	611	723
Saskatchewan[1]	73,008	39,664	33,344	52,965	30,178	22,787	20,043	9,486	10,557
1931 (5 mos.)	288	146	142	207	106	101	81	40	41
1926-30	5,878	3,085	2,793	4,212	2,258	1,954	1,666	827	839
1921-25	4,640	2,316	2,324	3,506	1,813	1,693	1,134	503	631
1916-20	8,980	4,386	4,594	6,789	3,477	3,312	2,191	909	1,282
1911-15	19,077	10,349	8,728	14,145	8,071	6,074	4,932	2,278	2,654
1901-10	30,697	17,509	13,188	22,180	13,368	8,812	8,517	4,141	4,376
Before 1901	3,039	1,676	1,363	1,830	1,048	782	1,209	628	581
Alberta[1]	78,959	43,166	35,793	55,824	32,286	23,538	23,135	10,880	12,255
1931 (5 mos.)	410	216	194	309	172	137	101	44	57
1926-30	7,640	4,021	3,619	5,495	2,979	2,516	2,145	1,042	1,103
1921-25	4,882	2,459	2,423	3,617	1,949	1,668	1,265	510	755
1916-20	11,691	6,025	5,666	8,904	4,777	4,127	2,787	1,248	1,539
1911-15	16,839	9,032	7,807	11,849	6,753	5,096	4,990	2,279	2,711
1901-10	31,804	18,247	13,557	22,243	13,612	8,631	9,561	4,635	4,926
Before 1901	5,558	3,105	2,453	3,306	1,995	1,311	2,252	1,110	1,142
British Columbia[1]	34,706	17,474	17,232	16,809	9,448	7,361	17,897	8,026	9,871
1931 (5 mos.)	605	313	292	366	205	161	239	108	131
1926-30	4,843	2,437	2,406	2,331	1,233	1,098	2,512	1,204	1,308
1921-25	3,201	1,549	1,652	1,556	817	739	1,645	732	913
1916-20	4,080	2,036	2,044	2,086	1,135	951	1,994	901	1,093
1911-15	6,200	3,044	3,156	2,973	1,673	1,300	3,227	1,371	1,856
1901-10	9,853	5,098	4,755	4,869	2,851	2,018	4,984	2,247	2,737
Before 1901	5,798	2,944	2,854	2,549	1,499	1,050	3,249	1,445	1,804
Yukon[1]	526	365	161	284	203	81	242	162	80
1931 (5 mos.)	23	20	3	5	4	1	18	16	2
1926-30	62	40	22	31	22	9	31	18	13
1921-25	40	30	10	15	10	5	25	20	5
1916-20	28	14	14	18	10	8	10	4	6
1911-15	43	25	18	27	16	11	16	9	7
1901-10	109	66	43	45	31	14	64	35	29
Before 1901	171	142	29	94	82	12	77	60	17

[1]Totals include immigrants for whom year of immigration was not reported.

THE AMERICAN-BORN IN CANADA

TABLE II—concluded

American-Born, Rural and Urban, by Sex, Classified by Period of Immigration, Canada: 1931

NOTE:—Figures exclude repatriated Canadians.

Province and Period of Immigration	Total			Rural			Urban		
	Both Sexes	Male	Female	Both Sexes	Male	Female	Both Sexes	Male	Female
	No.	No.	No.	No.	No.	No.	No.	No.	No.
Northwest Territories [1]..	145	108	37	145	108	37	......	......	......
1931 (5 mos.)...............	......	......	......	......	......	......	......	......	......
1926-30........................	......	......	......	......	......	......	......	......	......
1921-25........................	......	......	......	......	......	......	......	......	......
1916-20........................	......	......	......	......	......	......	......	......	......
1911-15........................	......	......	......	......	......	......	......	......	......
1901-10........................	......	......	......	......	......	......	......	......	......
Before 1901...............	30	22	8	30	22	8	......	......	......

[1]Totals include immigrants for whom year of immigration was not reported.

TABLE III

Percentage Distribution of Total Immigrant Population and Total American-Born and of Foreign-Born and American-Born 21 Years of Age or Over, by Sex and by Rural and Urban, Classified by Period of Immigration: 1931

NOTE.—Figures are for those immigrants who stated year of immigration only, and are exclusive of repatriated Canadians.

Period of Immigration	Total Immigrant Population [1]			Total American-Born				
	Total	Male	Female	Total	Rural	Urban	Male	Female
TOTALS........................	100.00	100.00	100.00	100.00	100.00	100.00	100.00	100.00
1931 (5 mos.).............	0.52	0.45	0.60	1.49	1.39	1.61	1.49	1.49
1926-30.......................	19.85	20.96	18.42	15.38	13.40	17.52	15.18	15.59
1921-25.......................	12.20	11.60	12.96	8.40	7.90	8.94	7.98	8.84
1916-20.......................	8.50	7.04	10.38	12.44	13.60	11.19	11.92	12.98
1911-15.......................	20.63	19.92	21.55	18.76	20.09	17.32	18.88	18.64
1901-10.......................	27.19	28.78	25.15	30.00	33.18	26.56	31.58	28.37
Before 1901.................	11.11	11.24	10.94	13.52	10.44	16.87	12.98	14.09

Period of Immigration	Foreign-Born [1] 21 Years or Over			American-Born 21 Years or Over				
	Total	Male	Female	Total	Rural	Urban	Male	Female
TOTALS........................	100.00	100.00	100.00	100.00	100.00	100.00	100.00	100.00
1931 (5 mos.).............	0.40	0.30	0.56	0.91	0.72	1.09	0.91	0.88
1926-30.......................	21.46	23.49	18.32	8.46	6.76	10.31	8.14	8.79
1921-25.......................	9.86	9.48	10.45	5.69	5.15	6.29	5.17	6.23
1916-20.......................	26.12	25.68	26.79	10.15	11.06	9.15	9.51	10.81
1911-15.......................				20.06	21.58	18.41	20.22	19.90
1901-10.......................	30.30	30.10	30.62	37.69	41.59	33.43	39.69	35.63
Before 1901.................	11.86	10.96	13.24	17.05	13.14	21.32	16.36	17.76

[1]British-born is included in "Total Immigrant Population" but is not included in "Foreign-Born 21 Years or Over."

TABLE IV

Percentage Distribution of Total American-Born for Each Province,
Classified by Period of Immigration: 1931

NOTE.—Figures are for those immigrants only who stated year of immigration, and are exclusive of repatriated Canadians.

Period of Immigration	American-Born								
	P.E.I.	N.S.	N.B.	Que.	Ont.	Man.	Sask.	Alta.	B.C.
TOTALS	100.00	100.00	100.00	100.00	100.00	100.00	100.00	100.00	100.00
1931 (5 mos.)	2.15	3.48	2.71	2.19	2.80	1.02	0.40	0.52	1.75
1926-30	33.53	28.92	25.67	21.47	23.19	12.72	8.10	9.69	14.01
1921-25	11.03	9.95	10.83	9.92	10.87	8.49	6.39	6.19	9.26
1916-20	13.99	10.72	12.03	9.46	11.62	15.91	12.37	14.83	11.80
1911-15	12.51	11.65	12.23	13.62	14.19	17.72	26.28	21.36	17.93
1901-10	12.36	15.94	16.57	20.60	17.34	28.09	42.28	40.35	28.49
Before 1901	14.43	19.33	19.96	22.74	19.99	16.06	4.19	7.05	16.77

THE AMERICAN STOCK

The United States Census records the number of persons of Canadian stock, the term including those native Americans who are children of Canadian-born parents. No similar compilation has been made in the Canadian Census, which includes all foreign parents in a single category. Through the medium of vital statistics, however, the number of births to American-born parents (births having one or both parents American-born) are available since 1921. (The figures do not cover Quebec prior to 1926, but a close estimate can be made for the whole of Canada by considering the number of births in Quebec from 1921 to 1926 as constant, which, there is reason to believe, is closely in accord with the facts.) By applying the 1931 life tables (the probabilities of children, born alive in each succeeding year, living till 1931) the probable number surviving in 1931 is obtained.

Omitting details of the calculation, the data of which, however, are given in the accompanying tables, the number of Canadian-born of American stock in 1931 is found to be 474,200. Adding the 344,574 American-born, a total American stock of 818,774 is obtained. The figure does not allow for emigration, but as this was probably not large, it may be accepted as giving a fair idea of the population in Canada who were of American birth or parentage in 1931.

TABLE V

American and Total Foreign Stock Born in Canada, by Certain Age Groups: 1931

Item	All Ages	0-9 Years	10-20 Years	21 Years or Over
	No.	No.	No.	No.
Total Canadian-Born—				
Number..............................	8,069,261	2,123,065	2,108,629	3,837,567
American Stock—				
Number................................	474,200	185,500	177,900	110,800
Percentage of total.............	....	8.74	8.44	2.89
Total Foreign Stock—				
Number..................	1,118,616	437,530	419,649	261,437
Percentage of total..............	....	20.61	19.90	6.81

Some interesting facts on the cognate subject of American-Canadian intermarriage (at least in so far as fertile marriages are concerned) are given in Table VI. It will be seen that 20.4 p.c. of the surviving children of American-born parentage under 10 years of age in 1931 had both parents American-born; 30.2 p.c. had the mother American-born and the father Canadian-born, while 28.9 p.c. had the father American-born and the mother Canadian-born. While the proportion of children with mother American-born and father Canadian-born was higher than the proportion with father American-born and mother Canadian-born up to 1928, the situation was reversed in 1929 and 1930. This is probably connected, in some degree, with the sex distribution at different periods. Thus from the period of immigration figures, the female immigrants of American-born exceeded the male during the years 1916-25, but the situation was reversed before and after that period.

In 1931 there were more children under 10 with American-born mothers than with American-born fathers, although the number of American-born males in Canada was greater than the number of American-born females. This was particularly noticeable in the case of children with American-born mothers and European-born fathers; these were double the number having American-born fathers and European-born mothers. The same held where the father was Asiatic because of the ban on the immigration of oriental females. If the marriages indicated in Table VI occurred in Canada and largely in the western provinces, the "preference" mentioned would be at least partly due to the pronounced masculinity of the European-born, but the degree of preference seems too large to be attributable to that alone.

TABLE VI

Children of American-Born Parents Surviving in 1931 from Births during 1921-31

Nativity of Parents	0-10 Years		0-9 Years	
	No.	*p.c.*	*No.*	*p.c.*
TOTALS	195,500	100.0	185,500	100.0
Father American-Born and Mother—				
American-born	39,800	20.4	37,460	20.2
Canadian-born	56,550	28.9	53,970	29.1
British-born	10,870	5.6	10,240	5.5
European-born	5,900	3.0	5,600	3.0
Asiatic-born	1	1	1	1
Other	190	0.1	170	0.1
Mother American-Born and Father—				
American-born	2	2	2	2
Canadian-born	59,070	30.2	56,160	30.3
British-born	10,900	5.6	10,330	5.6
European-born	11,750	6.0	11,180	6.0
Asiatic-born	1	1	1	1
Other	470	0.2	390	0.2

[1]Numbers insignificant.　　　[2]Same as for "Father American-born."

Tables VII and VIII show the nativity of the parents of the American-born population by provinces, while Table IX carries the breakdown to sex, and to rural and urban composition. Table X shows for 1891 the residents of Canada with one or both parents American-born.

The tendency of the American-born to be of Canadian or British stock is a highly significant feature and suggests other than economic reasons for their presence in Canada. Thus of the 344,574 American-born of 1931, 66,953 had both parents Canadian-born, 21,603 had both parents British-born, and 9,870 had one parent Canadian and the other British. Further, about 23,000 had one parent Canadian and the other foreign-born, while another 13,000 had one parent British and the other foreign-born. Only 199,000 had both parents foreign-born. From Ontario east the majority of the American-born were of Canadian or British stock. In Nova Scotia nearly 74 p.c. had one or both parents Canadian; in Manitoba and British Columbia the percentage with one or both parents British or Canadian was 40; only in Saskatchewan and Alberta were there large majorities of foreign stock. The rural and urban aspects of the nativity of parents do not appear important. All the stocks were more rural than urban in the Maritime and Prairie Provinces, and more urban than rural in Quebec, Ontario and British Columbia.

TABLE VII

American-Born, Classified by Nativity of Parents, Canada and Provinces: 1931

Nativity of Parents	CANADA	P.E.I.	N.S.	N.B.	Que.	Ont.
	No.	No.	No.	No.	No.	No.
TOTAL AMERICAN-BORN[1]	344,574	1,380	7,222	8,794	49,406	72,525
Both Parents—						
Canadian-born	66,953	814	3,489	4,057	26,107	15,424
British-born	21,603	25	378	230	1,717	7,576
Foreign-born	198,842	167	1,344	2,116	12,835	32,693
One or Both Parents—						
Canadian-born	110,128	1,177	5,319	6,282	33,874	28,649
British- or Canadian-born	144,970	1,212	5,867	6,668	36,507	39,661
Father Canadian and Mother—						
British-born	3,995	23	224	160	369	1,588
Foreign-born	19,508	130	656	1,057	4,072	5,065
Father British and Mother—						
Canadian-born	5,875	58	248	159	479	2,485
Foreign-born	8,510	7	99	96	564	2,076
Father Foreign and Mother—						
Canadian-born	13,797	152	702	849	2,847	4,087
British-born	4,729	3	71	60	352	1,360

	Man.	Sask.	Alta.	B.C.	Yukon	N.W.T.
	No.	No.	No.	No.	No.	No.
TOTAL AMERICAN-BORN[1]	17,903	73,008	78,959	34,706	526	145
Both Parents—						
Canadian-born	2,897	5,864	4,990	3,281	30	....
British-born	1,307	2,312	3,677	4,342	39	....
Foreign-born	10,641	57,169	61,087	20,280	369	141
One or Both Parents—						
Canadian-born	5,188	11,296	10,703	7,560	78	2
British- or Canadian-born	7,211	15,643	17,831	14,212	154	4
Father Canadian and Mother—						
British-born	258	368	447	553	5	....
Foreign-born	1,038	2,700	2,917	1,846	25	2
Father British and Mother—						
Canadian-born	358	619	660	805	4	....
Foreign-born	449	1,311	2,345	1,535	28	....
Father Foreign and Mother—						
Canadian-born	637	1,745	1,689	1,075	14	....
British-born	267	724	1,106	775	9	2

[1] Includes persons with parentage not stated.

TABLE VIII

Percentage Distribution of American-Born for Canada and Each Province,
Classified by Nativity of Parents: 1931

NOTE.—These figures do not include persons with parentage not stated.

Nativity of Parents	CANADA	P.E.I.	N.S.	N.B.	Que.	Ont.
	p.c.	p.c.	p.c.	p.c.	p.c.	p.c.
Both Parents—						
Canadian-born	19.47	59.03	48.38	46.19	52.91	21.32
British-born	6.28	1.81	5.24	2.62	3.48	10.47
Foreign-born	57.83	12.11	18.64	24.09	26.01	45.18
One or Both Parents—						
Canadian-born	32.03	85.35	73.76	71.52	68.65	39.60
British- or Canadian-born	42.17	87.89	81.36	75.91	73.99	54.82
Father Canadian and Mother—						
British-born	1.16	1.67	3.11	1.82	0.75	2.19
Foreign-born	5.67	9.43	9.10	12.03	8.25	7.00
Father British and Mother—						
Canadian-born	1.71	4.21	3.44	1.81	0.97	3.43
Foreign-born	2.48	0.51	1.37	1.09	1.14	2.87
Father Foreign and Mother—						
Canadian-born	4.01	11.02	9.74	9.67	5.77	5.65
British-born	1.38	0.22	0.98	0.68	0.71	1.88

	Man.	Sask.	Alta.	B.C.	Yukon	N.W.T.
	p.c.	p.c.	p.c.	p.c.	p.c.	p.c.
Both Parents—						
Canadian-born	16.23	8.05	6.32	9.51	5.74	......
British-born	7.32	3.18	4.66	12.59	7.46	......
Foreign-born	59.61	78.52	77.41	58.80	70.55	97.24
One or Both Parents—						
Canadian-born	29.06	15.51	13.56	21.92	14.91	1.38
British- or Canadian-born	40.39	21.48	22.59	41.20	29.45	2.76
Father Canadian and Mother—						
British-born	1.45	0.51	0.57	1.60	0.96	......
Foreign-born	5.81	3.71	3.70	5.35	4.78	1.38
Father British and Mother—						
Canadian-born	2.01	0.85	0.84	2.33	0.76	......
Foreign-born	2.52	1.80	2.97	4.45	5.35	......
Father Foreign and Mother—						
Canadian-born	3.57	2.40	2.14	3.12	2.66	......
British-born	1.50	0.99	1.40	2.25	1.72	1.38

TABLE IX

American-Born, Rural and Urban, by Sex, Classified by Nativity of Parents, Canada: 1931

Nativity of Parents	Rural			Urban		
	Both Sexes	Male	Female	Both Sexes	Male	Female
	No.	No.	No.	No.	No.	No.
TOTAL AMERICAN-BORN[1]	179,036	98,991	80,045	165,538	76,149	89,389
Both Parents—						
Canadian-born	28,016	14,850	13,166	38,937	17,832	21,105
British-born	8,245	4,641	3,604	13,358	6,370	6,988
Foreign-born	117,519	65,935	51,584	81,323	37,598	43,725
Father Canadian and Mother—						
British-born	1,518	837	681	2,477	1,131	1,346
Foreign-born	9,120	4,759	4,361	10,388	4,533	5,855
Father British and Mother—						
Canadian-born	2,229	1,163	1,066	3,646	1,637	2,009
Foreign-born	3,857	2,208	1,649	4,653	2,127	2,526
Father Foreign and Mother—						
Canadian-born	6,172	3,206	2,966	7,625	3,474	4,151
British-born	2,049	1,197	852	2,680	1,232	1,448

[1] Includes persons with parentage not stated.

TABLE X

Residents of Canada with One or Both Parents Born in the United States, Canada and Provinces: 1891

Province	Both Parents American-Born	Father American-Born	Mother American-Born
	No.	No.	No.
CANADA	80,915	111,627	111,165
Prince Edward Island	582	517	387
Nova Scotia	3,238	3,755	3,628
New Brunswick	4,278	6,363	6,542
Quebec	18,524	17,187	18,187
Ontario	42,702	75,070	72,858
Manitoba	3,063	2,286	2,755
Saskatchewan	710	694	667
Alberta	1,251	900	902
British Columbia	6,567	4,835	5,239
Yukon	......	......	......
Northwest Territories	......	......	......

CHAPTER II

DISTRIBUTION BY AREAS

THE geographical distribution of an immigrant population is of first importance not only for its direct repercussions, but also as indicating fundamental characteristics and causes. To illustrate this feature and to permit its study in detail for the American-born in Canada is the purpose of the present chapter.

Perhaps the most easily grasped demonstration is that of Table XI, which affords a measure, necessarily somewhat rough, of the spread by areas of the American-born in Canada in comparison with those born in other countries in 1931. The counties being of unequal size, and total population being, for other reasons, unevenly spread by counties, the distribution of the total population of Canada is shown as a control or general check upon comparisons.

The table is not intended to show the proportion of the population represented by each country of birth, but merely to give a comparison, as between the different birthplaces, of the extent of distribution over the same areas. It brings out, for example, the fact that, although there were almost exactly the same number of Icelandic-born as of Lithuanian-born in Canada in 1931—enough to give 26 persons of each to each county—there were 134 counties with no Icelandic-born, but only 90 with no Lithuanian-born. Again, the table definitely posits the problem of the effect of size in a population upon its distribution; it might appear equally probable, for example, to find 7 Bulgarians (out of a total of 1,467) in any one county, as to find 3,275 English-born (out of a total of 723,864), but this is not the case. Particularly does the number of counties that have no representatives of a country of birth depend upon the total population representing that country. The different columns, therefore, control one another. While Table XI does not measure distribution with complete adequacy, it does reveal clearly the manner of distribution. Taking for example the Scottish-born, relatively few counties have more than twice the average, while only five counties have none. The other 200 counties range between one and double the average, and all but 17 of these have between one and the average: there are few with very small numbers. In other words, the Scottish-born range between a moderately large number on the one hand and a

67

moderately small number on the other—they are the most evenly spread in Canada, neither concentrating nor losing touch with one another. This behaviour renders the Scottish-born extremely valuable as a control or standard of comparison. They are probably not so extremely individualistic as the Irish-born, but they are more consistently distributed in the sense that there is more likely to be a number near the average of Scottish-born in any county than of Irish-born. This may be a fact of considerable significance: since Quebec is the province that has the small extremes of both, the difference may probably be assigned to religion. Apart from Quebec, both Scottish- and Irish-born are found in every county.

As to the showing of the American-born in Table XI, it will again be seen, but from a different angle, that in 1931 they were the most widely distributed geographically of the native-born of any foreign country, and more widely distributed than the native-born of any British country with the single exception of England, this being borne out in particular by the final column of the table wherein the United States and England appear as the only countries without representation. The fact that, next to the English-born, the American-born are the largest single group, is, in part, accountable; neither they nor the English-born are so evenly (as distinguished from widely) distributed as are the Scottish-born. The findings of Table XI, eliminating the influence of size, have been reduced to index numbers, which have been already given at p. 7.

In Table XII the distribution of total population and American-born is brought together by provinces and counties for Eastern Canada and by provinces or territories for Western Canada, for the census years 1891, 1911, and 1931. The maps appearing as frontispiece of this study clarify the 1931 figures. It is unnecessary to repeat the description, based on these and on the remaining tables of the chapter. The omnipresence and the even distribution of the American-born in Canada are their outstanding features. The significance of this widespread and even distribution has also been discussed at some length (pp. 7-10).

The broad changes as between provinces (the 1931 data are shown graphically at p. 6) and between the urban and rural elements that took place in the distribution of the American-born in Canada between 1921 and 1931 are shown numerically in Table XIII. Prince Edward Island increased in American-born. On the other hand, Nova Scotia, which may be roughly divided into northern and southern, saw an almost general decrease in the northern parts, while the southern increased in every county. The increase cannot be attributed to urbanization (Halifax) as it took place almost wholly in rural areas and was caused by the return of Canadian-born emigrés and their children from the United States, and by the opening of roads and the improvement of rural facilities in general.

In New Brunswick there was an almost general increase, again predominantly in the rural regions. *Per contra*, Quebec greatly increased its American-born in urban localities, chiefly on Montreal and Jesus Islands and in the counties immediately adjacent—a heavily industrialized area comparatively close to the international border. In Gaspe and other counties between the St. Lawrence and the border, slight increases and decreases took place correlating closely with the movement from the United States in 1901-11.

In Ontario the situation is complex. At least 50 p.c. of the counties showed a decline in the number of American-born. The largest increases occurred in counties with large urban centres (except in the case of Wentworth), yet the cities themselves did not show a proportional increase—rather, in some cases, a decrease or an almost stationary condition. For example, the County of York increased its American-born population by 1,834, although the city of Toronto lost 180 American-born in the decade—a situation opposite to that of Montreal which absorbed a large proportion of the provincial increase. (It may be pointed out that Toronto had 20 p.c. of all the American-born in the Province of Ontario, and 79 p.c. of all in York County, while Montreal had 35 p.c. of those in Quebec, and 77 p.c. of those in the county.) The American-born in Ontario showed a tendency to settle in rural parts not far removed from the larger cities: the rural increase exceeded the urban increase by more than 100 p.c. in the Province. In northern Ontario the American-born were chiefly miners and prospectors.

The Prairie Provinces showed marked homogeneity, the southern sections declining, especially in western Saskatchewan and eastern Alberta, and the northern parts increasing. British Columbia's American-born were largely concentrated in Division No. 4, which lies along the international border west of the Rocky Mountains; Vancouver city contained about 64 p.c. of the American-born of this division, probably due to the presence of large United States interests; the district, also, is a haven for health seekers.

TABLE XI

Density of Distribution, by Birthplace, of the Immigrant Population Over the 221 Counties and Census Divisions[1] of Canada: 1931

Birthplace	Total	Average per County or Division	Twice the Average or More	Over but Less than Twice the Average	Less but More than Half the Average	Less than Half the Average	No Immigrant Population
	No.	No.	No.	No.	No.	No.	No.
TOTAL POPULATION	10,376,786	46,954	14	36	87	84	0
Total Immigrant Population	2,307,525	10,441	21	33	34	133	0
British Isles—							
England	723,864	3,275	17	26	39	139	0
Ireland	107,544	487	13	20	45	138	5
Scotland	279,765	1,266	16	17	46	137	5
Wales	22,348	101	21	26	30	101	43
United States	344,574	1,559	32	19	31	139	0
Other Foreign Countries—							
Austria	37,391	169	30	18	20	111	42
Belgium	17,033	77	22	16	23	122	38
Bulgaria	1,467	7	22	15	13	47	124
China	42,037	190	16	12	22	148	23
Czechoslovakia	22,835	103	24	26	21	87	63
Denmark	17,217	78	26	28	23	112	32
Finland	30,354	137	16	13	8	128	56
France	16,756	76	22	21	32	139	7
Germany	39,163	177	35	20	19	126	21
Greece	5,579	25	16	18	17	81	89
Holland	10,736	49	25	20	29	96	51
Hungary	28,523	129	26	12	18	96	69
Iceland	5,731	26	14	7	11	55	134
Italy	42,578	193	21	7	15	155	23
Japan	12,261	55	7	1	5	62	146
Lithuania	5,704	26	15	18	21	77	90
Norway	32,679	148	37	16	8	116	44
Poland[2]	171,169	775	27	18	18	127	31
Roumania	40,322	182	27	12	14	128	40
Russia	114,406	518	24	20	11	143	23
Sweden	34,415	156	36	21	8	122	34
Switzerland	6,076	27	27	24	28	90	52
Yugoslavia	17,110	77	26	13	13	78	91

[1] The Yukon and Northwest Territories are here considered as census divisions and Lennox and Addington one county. [2] Includes Galicia.

TABLE XII

Total Population and American-Born, by Provinces and Counties for the Maritime Provinces, Quebec and Ontario, and by Provinces or Territories for Western Canada: 1891, 1911, and 1931

Province and County	1891		1911		1931	
	Total Population	American-Born	Total Population	American-Born	Total Population	American-Born
	No.	No.	No.	No.	No.	No.
CANADA	4,833,239	80,915	7,206,643	303,680	10,376,786	344,574
Prince Edward Island	109,078	582	93,728	829	88,038	1,380
Kings	26,633	227	22,636	229	19,147	338
Prince	36,470	122	32,779	200	31,500	480
Queens	45,975	233	38,313	400	37,391	562
Nova Scotia	450,396	3,238	492,338	4,802	512,846	7,222
Annapolis	19,350	173	18,581	302	16,297	277
Antigonish	16,114	79	11,962	185	10,073	196
Cape Breton	46,676[1]	134[1]	83,240[1]	880[1]	92,419	964
Colchester	27,160	268	23,664	295	25,051	425
Cumberland	34,529	332	40,543	475	36,366	419
Digby	19,897	142	20,167	244	18,353	402
Guysborough	17,195	68	17,048	73	15,443	133
Halifax	71,358	813	80,257	612	100,204	1,493
Hants	22,052	169	19,703	199	19,393	306
Inverness	25,779	106	25,571	169	21,055	216
Kings	22,489	284	21,780	325	24,357	494
Lunenburg	31,075	56	33,260	75	31,674	234
Pictou	34,541	260	35,858	392	39,018	618
Queens	[2]	[2]	[2]	[2]	10,612	180
Richmond	14,399	49	13,273	62	11,098	116
Shelburne	25,566[2]	74[2]	24,211[2]	228[2]	12,485	210
Victoria	[1]	[1]	[1]	[1]	8,009	92
Yarmouth	22,216	231	23,220	286	20,939	447
New Brunswick	321,263	4,278	351,889	5,766	408,219	8,794
Albert	[3]	[3]	[3]	[3]	7,679	110
Carleton	22,529	559	21,446	595	20,796	760
Charlotte	23,752	988	21,147	824	21,337	1,096
Gloucester	24,897	30	32,662	118	41,914	257
Kent	23,845	60	24,376	213	23,478	414
Kings	34,058[3]	234[3]	30,285[3]	289[3]	19,807	364
Madawaska	[4]	[4]	[4]	[4]	24,527	1,190
Northumberland	25,713	82	31,194	164	34,124	290
Queens	[5]	[5]	[5]	[5]	11,219	150
Restigouche	8,308	64	15,687	142	29,859	507
St. John	49,574	680	53,572	959	61,613	1,232
Sunbury	17,914[5]	88[5]	17,116[5]	190[5]	6,999	64
Victoria	18,217[4]	887[4]	28,222[4]	1,311[4]	14,907	622
Westmorland	41,477	238	44,621	524	57,506	1,120
York	30,979	368	31,561	437	32,454	618

[1]Cape Breton includes Victoria.   [2]Shelburne includes Queens.   [3]Kings includes Albert.
[4]Victoria includes Madawaska.   [5]Sunbury includes Queens.

TABLE XII—continued

*Total Population and American-Born, by Provinces and Counties for the
Maritime Provinces, Quebec and Ontario, and by Provinces or Territories
for Western Canada: 1891, 1911, and 1931*

Province and County	1891		1911		1931	
	Total Population	American-Born	Total Population	American-Born	Total Population	American-Born
	No.	No.	No.	No.	No.	No.
Quebec	1,488,535	18,524	2,005,776	29,843	2,874,255	49,406
Abitibi	......	......	2,063	8	23,692	484
Argenteuil	15,158	125	16,766	128	18,976	170
Arthabaska	1	1	1	1	27,159	564
Bagot	21,695	333	18,206	311	16,914	398
Beauce	30,837	170	38,161	166	44,793	312
Beauharnois	16,662	101	20,802	279	25,163	459
Bellechasse	18,368	......	21,141	101	22,006	227
Berthier	20,399	122	20,606	91	19,506	397
Bonaventure	20,835	69	28,110	120	32,432	134
Brome	14,709	1,311	13,216	889	12,433	563
Chambly	23,961[2]	117[2]	28,715[2]	302[2]	26,801	547
Champlain	27,335	226	43,866	421	59,935	653
Charlevoix	19,038	2	20,637	32	22,940	78
Chateauguay	13,864	75	13,322	122	13,125	147
Chicoutimi	24,233[3]	16[3]	38,777[3]	124[3]	55,724	461
Compton	17,386	988	21,235	846	21,917	741
Deux-Montagnes	15,027	9	13,868	33	14,284	31
Dorchester	18,364	57	24,457	133	27,994	132
Drummond	39,893[1]	743[1]	41,590[1]	735[1]	26,179	833
Frontenac	12,431	86	22,272	171	25,681	362
Gaspe	26,875	21	35,001	84	45,617	142
Hull	37,712	223	48,332	302	63,870	580
Huntingdon	14,385	515	13,240	465	12,345	560
Iberville	4	4	4	4	9,402	309
Joliette	22,921	100	23,911	245	27,585	455
Kamouraska	20,454	20	20,888	129	23,954	219
Labelle	2,676	16	13,691	105	20,140	105
Lac-St-Jean	14,048	8	27,111	80	50,253	292
Laprairie	21,001[5]	218[5]	19,335[5]	210[5]	13,491	131
L'Assomption	13,674	2	15,164	104	15,323	88
Lévis	25,995	54	28,913	137	35,656	208
L'Islet	13,823	52	16,435	124	19,404	181
Lotbinière	20,688	43	22,158	152	23,034	280
Maskinongé	17,266	208	15,775	98	16,039	220
Matane	14,621	23	27,539	308	45,272	440
Mégantic	22,233	228	31,314	596	35,492	580
Missisquoi	18,549	1,119	17,466	942	19,636	889
Montcalm	12,131	57	13,342	55	13,865	81
Montmagny	14,726	13	17,356	119	20,239	194
Montmorency	12,309	7	13,215	26	16,955	60
Montreal—Jesus Islands	286,961	5,338	566,168	11,743	1,020,018	22,788
Napierville	5	5	5	5	7,600	133
Nicolet	28,735	164	30,055	153	28,673	337

[1] Drummond includes Arthabaska.   [2] Chambly includes Verchères.   [3] Chicoutimi includes Saguenay.   [4] St-Jean includes Iberville.   [5] Laprairie includes Napierville.

TABLE XII—continued

Total Population and American-Born, by Provinces and Counties for the
Maritime Provinces, Quebec and Ontario, and by Provinces or Territories
for Western Canada: 1891, 1911, and 1931

Province and County	1891		1911		1931	
	Total Population	American-Born	Total Population	American-Born	Total Population	American-Born
	No.	No.	No.	No.	No.	No.
Quebec—concluded						
Papineau	22,972	138	27,180	216	29,246	237
Pontiac	20,381	132	21,123	202	21,241	96
Portneuf	25,813	97	30,529	119	35,890	166
Quebec	82,593	288	104,554	546	170,915	1,591
Richelieu	21,652	179	20,686	408	21,483	549
Richmond	31,347[1]	648[1]	39,491[1]	962[1]	24,956	835
Rimouski	18,809	30	23,951	268	33,151	281
Rouville	16,012	405	13,131	266	13,776	359
St-Hyacinthe	21,135	387	22,342	599	25,854	869
St-Jean	24,175[2]	484[2]	21,882[2]	592[2]	17,649	635
St-Maurice	23,033	120	35,045	533	69,095	1,254
Saguenay	[3]	[3]	[3]	[3]	21,754	40
Shefford	23,263	692	23,976	750	28,262	739
Sherbrooke	16,088	12	23,211	792	37,386	1,454
Soulanges	9,608	29	9,400	39	9,099	59
Stanstead	18,067	1,493	20,765	1,508	25,118	1,260
Témiscouata	25,698	122	36,430	449	50,294	640
Temiskaming	1,903	13	8,293	80	20,609	357
Terrebonne	23,128	92	29,018	111	38,611	227
Vaudreuil	10,792	39	11,039	47	12,015	72
Verchères	[4]	[4]	[4]	[4]	12,603	101
Wolfe	[1]	[1]	[1]	[1]	16,911	317
Yamaska	20,088	145	19,511	167	16,820	303
Ontario	2,114,321	42,702	2,527,292	55,676	3,431,683	72,525
Addington	9,850	} 322 {	8,138	} 232 {	6,879	49
Lennox	14,900		12,248		12,004	127
Brant	36,445	783	45,876	1,110	53,476	873
Bruce	64,603	610	50,032	375	42,286	364
Carleton	77,630	1,289	119,384	2,292	170,040	2,806
Dufferin	22,332	35	17,740	85	14,892	116
Dundas	20,132	286	18,165	252	16,098	211
Durham	32,427	374	26,411	296	25,782	269
Elgin	43,377	1,219	44,312	990	43,436	1,076
Essex	55,545	3,514	67,547	4,210	159,780	7,956
Frontenac	47,009	1,027	42,604	705	45,756	840
Glengarry	22,447	364	21,259	178	18,666	230
Grenville	21,609	}1,564{	17,545	}1,059{	16,327	320
Leeds	39,279		36,753		35,157	742
Grey	71,214	588	65,891	524	57,699	492
Haldimand	23,440	319	21,562	318	21,428	313
Halton	21,982	330	22,208	333	26,558	457
Hastings	59,084	848	55,803	559	58,846	622

[1] Richmond includes Wolfe. [2] St-Jean includes Iberville. [3] Chicoutimi includes Saguenay.
[4] Chambly includes Verchères.

TABLE XII—concluded

Total Population and American-Born, by Provinces and Counties for the Maritime Provinces, Quebec and Ontario, and by Provinces or Territories for Western Canada: 1891, 1911, and 1931

Province and County	1891		1911		1931	
	Total Population	American-Born	Total Population	American-Born	Total Population	American-Born
Ontario—concluded	No.	No.	No.	No.	No.	No.
Huron	66,781	505	52,983	435	45,180	434
Kent	57,814	2,517	55,995	1,706	62,865	1,969
Lambton	58,810	1,483	51,332	1,428	54,674	1,433
Lanark	37,725	332	34,375	310	32,856	304
Lincoln	30,079	1,164	35,429	1,249	54,199	1,432
Middlesex	92,344	1,619	97,065	1,906	118,241	2,282
Norfolk	30,992	602	27,110	577	31,359	1,357
Northumberland	38,035	599	33,759	466	31,452	346
Ontario	45,355	871	41,006	375	59,667	717
Oxford	49,849	917	47,371	714	47,825	762
Peel	24,871	191	22,102	151	28,156	270
Perth	51,716	509	49,182	494	51,392	573
Peterborough	34,597	459	40,783	534	43,958	573
Prescott	24,173	173	26,968	174	24,596	148
Prince Edward	18,889	290	17,150	178	16,693	208
Renfrew	46,977	263	51,856	225	52,227	298
Russell	18,289	165	21,649	230	18,487	207
Simcoe	82,727	921	85,053	873	83,667	748
Stormont	27,156	1,059	24,775	602	32,524	708
Victoria	32,991	209	30,179	205	25,844	142
Waterloo	50,464	840	62,607	980	89,852	1,487
Welland	30,631	1,748	42,163	2,838	82,731	4,039
Wellington	59,350	621	54,492	525	58,164	640
Wentworth	77,114	2,221	111,706	3,501	190,019	4,599
York	245,101	6,975	444,234	12,317	856,955	18,619
Muskoka	15,666		21,233	271	20,985	312
Parry Sound	21,152		26,547	429	25,900	330
Haliburton	6,350		6,320		5,997	48
Nipissing	10,654		28,066		41,207	659
Sudbury	4,842	1,977	29,778		58,251	1,153
Manitoulin	10,794		11,324		10,734	100
Algoma	13,534		40,962	8,465	46,444	1,596
Thunder Bay	8,000		39,496		65,118	1,701
Rainy River	2,210		10,429		17,359	1,823
Kenora	4,984		15,490		21,946	627
Cochrane	......	......	12,236		58,033	1,253
Timiskaming	......	......	26,592		37,043	732
Patricia	......	......	4,017		3,973	33
Manitoba	152,506	3,063	461,394	16,328	700,139	17,903
Saskatchewan	41,522	710	492,432	69,628	921,785	73,008
Alberta	25,277	1,251	374,295	81,357	731,605	78,959
British Columbia	98,173	6,567	392,480	37,548	694,263	34,706
Yukon	32,168	......	8,512	1,891	4,230	526
Northwest Territories			6,507	12	9,723	145

TABLE XIII

American-Born, Rural and Urban, Canada and Provinces: 1921 and 1931

Province	1921		1931		Increase or Decrease		
	Rural	Urban	Rural	Urban	Rural	Urban	Net
	No.	No.	No,	No.	No.	No.	No.
CANADA	214,563	159,461	179,036	165,538	−35,527	+6,077	−29,450
Prince Edward Island..	945	270	999	381	+ 54	+ 111	+ 165
Nova Scotia	3,667	3,349	3,862	3,360	+ 195	+ 11	+ 206
New Brunswick	5,106	3,163	5,615	3,179	+ 509	+ 17	+ 526
Quebec	11,405	30,719	11,588	37,818	+ 183	+7,099	+ 7,282
Ontario	20,185	50,544	21,462	51,063	+ 1,277	+ 519	+ 1,796
Manitoba	11,907	9,737	9,483	8,420	− 2,424	−1,317	− 3,741
Saskatchewan	67,565	20,052	52,965	20,043	−14,600	− 9	−14,609
Alberta	74,030	25,849	55,824	23,135	−18,206	−2,714	−20,920
British Columbia	19,404	15,522	16,809	17,897	− 2,595	+2,375	− 220
Yukon and Northwest Territories	349	257	429	242	+ 80	− 15	+ 65

TABLE XIV

Percentages of American-Born and Immigrants of German Racial Origin to Total Population[1] Compared with those of Scottish Racial Origin, by Provinces: 1931

Province	Scottish Racial Origin[2]	American-Born	German Racial Origin
	p.c.	p.c.	p.c.
CANADA	12.97	3.32	4.56
Prince Edward Island	36.90	1.57	0.32
Nova Scotia	27.30	1.41	5.28
New Brunswick	13.86	2.15	0.65
Quebec	3.04	1.72	0.37
Ontario	16.02	2.11	5.07
Manitoba	16.04	2.56	5.44
Saskatchewan	13.18	7.92	14.02
Alberta	15.13	10.79	10.18
British Columbia	19.45	5.00	2.45
Yukon	13.62	12.43	2.32
Northwest Territories	2.21	1.49	0.40

[1]Figures of total population by counties are given for 1931 in Table XII. control or standard of comparison (see text, p. 67).   [2]This origin is the

TABLE XV

Counties and Census Divisions in Canada Grouped According to Percentage Distribution of American-Born and Immigrants of German Racial Origin as Compared with those of Scottish Racial Origin: 1931

Percentage of Total Population	Number of Counties and Census Divisions			Percentage of Total Population	Number of Counties and Census Divisions		
	Scottish Racial Origin [1]	American-Born	German Racial Origin		Scottish Racial Origin [1]	American-Born	German Racial Origin
0	....	....	1	22-22.99..............	3	....	1
0- 0.99.................	38	50	100	23-23.99..............	5	....	1
1- 1.99.................	14	72	20	24-24.99..............	1	....	....
2- 2.99.................	6	34	21	25-25.99..............	2	....	1
3- 3.99.................	8	13	15	26-26.99..............	1	....	....
4- 4.99.................	2	10	6	28-28.99..............	1	....	....
5- 5.99.................	8	8	8	30-30.99..............	1	....	....
6- 6.99.................	4	5	3	38-38.99..............	1	....	....
7- 7.99.................	....	3	4	39-39.99..............	1	....	....
8- 8.99.................	9	3	9	40-40.99..............	1	....	....
9- 9.99.................	6	4	4	42-42.99..............	1	....	....
10-10.99.................	7	4	3	49-49.99..............	....	....	1
11-11.99.................	4	1	3	50-50.99..............	....	....	1
12-12.99.................	11	5	7	52-52.99..............	1	....	....
13-13.99.................	11	2	2	58-58.99..............	1	....	....
14-14.99.................	13	1	3	63-63.99..............	1	....	....
15-15.99.................	19	3	....	64-64.99..............	1	....	....
16-16.99.................	11	1	1	68-68.99..............	1	....	....
17-17.99.................	9	1	3				
18-18.99.................	9	2	....	Totals.....................	222	222	222
19-19.99.................	6	....	1	Av. p.c., Canada....	12.97	3.32	4.56
20-20.99.................	2	....	1	Maximum...............	68.14	18.74	50.33
21-21.99.................	2	....	2	Minimum...............	0.01	0.18	0.00
				Number over Av...	105	63	62

[1] This origin is the control or standard of comparison (see text, p. 67).

CHAPTER III

AGE—SEX—RURAL AND URBAN

THE age, sex, and rural and urban attributes of the American-born in Canada are interlocked to such a degree that they are best considered in conjunction.* Of the 344,574 American-born of both sexes in Canada at the latest Census, 52 p.c. were in unincorporated rural areas; 24 p.c. in cities of 30,000 or over; 18 p.c. in urban localities of 1,000 to 30,000; and 6 p.c. in incorporated villages of less than 1,000. Of the total population of Canada in 1931, 46 p.c. was rural (15.1 p.c. non-farm) 29 p.c. was in cities of 30,000 or over; 21 p.c. in urban localities of 1,000 to 30,000; and 4 p.c. in incorporated villages of less than 1,000. This is in marked contrast with the Canadian-born in the United States, 92 p.c. of whom are in urban localities of 2,500 or over (*plus* rural non-farm). Table XXVII gives the general picture.

The sex distribution of the American-born by types of locality shows a greater urban tendency on the part of females than of males, but not so great as that of total Canadian females. In absolute numbers there were 18,946 more rural males than rural females, and 13,240 more urban females than urban males. The females gravitate to the larger urban centres in particular more readily than do the males, as would stand out more clearly were the classifications by smaller areas.

In further elucidation of the distribution of American-born by sex, and the disparity just referred to, Table XIX anticipates later data by showing the sex ratios at different ages. The predominance of males at all ages from 15 on, is not explained away by the fact that the total number of males is greater by 5,706 than the total number of females.

A higher male ratio is a familiar phenomenon in an immigrant population. Its modification, however, as between rural and urban is interesting. Briefly, in addition to a general tendency, it points to different years of immigration. A possible explanation is, of course, that American-born females moved into the cities from rural areas after coming to Canada at the same time as the males, but this could not have occurred on any major scale for the following reason: In 1911 the males and females of the American-born in Canada (Table XVI) were, respectively, 168,278 and 135,402, a male

---

*In the Canadian Census, "urban" population is that of cities, towns or incorporated villages, all outside such localities being "rural." The laws of the various provinces differ as to the population necessary before a municipality may be incorporated. For instance, as few as 50 people on an area of 640 acres may be incorporated in Saskatchewan. In the United States Census the term "urban" includes all places with a population of 2,500 or more, including such townships and other political sub-divisions that have a total population of 10,000 or more each and a population density of 1,000 or more per square mile. "Rural" population includes all other places.

excess of 32,876; in 1921 they compared as 196,425 and 177,597, respectively, a male increase in the decade of only 28,147 and a female increase of 42,195; in 1931 they compared as 175,140 males and 169,434 females, a male decrease of 21,285 in the decade and a female decrease of only 8,163; between 1911 and 1931 the males increased by 6,862 and the females by 34,032. The obvious explanation is that the United States males moved in before the appearance of a strong urbanizing tendency.

The segregation of the male and female movement may also be illustrated from the "year of immigration" figures of the 1931 Census. The percentages of each sex in the American-born population of Canada arriving in specific periods are given in Chapter i, p. 60. The female percentages, it will have been noted, were in excess from 1916 to 1931, while the male percentages were in excess from 1901 to 1915. That the pre-1901 female percentages were in excess of the male may reflect the stabilizing influence of marriage.

AGE DISTRIBUTION

In considering age distribution, a comparison is made between (1) the American-born in Canada and other immigrants; (2) the American-born and the total population of Canada; (3) the American-born and the Canadian-born population; and (4) the Canadian-born population of Canada and the American-born white population of the United States. Incidental intercomparisons among these follow. The native-born of both countries are brought into the picture in order to render the comparisons more concrete and measurable, since obviously an immigrant population will show differences in age distributions. What, however, is the extent of these differences, and at what parts of the age range do they occur? Generally, an immigrant population shows high proportions in the middle adult ages—also, to the extent to which immigrants move in families, a peak at the child ages as compared with the immediately pre-adult ages. This phenomenon is a result of the ages at which immigrants move, and its appearance at subsequent dates depends upon the volume and date of movement. Table XX makes all four comparisons; it reveals at once a clustering of percentages at certain adult ages in immigrants which is not found in natives, for whom a fairly definite decrease in percentages normally occurs from the child ages up.

Comparing, first, the natives of Canada with those of the United States, the former are younger, i.e., they have higher percentages in the ages below 20, and lower afterwards. This is interesting as well as important as background. It is probably due largely to the fact that the native population of Canada contains a large element of the children of immigrants, and that immigrants, more or less recently arrived, form a larger proportion of the population of Canada than of the United States.

The next comparison inviting attention is between the American-born in Canada and the total population of Canada including natives and immigrants. The age distribution of the latter is clearly affected by the immigrant element; it is a composite distribution in which one population (immigrant) is superimposed upon another. The superimposed population contains a much higher proportion than normal above the age of 40, but if the examination had been made as in 1921 instead of 1931 the abnormal proportion would have applied to ages above 35, while if it had been made as in 1911 the abnormal proportion would have begun about age 30. Thus the superimposed population travels upwards with time, being as yet little affected by deaths. The American-born in Canada, a purely immigrant population, naturally compare more closely with the superimposed population (of which they form a part), and consequently show the same characteristics, only somewhat exaggerated. However, the main clustering of the American-born is found between 35 and 39, somewhat lower than that of the "other immigrant" population (see chart, p. 35).

The third comparison lies between the American-born and the other immigrant population of Canada. In the first place the American-born are considerably younger than the "other immigrant" population, ages up to 25 being definitely in excess. Thereafter, a United States peak occurs around 35, while the "other immigrant" peak occurs around 40. These facts suggest that the "other immigrants" arrived on the whole more recently than the American-born.

An explanation of the younger age of the American-born lies, especially in 1931, in the considerable element they contain of persons born of Canadian parentage. In that year as many as 66,953 of the 344,574 American-born population of Canada were of Canadian parentage, and came largely to the Maritime Provinces and Quebec. Consequently the age distribution of the American-born depends pre-eminently upon what part of Canada is studied. Table XXII compares the American-born age distribution of Quebec and the Maritime Provinces on the one hand and the Prairie Provinces on the other; the former are definitely younger—the explanation need not be elaborated.

CHANGES IN THE AGE DISTRIBUTION OF THE AMERICAN-BORN IN CANADA

As a measure of the changes taking place in the age distribution of the American-born in Canada, Table XXIII compares on an absolute basis and Table XXIV on a percentage basis (see also the chart at p. 16) the ages by sex in the Prairie Provinces in 1926 and 1936. Canada as a whole is not covered, as ages by birthplace are not tabulated for the Dominion until 1931, but the Prairie Provinces have the bulk of miscellaneous American-born and the eastern provinces the American-born children of Canadian-born parents (see Chapter I, p. 57).

Considering the Prairies as a whole the median ages in 1926 and 1936 were: males, 32.5 and 41.0, respectively; females, 31.3 and 38.4, respectively. The ageing index was 8.15 for males and 7.1 for females for that period.

Even in a population not under process of renewal one would not expect an ageing of ten years in a decade, but the American-born population of Canada was under such process, for, of the 1931 American-born, 16.87 p.c. arrived between 1926 and 1931. Consequently the ageing shown above was very rapid. This is due to the behaviour of the age-cluster. The male cluster in 1926 was between 15 and 50 and included 75.74 p.c. of the male population; in 1936 it was between 25 and 60 and included 75.46 p.c. with no evidence of 'weathering' through deaths. The female cluster in 1926 was between 15 and 45 and included 72.65 p.c. of the female population; in 1936 it lay between 25 and 55 and included 71.40 p.c., again with little evidence of the influence of deaths or emigration. Now there was a considerable decrease in the American-born in the Prairies between 1926 and 1936, and this makes the phenomenon of the ageing of the clusters striking; in other words, it is remarkable that the proportions should have remained consistent considering that they represented different absolute numbers and different individuals through arrivals and replacements. Again, both the age distribution and the changes of the decade are quite different in Manitoba from Saskatchewan and Alberta. Manitoba, of course, has a small American-born population compared with the other two Prairie Provinces, and this alone could cause a considerable difference. However, interprovincial migration is also suggested. Thus the proportions of American-born in the different provinces in 1926, 1931, and 1936 were as follows:—

	1926	1931	1936
Alberta	45.6	46.5	47.6
Saskatchewan	44.0	43.0	41.8
Manitoba	10.5	10.5	10.6
Totals	100.0	100.0	100.0

AGE-SEX COMPARISON

In the table on sex ratios (XIX) the male ratio in rural parts appears greatly in excess of 100 throughout the age range, with an abrupt rise between the late 30's and the early 40's; in the urban parts the male ratio is over 100 at ages under 15 and below 100 after this age, except for a slight disturbance at ages 50-54 where it is exactly 100. These ratios are not altogether explained by the fact that total American-born males are in excess in rural and in defect in urban parts. The general population of Canada behaves in somewhat the same way. The abrupt rise at the late 30's in the rural, and the lack of such a tendency of the female at the same ages in the urban, seem to be significant, especially in view of the resemblance in behaviour to the general population. There is little doubt that it has to do with the differential movement of single and married females into the cities.

Since sex ratios as in Table XIX disguise certain age tendencies when the absolute numbers of the sexes are so different (as in the case of the American-born in Canada) the sex comparison is shown in another way in Table XX, viz., the number of each sex in each quinquennial age group as a percentage of the total of the sex. This table gives not only a comparison of American-born by sex, but also as between American-born and Canadian-born. Taking the former living in Canada in 1931 we find among both males and females a clustering between the ages of 20 and 50, the peak of the cluster coming in the same age group, viz., 35-39. The 30-year span includes 60.9 p.c. of the males and 64.2 p.c. of the females compared to 42.2 p.c. of the males and 41.1 p.c. of the females in the total population. A significant feature is that in every quinquennial group from 20 to 40 the female proportion is in excess of the male while from 40 onwards the male is in excess. This is in line with what has already been said regarding the year of arrival, the larger cluster of the females being probably because more arrived within a shorter period than in the case of males, who tended to arrive gradually. While the explanation of the differential clustering may be thus simple, the consequences may be important. The fact that the females are bulked within a 30-year range makes them a rather abnormal element, with possible important consequences in years to come.

TABLE XVI

American-Born, by Sex, Canada and Provinces: 1911, 1921, and 1931

Province	1911		1921		1931	
	Male	Female	Male	Female	Male	Female
	No.	No.	No.	No.	No.	No.
CANADA	168,278	135,402	196,425[1]	177,597	175,140	169,434
Prince Edward Island	391	438	625	590	680	700
Nova Scotia	2,345	2,457	3,311	3,705	3,355	3,867
New Brunswick	2,741	3,025	3,771	4,497	4,037	4,757
Quebec	14,605	15,238	20,158	21,964	23,247	26,159
Ontario	27,880	27,796	34,325	36,404	34,017	38,508
Manitoba	8,577	7,751	11,258	10,386	9,027	8,876
Saskatchewan	40,529	29,099	48,390	39,227	39,664	33,344
Alberta	47,500	33,857	55,699	44,180	43,166	35,793
British Columbia	22,330	15,218	18,450	16,476	17,474	17,232
Yukon	1,369	522	394	163	365	161
Northwest Territories	11	1	41	5	108	37

[1]Includes 3 in Royal Canadian Navy.

TABLE XVII

American-Born, Rural and Urban, by Sex, Canada and Provinces: 1931

Province	Rural			Urban		
	Male	Female	Male Excess	Male	Female	Male Excess
	No.	No.	No.	No.	No.	No.
CANADA	98,991	80,045	18,946	76,149	89,389	−13,240
Prince Edward Island	498	501	−3	182	199	−17
Nova Scotia	1,859	2,003	−144	1,496	1,864	−368
New Brunswick	2,633	2,982	−349	1,404	1,775	−371
Quebec	5,881	5,707	174	17,366	20,452	−3,086
Ontario	10,749	10,713	36	23,268	27,795	−4,527
Manitoba	5,148	4,335	813	3,879	4,541	−662
Saskatchewan	30,178	22,787	7,391	9,486	10,557	−1,071
Alberta	32,286	23,538	8,748	10,880	12,255	−1,375
British Columbia	9,448	7,361	2,087	8,026	9,871	−1,845
Yukon	203	81	122	162	80	82
Northwest Territories	108	37	71	....	....	....

TABLE XVIII

*Percentage Distribution of American-Born Compared with that of the
Total Population, by Sex, Classified by Rural and by Urban
Size Groups: 1931*

Locality	Total Population		American-Born	
	Male	Female	Male	Female
TOTAL	100.0	100.0	100.0	100.0
Rural	48.4	44.0	56.5	47.2
Urban—				
30,000 or over	27.9	30.5	21.5	27.1
1,000-30,000	19.9	21.4	16.2	19.3
Under 1,000	3.9	4.1	5.8	6.3

TABLE XIX

American-Born Males per 100 Females, Rural and Urban, by Age Groups: 1931

Age Group	Rural	Urban	Age Group	Rural	Urban
	No.	No.		No.	No.
ALL AGES	124	85	50-54	146	100
			55-59	154	97
0- 4	107	106	60-64	162	94
5- 9	109	105	65-69	169	93
10-14	110	102	70-74	170	88
15-19	116	86	75-79	154	85
20-24	119	70	80-84	137	89
25-29	113	69	85-89	129	59
30-34	111	75	90-94	153	62
35-39	114	78	95-99	57	50
40-44	129	90	100 or over	......	......
45-49	139	98	Not stated	200	100

TABLE XX

Percentage Distribution, by Sex, Classified by Age Groups, of American-Born, Other Immigrants, Total Population and Canadian-Born Population, 1931, and American-Born White Population of United States, 1930

Age Group	American-Born in Canada		Other Immigrants		Total Population of Canada		Canadian-Born Population of Canada		American-Born White Population of United States	
	Male	Female	Male	Female	Male	Female	Male	Female	Male	Female
ALL AGES	100.00	100.00	100.00	100.00	100.00	100.00	100.00	100.00	100.00	100.00
0- 4	3.25	3.15	0.52	0.68	10.11	10.62	13.04	13.03	10.49	10.24
5- 9	4.66	4.50	2.07	2.67	10.65	11.20	13.27	13.28	11.45	11.24
10-14	4.71	4.58	2.39	3.03	10.10	10.62	12.46	12.47	10.97	10.81
15-19	6.46	6.61	3.54	3.86	9.77	10.28	11.63	11.79	10.22	10.28
20-24	9.44	10.51	7.77	8.68	8.63	8.95	8.83	8.93	9.05	9.39
25-29	10.08	11.56	11.38	10.84	7.63	7.52	6.49	6.65	7.77	8.05
30-34	10.45	11.77	11.31	11.46	6.85	6.81	5.47	5.62	7.10	7.27
35-39	11.38	12.36	11.48	11.82	6.68	6.58	5.16	5.24	6.83	6.89
40-44	10.57	10.04	12.25	11.37	6.47	5.96	4.70	4.65	5.77	5.75
45-49	9.00	7.93	11.66	10.33	5.98	5.27	4.29	4.09	5.02	4.94
50-54	6.49	5.51	8.91	8.17	4.97	4.42	3.82	3.59	4.36	4.21
55-59	4.81	4.06	5.82	5.42	3.71	3.36	3.08	2.89	3.48	3.36
60-64	3.44	2.88	4.24	4.14	2.92	2.75	2.53	2.46	2.72	2.66
65-69	2.27	1.86	2.93	3.08	2.25	2.21	2.06	2.04	1.97	1.97
70-74	1.64	1.38	1.88	2.14	1.65	1.66	1.59	1.57	1.44	1.45
75 or over	1.34	1.29	1.79	2.29	1.58	1.76	1.54	1.67	1.28	1.43
Not stated	0.03	0.02	0.05	0.02	0.05	0.02	0.05	0.02	0.08	0.07

TABLE XXI

American-Born in United States, 1930, Compared with those in Canada, 1931, by Sex, Classified by Age Groups

Age Group	Both Sexes		Male		Female	
	In United States	In Canada	In United States	In Canada	In United States	In Canada
	No.	No.	No.	No.	No.	No.
ALL AGES	95,497,800	344,574	48,010,145	175,140	47,487,655	169,434
Under 5 years	9,899,608	11,030	5,036,989	5,687	4,862,619	5,343
5- 9	10,834,453	15,777	5,497,255	8,159	5,337,198	7,618
10-14	10,398,546	16,000	5,265,795	8,248	5,132,751	7,752
15-19	9,786,954	22,499	4,907,316	11,307	4,879,638	11,192
20-24	8,804,163	34,344	4,346,913	16,531	4,457,250	17,813
25-29	7,552,690	37,245	3,731,794	17,661	3,820,896	19,584
30-34	6,862,936	38,234	3,408,584	18,297	3,454,352	19,937
35-39	6,551,953	40,882	3,278,767	19,936	3,273,186	20,946
40-44	5,504,331	35,522	2,771,481	18,504	2,732,850	17,018
45-49	4,757,775	29,199	2,411,909	15,755	2,345,866	13,444
50-54	4,091,686	20,706	2,092,785	11,371	1,998,901	9,335
55-59	3,264,494	15,296	1,670,570	8,425	1,593,924	6,871
60-64	2,566,416	10,901	1,305,260	6,024	1,261,156	4,877
65-69	1,882,526	7,115	944,823	3,970	937,703	3,145
70-74	1,377,436	5,219	690,036	2,875	687,400	2,344
75 or over	1,294,328	4,519	613,379	2,339	680,949	2,180
Not stated	67,505	86	36,489	51	31,016	35
Under 15 years	31,132,607	42,807	15,800,039	22,094	15,332,568	20,713
15-24	18,591,117	56,843	9,254,229	27,838	9,336,888	29,005
25-44	26,471,910	151,883	13,190,626	74,398	13,281,284	77,485
45-64	14,680,371	76,102	7,480,524	41,575	7,199,847	34,527
65 or over	4,554,290	16,853	2,248,238	9,184	2,306,052	7,669

TABLE XXII

Distribution of American-Born in the Maritime Provinces and Quebec Compared with the Prairie Provinces, by Sex, Classified by Age Groups: 1931

Age Group	Maritime Provinces and Quebec			Prairie Provinces		
	Total	Male	Female	Total	Male	Female
	No.	No.	No.	No.	No.	No.
ALL AGES	66,802	31,319	35,483	169,870	91,857	78,013
0- 4	4,348	2,246	2,102	2,145	1,105	1,040
5- 9	5,237	2,754	2,483	4,376	2,234	2,142
10-14	3,697	1,907	1,790	6,205	3,189	3,016
15-19	4,768	2,272	2,496	10,367	5,337	5,030
20-24	6,685	2,983	3,702	17,925	9,102	8,823
25-29	6,948	3,042	3,906	20,653	10,433	10,220
30-34	7,074	3,211	3,863	20,931	10,497	10,434
35-39	7,445	3,438	4,007	21,766	11,272	10,494
40-44	5,793	2,699	3,094	19,565	11,002	8,563

TABLE XXII—concluded

Distribution of American-Born in the Maritime Provinces and Quebec Compared with the Prairie Provinces, by Sex, Classified by Age Groups: 1931

Age Group	Maritime Provinces and Quebec			Prairie Provinces		
	Total	Male	Female	Total	Male	Female
	No.	No.	No.	No.	No.	No.
45-49	4,504	2,048	2,456	15,887	9,292	6,595
50-54	3,153	1,456	1,697	10,931	6,584	4,347
55-59	2,636	1,204	1,432	7,301	4,468	2,833
60-64	1,794	847	947	4,950	3,047	1,903
65-69	1,072	496	576	3,212	1,998	1,214
70-74	785	344	441	2,146	1,363	783
75-79	511	226	285	1,011	634	377
80-84	225	103	122	334	202	132
85-89	79	30	49	101	59	42
90-94	25	6	19	23	14	9
95-99	8	4	4	5	3	2
100 or over	1	....	1	1	....	1
Not stated	14	3	11	35	22	13

TABLE XXIII

American-Born in the Prairie Provinces, by Sex, Classified by Age Groups: 1926 and 1936

Age Group	1926		1936	
	Male	Female	Male	Female
	No.	No.	No.	No.
ALL AGES	92,999	78,435	81,915	70,993
0- 9	3,613	3,510	1,323	1,324
10-14	5,024	4,677	1,988	1,877
15-19	9,576	9,093	2,787	2,721
20-24	11,008	10,784	4,528	4,573
25-29	10,744	10,778	7,968	7,880
30-34	10,935	10,331	9,223	9,269
35-39	11,484	9,267	10,040	10,049
40-44	9,687	6,731	10,190	9,439
45-49	6,994	4,719	10,089	8,117
50-54	5,137	3,249	8,481	5,932
55-59	3,301	2,082	5,806	3,771
60-64	2,329	1,417	3,954	2,507
65-69	1,680	986	2,599	1,674
70-74	919	450	1,559	957
75-79	388	227	911	565
80-84	108	80	338	244
85-89	42	35	88	68
90 or over	12	9	20	17
Not stated	18	10	23	9

TABLE XXIV

*Percentage Distribution of American-Born in the Prairie Provinces,
by Sex, Classified by Age Groups: 1926 and 1936*

Age Group	1926		1936	
	Male	Female	Male	Female
ALL AGES	100.00	100.00	100.00	100.00
0- 9	3.88	4.48	1.62	1.86
10-14	5.40	5.96	2.43	2.64
15-19	10.30	11.59	3.40	3.83
20-24	11.84	13.75	5.53	6.44
25-29	11.55	13.74	9.73	11.10
30-34	11.76	13.17	11.26	13.06
35-39	12.35	11.81	12.26	14.15
40-44	10.42	8.58	12.44	13.30
45-49	7.52	6.02	12.32	11.43
50-54	5.52	4.14	10.35	8.36
55-59	3.55	2.65	7.09	5.31
60-64	2.50	1.81	4.83	3.53
65-69	1.81	1.26	3.17	2.36
70-74	0.99	0.57	1.90	1.35
75-79	0.42	0.29	1.11	0.80
80-84	0.12	0.10	0.41	0.34
85-89	0.05	0.04	0.11	0.10
90 or over	0.01	0.01	0.02	0.02
Not stated	0.02	0.01	0.03	0.01

TABLE XXV

*American-Born in the Prairie Provinces, Rural and Urban, by Sex,
Classified by Age Groups: 1936*

Age Group	Rural		Urban	
	Male	Female	Male	Female
	No.	No.	No.	No.
ALL AGES	60,714	46,210	21,201	24,783
0- 4	122	109	82	66
5- 9	703	736	416	413
10-14	1,384	1,304	604	573
15-19	2,161	1,947	626	774
20-24	3,653	3,091	875	1,482
25-29	6,144	5,033	1,824	2,847
30-34	7,015	5,937	2,208	3,332
35-39	7,515	6,469	2,525	3,580
40-44	7,449	6,015	2,741	3,424
45-49	7,346	5,344	2,743	2,773
50-54	6,163	3,940	2,318	1,992

TABLE XXV—concluded

American-Born in the Prairie Provinces, Rural and Urban, by Sex,
Classified by Age Groups: 1936

Age Group	Rural		Urban	
	Male	Female	Male	Female
	No.	No.	No.	No.
55-59	4,196	2,527	1,610	1,244
60-64	2,930	1,626	1,024	881
65-69	1,907	1,066	692	608
70-74	1,120	535	439	422
75-79	625	329	286	236
80-84	190	144	148	100
85-89	57	44	31	24
90 or over	17	10	3	7
Not stated	17	4	6	5

TABLE XXVI

Percentage Distribution of American-Born in the Prairie Provinces,
Rural and Urban, by Sex, Classified by Age Groups: 1936

Age Group	Rural		Urban	
	Male	Female	Male	Female
ALL AGES	100.00	100.00	100.00	100.00
0- 4	0.20	0.24	0.39	0.27
5- 9	1.16	1.59	1.96	1.67
10-14	2.28	2.82	2.85	2.31
15-19	3.56	4.21	2.95	3.12
20-24	6.02	6.69	4.13	5.98
25-29	10.12	10.89	8.60	11.49
30-34	11.55	12.85	10.41	13.44
35-39	12.38	14.00	11.91	14.45
40-44	12.27	13.02	12.93	13.82
45-49	12.10	11.56	12.94	11.19
50-54	10.15	8.53	10.93	8.04
55-59	6.91	5.47	7.59	5.02
60-64	4.83	3.52	4.83	3.55
65-69	3.14	2.31	3.26	2.45
70-74	1.84	1.16	2.07	1.70
75-79	1.03	0.71	1.35	0.95
80-84	0.31	0.31	0.70	0.40
85-89	0.09	0.10	0.15	0.10
90 or over	0.03	0.02	0.01	0.03
Not stated	0.03	0.01	0.03	0.02

TABLE XXVII

American-Born, Rural and Urban, by Sex, Classified by Age Groups,
Canada: 1931

| Age Group | Rural | | Total Urban | | Urban Localities | | | | | |
| | | | | | 30,000 or Over | | 1,000- 30,000 | | Under 1,000 | |
	Male	Female	Male	Female	Male	Female	Male	Female	Male	Female
					CANADA					
	No.	No.	No.	No.	No.	No.	No.	No.	No.	No.
ALL AGES	98,991	80,045	76,149	89,389	37,599	45,980	28,398	32,699	10,152	10,710
0- 4	2,742	2,560	2,945	2,783	1,418	1,369	1,271	1,214	256	200
5- 9	4,054	3,719	4,105	3,899	1,976	1,873	1,782	1,644	347	382
10-14	4,369	3,955	3,879	3,797	1,924	1,814	1,604	1,586	351	397
15-19	6,513	5,616	4,794	5,576	2,344	2,759	1,918	2,211	532	606
20-24	9,889	8,318	6,642	9,495	3,474	5,065	2,448	3,408	720	1,022
25-29	10,495	9,252	7,166	10,332	3,722	5,462	2,522	3,560	922	1,310
30-34	10,493	9,495	7,804	10,442	3,849	5,383	2,870	3,681	1,085	1,378
35-39	11,175	9,785	8,761	11,161	4,393	5,649	3,113	4,027	1,255	1,485
40-44	10,487	8,107	8,017	8,911	3,855	4,670	2,892	3,121	1,270	1,120
45-49	8,844	6,377	6,911	7,067	3,408	3,735	2,460	2,513	1,043	819
50-54	6,438	4,399	4,933	4,936	2,463	2,603	1,709	1,719	761	614
55-59	4,797	3,124	3,628	3,747	1,798	1,957	1,298	1,349	532	441
60-64	3,416	2,108	2,608	2,769	1,304	1,450	921	987	383	332
65-69	2,314	1,372	1,656	1,773	715	875	646	642	295	256
70-74	1,683	988	1,192	1,356	484	667	486	502	222	187
75-79	832	541	708	835	316	414	267	313	125	108
80-84	298	217	273	307	111	147	127	129	35	31
85-89	93	72	74	126	25	56	37	59	12	11
90-94	23	15	28	45	11	18	14	22	3	5
95-99	4	7	6	12	1	2	5	9	....	1
100 or over	....	2	....	1	....	1	....	....	....	....
Not stated	32	16	19	19	8	11	8	3	3	5

| | | | | | *PRINCE EDWARD ISLAND* | | | | | |
	No.	No.	No.	No.	No.	No.	No.	No.	No.	No.
ALL AGES	498	501	182	199	....	....	160	166	22	33
0- 4	60	58	15	22	....	....	8	19	7	3
5- 9	73	72	27	22	....	....	23	17	4	5
10-14	65	59	15	17	....	....	14	13	1	4
15-19	70	63	18	23	....	....	18	17	....	6
20-24	60	49	21	16	....	....	20	15	1	1
25-29	34	39	15	21	....	....	13	20	2	1
30-34	27	45	17	13	....	....	17	8	....	5
35-39	29	27	12	17	....	....	11	16	1	1
40-44	21	25	3	11	....	....	2	9	1	2
45-49	8	24	7	10	....	....	7	8	....	2

TABLE XXVII—continued

*American-Born, Rural and Urban, by Sex, Classified by Age Groups,
Canada: 1931*

| Age Group | Rural | | Total Urban | | Urban Localities | | | | | |
| | | | | | 30,000 or Over | | 1,000- 30,000 | | Under 1,000 | |
	Male	Female	Male	Female	Male	Female	Male	Female	Male	Female
			PRINCE	*EDWARD*	*ISLAND*—concluded					
	No.	No.	No.	No.	No.	No.	No.	No.	No.	No.
50-54	10	10	13	9	....	....	13	8	....	1
55-59	13	9	4	7	....	....	2	7	2	....
60-64	11	7	7	4	....	....	6	3	1	1
65-69	8	4	2	3	....	....	1	2	1	1
70-74	4	7	3	3	....	....	3	3	....	....
75-79	5	1	3	1	....	....	2	1	1	....
80-84	....	1	....	....	....	....	....	....	....	....
85-89	....	....	....	....	....	....	....	....	....	....
90-94	....	1	....	....	....	....	....	....	....	....
95-99	....	....	....	....	....	....	....	....	....	....
100 or over	....	....	....	....	....	....	....	....	....	....
Not stated	....	....	....	....	....	....	....	....	....	....

NOVA SCOTIA

| Age Group | Rural | | Total Urban | | 30,000 or Over | | 1,000-30,000 | | Under 1,000 | |
	Male	Female	Male	Female	Male	Female	Male	Female	Male	Female
	No.	No.	No.	No.	No.	No.	No.	No.	No.	No.
ALL AGES	1,859	2,003	1,496	1,864	402	539	1,048	1,261	46	64
0- 4	284	248	173	167	45	52	118	110	10	5
5- 9	259	222	146	167	33	39	113	123	....	5
10-14	173	123	68	90	15	20	51	67	2	3
15-19	192	184	125	145	29	36	90	103	6	6
20-24	155	218	156	207	40	71	114	125	2	11
25-29	101	144	148	181	51	62	92	110	5	9
30-34	129	161	140	198	32	56	102	137	6	5
35-39	151	182	147	223	52	46	92	172	3	5
40-44	113	136	117	133	28	38	87	92	2	3
45-49	74	115	81	115	17	27	58	84	6	4
50-54	48	66	63	50	21	21	41	28	1	1
55-59	67	73	55	62	17	17	36	41	2	4
60-64	25	49	30	45	8	14	21	29	1	2
65-69	32	22	24	33	8	15	16	18	....	....
70-74	33	25	10	30	2	15	8	14	....	1
75-79	15	24	10	8	3	3	7	5	....	....
80-84	3	6	3	5	1	5	2	....	....	....
85-89	3	2	....	3	....	....	....	3	....	....
90-94	1	2	....	1	....	1	....	....	....	....
95-99	1	....	....	....	....	....	....	....	....	....
100 or over	....	....	....	....	....	....	....	....	....	....
Not stated	....	1	....	1	....	1	....	....	....	....

TABLE XXVII—continued

American-Born, Rural and Urban, by Sex, Classified by Age Groups, Canada: 1931

Age Group	Rural		Total Urban		Urban Localities					
					30,000 or Over		1,000- 30,000		Under 1,000	
	Male	Female	Male	Female	Male	Female	Male	Female	Male	Female
						NEW BRUNSWICK				
	No.	No.	No.	No.	No.	No.	No.	No.	No.	No.
ALL AGES	2,633	2,982	1,404	1,775	408	547	982	1,201	14	27
0- 4	320	303	121	96	35	28	85	68	1	....
5- 9	346	285	135	109	25	25	109	83	1	1
10-14	240	232	99	107	21	24	77	82	1	1
15-19	244	222	124	161	43	51	80	108	1	2
20-24	218	286	136	189	49	62	86	126	1	1
25-29	194	271	115	174	40	55	74	116	1	3
30-34	174	246	109	166	33	57	75	103	1	6
35-39	190	274	130	213	33	64	96	146	1	3
40-44	163	206	111	130	32	36	77	93	2	1
45-49	118	165	74	116	20	34	54	78	....	4
50-54	86	115	57	88	19	24	37	62	1	2
55-59	95	113	66	63	22	24	43	39	1	....
60-64	73	75	41	50	10	18	30	32	1	....
65-69	62	69	36	44	12	20	23	23	1	1
70-74	55	63	24	31	5	13	19	17	....	1
75-79	30	41	15	18	5	6	10	11	....	1
80-84	19	11	8	17	4	6	4	11	....	....
85-89	5	3	3	1	....	....	3	1	....	....
90-94	....	1	....	2	....	....	....	2	....	....
95-99	1	1	....	....	....	....	....	....	....	....
100 or over	....	....	....	....	....	....	....	....	....	....
Not stated	....	....	....	....	....	....	....	....	....	....
						QUEBEC				
	No.	No.	No.	No.	No.	No.	No.	No.	No.	No.
ALL AGES	5,881	5,707	17,366	20,452	9,698	11,150	6,580	7,913	1,088	1,389
0- 4	483	424	790	784	341	376	362	321	87	87
5- 9	630	572	1,138	1,034	514	458	528	454	96	122
10-14	353	297	894	865	435	376	398	407	61	82
15-19	414	392	1,085	1,306	527	630	482	571	76	105
20-24	564	466	1,673	2,271	991	1,269	609	889	73	113
25-29	541	541	1,894	2,535	1,176	1,519	650	895	68	121
30-34	580	569	2,035	2,465	1,194	1,429	726	914	115	122
35-39	631	658	2,148	2,413	1,269	1,341	760	948	119	124
40-44	469	508	1,702	1,945	998	1,083	597	739	107	123
45-49	336	411	1,350	1,500	823	848	461	561	66	91
50-54	269	250	910	1,109	508	629	342	400	60	80

TABLE XXVII—continued

American-Born, Rural and Urban, by Sex, Classified by Age Groups, Canada: 1931

Age Group	Rural		Total Urban		Urban Localities					
					30,000 or Over		1,000- 30,000		Under 1,000	
	Male	Female	Male	Female	Male	Female	Male	Female	Male	Female
					QUEBEC—*concluded*					
	No.	No.	No.	No.	No.	No.	No.	No.	No.	No.
55-59	218	235	686	870	382	480	256	327	48	63
60-64	157	148	503	569	290	313	180	200	33	56
65-69	88	99	244	302	106	165	103	106	35	31
70-74	65	68	150	214	75	103	56	84	19	27
75-79	50	39	98	153	46	70	35	54	17	29
80-84	24	16	46	66	18	36	22	25	6	5
85-89	8	6	11	34	2	17	7	14	2	3
90-94	1	1	4	11	2	6	2	2	....	3
95-99	....	2	2	1	....	....	2	....	....	1
100 or over	....	1	....	....	....	....	....	....	....	....
Not stated	....	4	3	5	1	2	2	2	....	1

ONTARIO

Age Group	Rural		Total Urban		30,000 or Over		1,000- 30,000		Under 1,000	
	Male	Female	Male	Female	Male	Female	Male	Female	Male	Female
	No.	No.	No.	No.	No.	No.	No.	No.	No.	No.
ALL AGES	10,749	10,713	23,268	27,795	12,263	15,032	10,334	11,958	671	805
0- 4	657	623	1,250	1,204	657	613	553	554	40	37
5- 9	808	708	1,592	1,512	808	779	728	679	56	54
10-14	702	646	1,585	1,507	789	764	746	695	50	48
15-19	897	751	1,804	1,906	928	1,000	823	848	53	58
20-24	982	928	2,009	2,727	1,097	1,525	869	1,147	43	55
25-29	850	984	1,878	2,768	1,035	1,521	796	1,178	47	69
30-34	918	1,037	2,195	2,820	1,142	1,574	1,004	1,194	49	52
35-39	1,044	1,141	2,365	3,093	1,283	1,698	1,030	1,310	52	85
40-44	891	879	2,103	2,440	1,135	1,356	918	1,013	50	71
45-49	710	743	1,827	1,998	955	1,100	824	852	48	46
50-54	554	596	1,302	1,482	709	817	549	619	44	46
55-59	497	510	1,086	1,261	580	669	472	551	34	41
60-64	417	362	800	1,073	457	588	315	443	28	42
65-69	290	275	561	715	270	372	268	309	23	34
70-74	274	250	441	617	199	331	220	254	22	32
75-79	169	165	279	423	143	218	116	183	20	22
80-84	51	76	129	152	52	70	67	73	10	9
85-89	24	31	35	60	13	23	20	34	2	3
90-94	11	6	16	22	7	8	9	13	....	1
95-99	....	2	3	9	....	....	3	9	....	....
100 or over	....	....	....	1	....	1	....	....	....	....
Not stated	3	....	8	5	4	5	4	....	....	....

TABLE XXVII—continued

American-Born, Rural and Urban, by Sex, Classified by Age Groups,
Canada: 1931

Age Group	Rural		Total Urban		Urban Localities					
					30,000 or Over		1,000- 30,000		Under 1,000	
	Male	Female	Male	Female	Male	Female	Male	Female	Male	Female
	MANITOBA									
	No.	No.	No.	No.	No.	No.	No.	No.	No.	No.
ALL AGES........	5,148	4,335	3,879	4,541	2,654	3,248	974	1,023	251	270
0- 4..............	124	119	113	95	79	65	28	26	6	4
5- 9..............	197	148	142	133	98	95	40	31	4	7
10-14..............	282	242	172	156	128	120	37	33	7	3
15-19..............	401	369	211	245	150	176	49	58	12	11
20-24..............	474	403	357	488	255	366	87	101	15	21
25-29..............	479	494	346	525	238	386	81	108	27	31
30-34..............	570	544	390	543	253	386	101	119	36	38
35-39..............	634	571	453	618	310	438	114	135	29	45
40-44..............	580	471	457	515	305	357	117	125	35	33
45-49..............	459	355	411	442	278	316	108	104	25	22
50-54..............	336	234	331	284	233	200	77	64	21	20
55-59..............	246	154	213	190	143	130	57	46	13	14
60-64..............	148	97	144	131	96	92	41	32	7	7
65-69..............	93	55	66	68	44	46	18	15	4	7
70-74..............	79	35	41	52	21	36	11	12	9	4
75-79..............	27	28	20	35	14	22	5	10	1	3
80-84..............	10	12	9	11	7	10	2	1	....	....
85-89..............	5	3	2	7	2	5	....	2	....	....
90-94..............	2	....	1	2	....	1	1	1	....	....
95-99..............	....	....	....	1	....	1	....	....	....	....
100 or over......	....	....	....	....	....	....	....	....	....	....
Not stated......	2	1	....	....	....	....	....	....	....	....
	SASKATCHEWAN									
	No.	No.	No.	No.	No.	No.	No.	No.	No.	No.
ALL AGES........	30,178	22,787	9,486	10,557	2,317	2,796	2,931	3,355	4,238	4,406
0- 4..............	281	279	130	100	41	30	33	34	56	36
5- 9..............	686	613	245	240	73	67	65	80	107	93
10-14..............	1,006	941	294	325	86	82	89	99	119	144
15-19..............	1,866	1,575	433	563	114	157	126	180	193	226
20-24..............	3,417	2,750	755	1,268	214	398	249	412	292	458
25-29..............	3,880	3,184	1,010	1,530	285	439	319	471	406	620
30-34..............	3,546	3,077	1,100	1,566	283	412	313	500	504	654
35-39..............	3,720	2,933	1,205	1,549	283	384	348	493	574	672
40-44..............	3,537	2,533	1,310	1,132	274	290	434	373	602	469
45-49..............	2,986	1,887	1,072	828	255	202	338	275	479	351

TABLE XXVII—continued

American Born, Rural and Urban, by Sex, Classified by Age Groups, Canada: 1931

Age Group	Rural		Total Urban		Urban Localities					
					30,000 or Over		1,000-30,000		Under 1,000	
	Male	Female	Male	Female	Male	Female	Male	Female	Male	Female

SASKATCHEWAN—concluded

Age Group	No.	No.	No.	No.	No.	No.	No.	No.	No.	No.
50-54	1,974	1,172	715	529	165	131	235	179	315	219
55-59	1,312	729	450	340	106	83	135	93	209	164
60-64	833	504	308	238	67	59	92	72	149	107
65-69	541	290	221	173	36	32	75	46	110	95
70-74	353	189	149	104	25	15	47	26	77	63
75-79	149	82	68	49	9	12	23	14	36	23
80-84	64	30	14	15	....	2	8	6	6	7
85-89	17	10	3	3	1	....	1	1	1	2
90-94	3	4	1	2	....	....	....	1	1	1
95-99	....	1	....	....	....	....	....	....	....	....
100 or over	....	1	....	....	....	....	....	....	....	....
Not stated	7	3	3	3	....	1	1	....	2	2

ALBERTA

Age Group	No.	No.	No.	No.	No.	No.	No.	No.	No.	No.
ALL AGES	32,286	23,538	10,880	12,255	4,535	5,700	3,093	3,330	3,252	3,225
0- 4	319	323	138	124	61	68	41	36	36	20
5- 9	701	722	263	286	126	131	72	77	65	78
10-14	1,109	1,009	326	343	142	156	100	94	84	93
15-19	1,917	1,609	509	669	229	324	125	180	155	165
20-24	3,251	2,531	848	1,383	399	711	204	350	245	322
25-29	3,636	2,893	1,082	1,594	469	779	289	401	324	414
30-34	3,745	3,039	1,146	1,665	478	769	325	453	343	443
35-39	3,842	3,068	1,418	1,755	607	786	392	480	419	489
40-44	3,717	2,518	1,401	1,394	559	653	410	386	432	355
45-49	3,128	2,023	1,236	1,060	504	490	363	317	369	253
50-54	2,353	1,433	875	695	356	316	257	178	262	201
55-59	1,658	936	589	484	238	212	174	138	177	134
60-64	1,197	612	417	321	158	130	136	91	123	100
65-69	804	406	273	222	93	81	90	67	90	74
70-74	540	244	201	159	64	55	67	56	70	48
75-79	264	114	106	69	32	28	36	17	38	24
80-84	74	45	31	19	13	6	7	5	11	8
85-89	19	9	13	10	4	5	3	3	6	2
90-94	3	....	4	1	1	....	1	1	2	....
95-99	2	....	1	....	1	....	....	....	....	....
100 or over	....	....	....	....	....	....	....	....	....	....
Not stated	7	4	3	2	1	....	1	....	1	2

TABLE XXVII—continued

American-Born, Rural and Urban, by Sex, Classified by Age Groups, Canada: 1931

| Age Group | Rural | | Total Urban | | Urban Localities | | | | | |
| | | | | | 30,000 or Over | | 1,000-30,000 | | Under 1,000 | |
	Male	Female	Male	Female	Male	Female	Male	Female	Male	Female
					BRITISH COLUMBIA					
ALL AGES	No. 9,448	No. 7,361	No. 8,026	No. 9,871	No. 5,322	No. 6,968	No. 2,296	No. 2,492	No. 408	No. 411
0- 4	210	180	215	188	159	137	43	46	13	5
5- 9	349	371	416	395	299	279	104	100	13	16
10-14	434	401	423	383	308	272	92	96	23	15
15-19	506	449	477	557	324	385	125	146	28	26
20-24	751	679	666	944	429	663	210	243	27	38
25-29	766	695	663	1,001	428	701	208	261	27	39
30-34	781	760	663	997	434	700	207	253	22	44
35-39	907	916	872	1,269	556	892	270	327	46	50
40-44	966	821	808	1,203	524	857	250	291	34	55
45-49	991	643	847	985	556	718	247	234	44	33
50-54	770	510	652	684	452	465	158	181	42	38
55-59	656	357	457	462	310	342	123	107	24	13
60-64	519	248	343	333	218	236	100	85	25	12
65-69	375	149	216	212	146	144	52	56	18	12
70-74	269	106	161	143	93	99	55	36	13	8
75-79	120	47	105	78	64	55	33	18	8	5
80-84	52	19	31	21	16	12	15	8	....	1
85-89	12	8	7	8	3	6	3	1	1	1
90-94	2	....	2	4	1	2	1	2	....	....
95-99	....	....	....	1	....	1	....	....	....	....
100 or over	....	....	....	....	....	....	....	....	....	....
Not stated	12	2	2	3	2	2	....	1	....	....
					YUKON					
ALL AGES	No. 203	No. 81	No. 162	No. 80	No.	No.	No.	No.	No. 162	No. 80
0- 4	4	1	....	3	....	....	....	....	....	3
5- 9	4	6	1	1	....	....	....	....	1	1
10-14	3	3	3	4	....	....	....	....	3	4
15-19	2	1	8	1	....	....	....	....	8	1
20-24	8	5	21	2	....	....	....	....	21	2
25-29	6	5	15	3	....	....	....	....	15	3
30-34	10	12	9	9	....	....	....	....	9	9
35-39	8	8	11	11	....	....	....	....	11	11
40-44	17	7	5	8	....	....	....	....	5	8

TABLE XXVII—concluded

American-Born, Rural and Urban, by Sex, Classified by Age Groups, Canada: 1931

Age Group	Rural		Total Urban		Urban Localities					
					30,000 or Over		1,000- 30,000		Under 1,000	
	Male	Female	Male	Female	Male	Female	Male	Female	Male	Female
					YUKON—concluded					
	No.	No.	No.	No.	No.	No.	No.	No.	No.	No.
45-49	23	8	6	13	....	....	....	....	6	13
50-54	26	9	15	6	....	....	....	....	15	6
55-59	26	8	22	8	....	....	....	....	22	8
60-64	33	4	15	5	....	....	....	....	15	5
65-69	18	2	13	1	....	....	....	....	13	1
70-74	10	1	12	3	....	....	....	....	12	3
75-79	3	....	4	1	....	....	....	....	4	1
80-84	1	....	2	1	....	....	....	....	2	1
85-89	....	....	....	....	....	....	....	....	....	....
90-94	....	....	....	....	....	....	....	....	....	....
95-99	....	1	....	....	....	....	....	....	....	....
100 or over	....	....	....	....	....	....	....	....	....	....
Not stated	1	....	....	....	....	....	....	....	....	....
					NORTHWEST TERRITORIES					
	No.	No.	No.	No.	No.	No.	No.	No.	No.	No.
ALL AGES	108	37	....	....	....	....	....	....	....	....
0- 4	....	2	....	....	....	....	....	....	....	....
5- 9	1	....	....	....	....	....	....	....	....	....
10-14	2	2	....	....	....	....	....	....	....	....
15-19	4	1	....	....	....	....	....	....	....	....
20-24	9	3	....	....	....	....	....	....	....	....
25-29	8	2	....	....	....	....	....	....	....	....
30-34	13	5	....	....	....	....	....	....	....	....
35-39	19	7	....	....	....	....	....	....	....	....
40-44	13	3	....	....	....	....	....	....	....	....
45-49	11	3	....	....	....	....	....	....	....	....
50-54	12	4	....	....	....	....	....	....	....	....
55-59	9	....	....	....	....	....	....	....	....	....
60-64	3	2	....	....	....	....	....	....	....	....
65-69	3	1	....	....	....	....	....	....	....	....
70-74	1	....	....	....	....	....	....	....	....	....
75-79	....	....	....	....	....	....	....	....	....	....
80-84	....	1	....	....	....	....	....	....	....	....
85-89	....	....	....	....	....	....	....	....	....	....
90-94	....	....	....	....	....	....	....	....	....	....
95-99	....	....	....	....	....	....	....	....	....	....
100 or over	....	....	....	....	....	....	....	....	....	....
Not stated	....	1	....	....	....	....	....	....	....	....

CHAPTER IV

CONJUGAL CONDITION—FAMILY COMPOSITION—
VITAL STATISTICS

As in Chapter III, the attributes herein discussed are so intermingled that they cannot usefully be separated.

Conjugal Condition

As introductory to the study of the conjugal condition of the American-born in Canada, Table XXVIII compares, on numerical and percentage bases, the conjugal state of the total population of Canada with that of the total immigrant population and of the American-born. Comparable data for the total White population of the United States is also shown. It is interesting to note that the American-born living in Canada have a larger percentage married than the White population of the United States and that in every classification the percentage of widows far surpasses that of widowers, the main reasons being that widowers remarry more than widows, and that the husband is older than the wife and consequently dies earlier. Divorce among the United States population is much greater than among the Canadian; the high percentage divorced among the American-born in Canada is probably accounted for by the numbers who have been divorced prior to entry into the country. This also explains the higher percentage among the total immigrant population, which, of course, includes the American-born.

The conjugal condition of that section of the total population 15 years of age or over, rural and urban, is then compared, on a percentage basis, with the American-born and the total immigrants within the same age limits in Table XXIX. Probably the most significant revelation of this table is that the American-born increase our percentage of married less than do other immigrants. This is true of both males and females, but more so of urban than of rural females. Age distribution is, of course, mainly account-able. The American-born add more than do the other foreign-born to the divorced population. The widowed are less prominent among the American-born than among either of the other classes—age again being probably responsible. Noteworthy is the similar tendency in all three populations to have a larger proportion married among the urban than among the rural males, and among the rural than among the urban females. In the case

96

of females, the explanation is that the unmarried rural who move into the cities increase the proportion of the married rural while adding to the unmarried urban; the converse, however, cannot be said to hold for males.

Following the above analyses, Table XXX gives, by sex, the conjugal condition of the American-born 15 years of age or over.

TABLE XXVIII

Numerical and Percentage Distributions, by Sex, Classified by Conjugal Condition, of Total Population, Total Immigrant Population and American-Born in Canada, 1931, and Total White Population of the United States, 1930

Conjugal Condition	Total Population of Canada				Immigrant Population of Canada			
	Male		Female		Male		Female	
	No.	p. c.	No.	p. c.	No.	p. c.	No.	p. c.
ALL CLASSES	5,374,541	100.00	5,002,245	100.00	1,298,540	100.00	1,008,985	100.00
Single	3,179,444	59.16	2,771,968	55.41	449,382	34.61	239,035	23.69
Married	2,033,240	37.83	1,937,950	38.74	792,714	61.05	680,505	67.44
Widowed	148,954	2.77	288,641	5.77	46,709	3.60	87,867	8.71
Divorced	4,049	0.08	3,392	0.07	2,083	0.16	1,506	0.15
Not stated	8,854	0.16	294	0.01	7,652	0.59	72	0.01

	American-Born in Canada				Total White Population of United States			
	Male		Female		Male		Female	
	No.	p. c.	No.	p.c.	No.	p. c.	No.	p. c.
ALL CLASSES	175,140	100.00	169,434	100.00	55,163,854	100.00	53,700,353	100.00
Single	75,653	43.20	51,500	30.40	29,313,557	53.14	25,706,178	47.87
Married	93,276	53.26	107,040	63.18	23,603,919	42.79	23,447,330	43.66
Widowed	5,647	3.22	10,487	6.19	1,745,239	3.16	4,023,477	7.49
Divorced	543	0.31	404	0.24	428,090	0.78	477,684	0.89
Not stated	21	0.01	3	....	73,049	0.13	45,684	0.09

TABLE XXIX

Percentage Distribution of the Total Population 15 Years of Age or Over,
Compared with the American-Born and the Immigrant Population
15 Years of Age or Over, Rural and Urban, by Sex, Classified by
Conjugal Condition: 1931

Conjugal Condition	Rural		Urban	
	Male	Female	Male	Female
TOTAL POPULATION (15 Years or Over)				
ALL CLASSES	100.00	100.00	100.00	100.00
Single	44.33	30.39	38.09	36.49
Married	51.36	62.06	57.95	54.12
Widowed	4.21	7.49	3.85	9.26
Divorced	0.10	0.06	0.12	0.13
Not stated[1]	....	....	....	....
AMERICAN-BORN (15 Years or Over)				
ALL CLASSES	100.00	100.00	100.00	100.00
Single	38.86	17.34	29.80	23.67
Married	57.12	77.18	66.12	67.37
Widowed	3.65	5.30	3.74	8.60
Divorced	0.37	0.17	0.33	0.36
Not stated[1]	....	....	....	....
IMMIGRANT POPULATION (15 Years or Over)				
ALL CLASSES	100.00	100.00	100.00	100.00
Single	35.64	12.49	26.88	20.53
Married	60.27	79.67	69.14	68.93
Widowed	3.91	7.73	3.81	10.35
Divorced	0.18	0.11	0.17	0.19
Not stated[1]	....	....	....	....

[1] Percentage very small.

TABLE XXX

American-Born 15 Years of Age or Over, by Sex, Classified by Conjugal Condition, Canada: 1931

Conjugal Condition	Totals			Rural			Urban		
	Both Sexes	Male	Female	Both Sexes	Male	Female	Both Sexes	Male	Female
	No.	No.	No.	No.	No.	No.	No.	No.	No.
CANADA	301,767	153,046	148,721	157,637	87,826	69,811	144,130	65,220	78,910
Single	84,346	53,559	30,787	46,234	34,127	12,107	38,112	19,432	18,680
Married	200,316	93,276	107,040	104,039	50,160	53,879	96,277	43,116	53,161
Widowed	16,134	5,647	10,487	6,906	3,205	3,701	9,228	2,442	6,786
Divorced	947	543	404	447	325	122	500	218	282
Not stated	24	21	3	11	9	2	13	12	1

FAMILY COMPOSITION

Table XXXI shows the composition of families with American-born heads in Canada compared with that of all families. Several points of difference are easily discernible; some at least are due to the fact that the comparison is of an immigrant with a total population. From the third column it will be observed that the families with American-born heads exceed the total families in the proportion of families with one person, the proportions of their own children under 15 years of age and the earnings of wives, while they fall below in all the other features tabulated—most notably in the proportion of children gainfully occupied, which is explained by the youth of the children. Families with American-born heads evidently avoid the responsibilities of guardianship and of dependants other than children. Owners and tenants are in about the same proportion as in the total population.

TABLE XXXI

*Family Composition and Related Data for American-Born Heads of
Families and All Heads of Families: 1931*

Item	American-Born Heads of Families (1)	All Heads of Families (2)	Ratio (2) ÷ (1)
Families..............No.	115,474	2,419,360	21.0
Owners..............No.	65,679	1,370,622	20.9
Tenants..............No.	49,795	1,048,738	21.1
Persons in families..............No.	433,713	9,346,195	21.5
Heads of families[1]..............No.	202,295	4,276,465	21.1
Families of one person..............No.	16,784	270,312	16.1
p.c.	14.53	11.17	
Families with children..............No.	77,150	1,669,634	21.6
p.c.	66.81	69.01	
Persons per family..............No.	3.76	3.86	
Children per family..............No.	1.94	2.02	
Own children living at home—			
All ages..............No.	224,053	4,881,050	21.8
0- 6 years..............No.	76,789	1,493,881	19.5
7-14 years..............No.	84,741	1,686,358	19.9
15 or over..............No.	62,523	1,700,811	27.2
Guardianship children—			
All ages..............No.	3,651	84,108	23.0
0- 6 years..............No.	802	19,146	23.9
7-14 years..............No.	1,613	37,772	23.4
15 or over..............No.	1,236	27,190	22.0
Dependants other than wives or children..No.	3,714	104,572	28.2
Wives gainfully occupied—			
Total..............No.	1,569	38,890	24.8
With earnings stated..............No.	906	21,517	23.7
Earnings..............$	577,310	11,426,350	19.8
Children gainfully occupied—			
Total..............No.	20,315	725,549	35.7
With earnings stated..............No.	16,121	609,109	37.8
Earnings..............$	9,033,960	345,258,260	38.2

[1] Families with husband and wife living together are considered to have two heads.

Vital Statistics

While it is important to have records of births, marriages, and deaths for the American-born in Canada as compared with the remainder of the population, it appears even more important to ascertain the relationship of these between different elements of the American-born themselves. One of the best tests of the latter is the tendency or lack of tendency in the American-born to marry other American-born. The data on the birthplaces of grooms and brides illustrate recent behaviour in this respect. Table XXXII shows that, in 1931, American-born males were exceeded by the males of only three of the countries there listed in the tendency to marry brides born elsewhere than in the country of birth of the husband. Table XXXIII is interesting as showing the birthplace of the brides of 3,829 American-born grooms, marrying in the different provinces of Canada. On the other hand, the birthplaces of the father and mother shown in current birth statistics include and throw light on cases where the marriages took place before emigration to Canada.

Table XXXII

Percentages of Males of Various Countries of Birth Marrying in 1931 Brides from the Same Country

Country of Birth	Percentage Marrying Brides Born in Same Country	Country of Birth	Percentage Marrying Brides Born in Same Country
Finland	82.4	Germany	30.7
Poland	65.7	Denmark	29.9
Hungary	62.3	England	28.0
Russia	40.9	Ireland	26.5
Austria	38.2	Sweden	22.6
Italy	35.6	United States	21.1
Belgium	34.1	Holland	16.9
Roumania	32.7	Wales	12.0
Scotland	32.6	France	10.5
Norway	31.9		

Table XXXIII

American-Born Males Marrying in 1931 in the Different Provinces of Canada, by Birthplace of Bride

Province	American-Born Grooms	Birthplaces of Brides			
		United States	Province where Married	Elsewhere in Canada	Elsewhere
	No.	No.	No.	No.	No.
CANADA...................................	3,829	807	1,919	539	564
Prince Edward Island..........	13	1	10	2	Nil
Nova Scotia..........................	99	11	79	3	6
New Brunswick....................	190	69	106	9	6
Quebec.................................	517	79	352	33	53
Ontario................................	985	161	590	96	138
Manitoba..............................	200	46	96	29	29
Saskatchewan......................	763	197	315	140	111
Alberta................................	805	201	301	155	148
British Columbia................	257	42	70	72	73

Table XXXIV

Percentage Distribution of Marriages of and Legitimate Births to American-Born, by Sex, Classified by Birthplace of Spouse: 1931

Birthplace of Spouse	Marriages of American-Born		Legitimate Births to American-Born	
	Bridegrooms	Brides	Fathers	Mothers
ALL BIRTHPLACES................	100.00	100.00	100.00	100.00
Canada.................................	64.21	46.76	55.25	50.02
British Isles........................	9.04	11.88	8.34	9.69
United States......................	21.08	27.40	30.10	29.03
Other...................................	5.67	13.96	6.31	11.25

Table XXXIV shows that of children born to American-born fathers, 55 p.c. had Canadian-born mothers and only 30 p.c. had American-born mothers. Of the births to American-born mothers, 50 p.c. were of Canadian-born fathers and 29 p.c. of American-born fathers. Thus, the American-born female immigrant is slightly less apt to have children by an American spouse than is the American-born male, although she is also less apt to have a Canadian spouse, and shows a stronger preference than the male for a British-born or a foreign-born (other than American-born) immigrant. From the marriage statistics the tendency to marry a compatriot is shown to be less in recent than in earlier marriages, only 21 p.c. of the males and 27 p.c. of the females currently marrying American-born. Since the American-born are only about 3 p.c. of the population of Canada, it would seem— at least superficially—that there is a preference for a compatriot even though only 21 p.c. so marry (yet this may be due to opportunity rather than to preference: in the nature of things the American-born male would have more acquaintances among the American-born females). In point of fact it is the low percentage of those marrying compatriots that is striking— no doubt due, to some extent, to the circumstance that so many of the American-born have Canadian-born or British-born parents, though race and religion may also enter. To fulfil the condition of being at one and the same time of the same race, religion and country of birth, and of suitable ages, would reduce the number of available mates considerably. Also, on the evidence of birth statistics, a considerable number were married before coming to Canada; this alone would account for a higher proportion marrying compatriots than is shown by the statistics of marriages (in Canada). Altogether the facts of Table XXXIV appear to indicate more strongly than almost any other data that the American-born did not come to Canada to settle in groups.

Turning to the incidence of death on the American-born as compared with the total population (Table XXXVII), it is seen that the death rate of the former is much lower, indeed it is lower than that of either Canada or the United States, being 8.76 per 1,000 compared with 10.24 (1930-32 averages) and 11.1 (10.6 White and 15.5 Coloured) (United States Census, 1930). Age is a factor to be considered here: it is at the extreme ages, where death rates are highest, that the American-born numbers are low.

TABLE XXXV

Legitimate Births (Exclusive of Stillbirths) to All Fathers and Mothers and to American-Born Fathers and Mothers, Classified by Birthplace of Other Parent: 1931

Birthplace of Other Parent	All Fathers	All Mothers	American-Born Father	American-Born Mother
	No.	No.	No.	No.
ALL BIRTHPLACES	232,108	232,108	10,712	11,108
Canada	164,263	171,479	5,915	5,552
Prince Edward Island	2,199	2,024	54	98
Nova Scotia	10,242	10,211	214	305
New Brunswick	9,696	9,497	261	374
Quebec	78,922	78,756	1,310	1,452
Ontario	46,481	46,263	1,679	2,126
Manitoba	7,688	9,674	622	491
Saskatchewan	3,808	7,079	813	286
Alberta	2,677	4,770	742	274
British Columbia	2,019	2,606	188	109
Not specified	531	599	32	37
British Isles	26,466	24,294	893	1,076
England	16,522	14,691	591	718
Ireland	2,860	2,394	73	91
Scotland	6,391	6,663	204	236
Wales	612	501	23	26
Other	81	45	2	5
British Possessions	1,653	1,366	22	58
Newfoundland	1,126	1,007	12	24
Other	527	359	10	34
Europe	27,341	22,427	638	1,164
Austria	3,016	2,291	23	44
Belgium	565	468	15	33
Denmark	554	361	12	35
Finland	675	677	22	34
France	388	305	17	31
Germany	1,119	1,029	82	93
Holland	425	299	7	19
Hungary	1,215	1,102	16	29
Italy	2,289	1,602	9	71
Norway	938	676	105	177
Poland	6,152	5,708	38	66
Roumania	1,380	985	22	50
Russia	5,514	4,549	179	282
Sweden	894	573	59	133
Other	2,217	1,802	32	67
Asia	1,354	1,151	9	17
China	254	169	2	3
Japan	807	781	1	2
Other	293	201	6	12
United States	10,712	11,108	3,222	3,222
Other	83	80	7	10
Not specified	236	203	6	9

Table XXXVI

Marriages of Total and of American-Born Bridegrooms and Brides,
Classified by Birthplace of Bridegroom or Bride: 1931

Birthplace of Bridegroom or Bride	All Bridegrooms	All Brides	American-Born Bridegrooms	American-Born Brides
	No.	No.	No.	No.
ALL BIRTHPLACES	66,591	66,591	3,829	2,946
Canada	44,397	49,289	2,458	1,377
Prince Edward Island	589	546	16	27
Nova Scotia	3,207	3,355	111	79
New Brunswick	2,341	2,348	123	75
Quebec	14,644	15,007	420	250
Ontario	15,766	16,508	737	530
Manitoba	2,958	3,700	200	127
Saskatchewan	1,997	3,452	378	124
Alberta	1,356	2,385	348	100
British Columbia	1,005	1,359	96	51
Not specified	534	629	29	14
British Isles	9,557	7,820	346	350
England	5,791	4,380	217	230
Ireland	1,056	869	31	25
Scotland	2,478	2,414	91	87
Wales	225	153	6	8
Other	7	4	1	....
British Possessions	480	370	8	18
Newfoundland	279	244	3	7
Other	201	126	5	11
Europe	8,098	6,057	206	384
Austria	432	286	7	15
Belgium	129	104	6	11
Denmark	261	107	5	29
Finland	459	524	12	15
France	114	74	5	7
Germany	475	280	18	25
Holland	154	55	3	11
Hungary	300	237	2	20
Italy	436	199	3	31
Norway	304	190	28	38
Poland	2,205	2,043	29	36
Roumania	425	301	12	12
Russia	1,292	978	47	45
Sweden	337	161	16	31
Other	775	518	13	58
Asia	171	66	1	2
China	64	16	....	1
Japan	49	20	....	....
Other	58	30	1	1
United States	3,829	2,946	807	807
Other	49	27	2	7
Not specified	10	16	1	1

TABLE XXXVII

Average Death Rates (1930–32) for Total Population and American-Born, by Sex, Classified by Provinces

Province, City or Town	All Deaths			Deaths of American-Born		
	Both Sexes	Male	Female	Both Sexes	Male	Female
CANADA	10.24	10.67	9.77	8.76	9.50	8.01
Prince Edward Island	11.07	11.27	10.86	5.31	6.37	4.29
Nova Scotia	11.92	12.17	11.65	10.48	9.94	10.95
New Brunswick	11.59	11.96	11.19	13.19	13.79	12.68
Quebec	12.01	12.48	11.53	9.76	10.84	8.81
Ontario	10.63	11.09	10.17	12.54	14.00	11.25
Manitoba	7.78	8.40	7.10	8.02	8.94	7.10
Saskatchewan	6.66	7.06	6.19	5.36	5.60	5.08
Alberta	7.44	7.92	6.84	6.97	7.48	6.35
British Columbia	8.96	9.93	7.76	9.73	12.09	7.33
CITIES AND TOWNS OF 10,000 OR OVER—						
Belleville, Ont	17.31	19.55	15.21	28.42	40.40	15.87
Brandon, Man	13.85	15.97	11.76	20.44	29.96	11.84
Brantford, Ont	12.48	12.71	12.26	19.57	28.02	13.89
Calgary, Alta	8.85	9.90	7.73	11.48	13.43	9.87
Charlottetown, P.E.I	22.25	26.02	18.89	8.13	8.40	7.87
Chatham, N.B	21.60	24.95	18.43	28.52	31.29	26.10
Chicoutimi, Que	16.29	16.05	16.54	15.87	18.52	13.89
Cornwall, Ont	21.57	21.35	21.79	26.32	20.00	32.47
East Windsor, Ont	3.75	3.76	3.75	3.37	1.71	4.98
Edmonton, Alta	10.92	12.76	9.05	14.01	18.30	10.75
Fort William, Ont	7.93	8.89	6.85	9.56	11.15	8.07
Galt, Ont	12.57	13.87	11.37	13.99	13.02	14.93
Glace Bay, N.S	13.49	13.22	13.79	8.13	10.64	6.01
Granby, Que	12.56	12.81	12.32	16.03	17.01	15.15
Guelph, Ont	11.07	12.60	9.67	15.58	21.43	11.05
Halifax, N.S	15.01	16.60	13.52	15.94	17.41	14.84
Hamilton, Ont	9.75	10.21	9.28	10.76	10.90	10.64
Hull, Que	12.37	13.21	11.52	16.67	17.81	15.50
Joliette, Que	16.16	18.54	14.00	4.22	4.90	3.70
Kingston, Ont	20.79	24.11	17.78	25.38	27.78	23.73
Kitchener, Ont	11.38	12.07	10.70	10.64	9.84	11.33
Lachine, Que	10.22	9.93	10.50	6.70	10.89	3.42
Lethbridge, Alta	13.89	15.02	12.65	23.47	24.57	22.32
Lévis, Que	19.93	20.79	19.10	31.01	35.09	27.78
London, Ont	14.55	14.93	14.21	16.92	15.83	17.74
Medicine Hat, Alta	13.20	13.73	12.66	16.23	20.53	12.82
Moncton, N.B	12.02	13.20	10.96	16.98	17.36	16.67
Montreal, Que	13.01	13.68	12.34	13.58	16.41	11.10
Moose Jaw, Sask	9.73	11.28	8.10	14.35	21.51	8.83
New Westminster, B.C	16.19	18.35	13.79	22.65	29.13	17.04
Niagara Falls, Ont	10.73	11.12	10.33	17.20	16.32	17.98
North Bay, Ont	10.09	10.96	9.14	15.47	31.75	2.53

TABLE XXXVII—concluded

Average Death Rates (1930-32) for Total Population of American-Born, by Sex, Classified by Provinces

Province, City or Town	All Deaths			Deaths of American-Born		
	Both Sexes	Male	Female	Both Sexes	Male	Female
Oshawa, Ont.	8.89	8.97	8.81	9.78	6.98	12.68
Ottawa, Ont.	13.62	14.94	12.46	15.07	18.27	12.56
Outremont, Que.	4.85	4.54	5.10	5.46	3.42	6.83
Owen Sound, Ont.	13.79	15.08	12.56	20.20	35.56	7.41
Peterborough, Ont.	14.27	14.92	13.67	13.64	17.34	10.70
Port Arthur, Ont.	11.08	12.66	9.29	9.55	9.72	9.39
Quebec, Que.	16.99	18.48	15.67	10.79	7.81	12.94
Regina, Sask.	8.96	9.82	8.10	11.47	13.78	9.68
St. Boniface, Man.	27.62	34.21	21.18	30.92	44.54	20.63
St. Catharines, Ont.	11.93	12.42	11.46	16.37	20.20	13.15
St. Hyacinthe, Que.	23.47	26.27	21.16	11.00	11.59	10.60
St. Jean, Que.	11.73	12.67	10.72	10.32	9.62	10.96
St. Thomas, Ont.	14.37	16.25	12.62	16.63	18.83	14.88
Saint John, N.B.	14.59	14.83	14.37	17.80	17.16	18.28
Sandwich, Ont.	5.09	4.88	5.30	5.57	4.72	6.45
Sarnia, Ont.	12.90	14.27	11.49	19.39	15.59	22.35
Saskatoon, Sask.	10.76	12.33	9.15	14.10	14.90	13.40
Sault Ste. Marie, Ont.	9.66	10.78	8.47	5.45	6.39	4.67
Shawinigan Falls, Que.	11.21	11.20	11.22	6.56	6.25	6.90
Sherbrooke, Que.	15.32	16.62	14.15	11.31	10.14	12.31
Sorel, Que.	13.86	14.35	13.33	2.51	....	5.21
Stratford, Ont.	11.16	12.67	9.71	11.34	10.10	12.35
Sudbury, Ont.	13.37	14.81	11.56	7.41	7.11	7.73
Sydney, N.S.	8.86	9.88	7.82	4.08	4.76	3.57
Thetford Mines, Que.	12.20	12.50	11.90	2.23	....	4.55
Timmins, Ont.	11.94	12.73	10.96	11.55	13.89	9.43
Toronto, Ont.	10.79	11.54	10.08	11.65	13.30	10.35
Three Rivers, Que.	15.98	16.96	15.05	7.81	9.86	5.89
Valleyfield, Que.	14.24	15.59	12.91	9.26	4.35	12.90
Vancouver, B.C.	9.30	10.42	8.03	10.18	13.52	7.58
Verdun, Que.	7.31	7.21	7.41	7.37	6.86	7.84
Victoria, B.C.	14.28	15.57	12.90	16.67	23.05	12.46
Walkerville, Ont.	17.91	18.07	17.75	19.81	17.86	21.58
Welland, Ont.	13.07	14.71	11.36	5.24	5.62	4.90
Westmount, Que.	10.33	9.76	10.73	8.99	6.16	10.87
Windsor, Ont.	9.04	9.45	8.62	13.22	16.35	10.37
Winnipeg, Man.	7.95	8.68	7.21	9.60	10.93	8.52
Woodstock, Ont.	14.57	15.06	14.10	10.78	8.93	12.50

CHAPTER V

RACIAL ORIGIN*

SINCE the Census of the United States has no rubric on racial origins (except in the sense of colour), it is impossible to assess the racial proportions of the American-born that have emigrated to Canada. However, some valuable comparisons, by sex and by rural and urban residence, can be deduced within the Canadian data.

Table XXXVIII shows the races in Canada which have been increased by American-born immigrants. Those that constituted larger proportions of the American-born than of the total Canadian population in 1931 were: Irish, British other than English, Irish and Scottish, Czechoslovak, Dutch, Finnish, Russian, German, Scandinavian, and Negro. These comprised 43.74 p.c. of the American-born in Canada, whereas they made up only 22.41 p.c. of the total Canadian population. The English, Scottish, and French races, on the other hand, constituted 52.01 p.c. of the American-born and 67.61 p.c. of the total population.

Racially, then, the American-born differ considerably from the total Canadian population, though the proportions of British in each are almost exactly the same (about 51 p.c.). The French element is considerably smaller in the American-born than in the total (16.15 p.c. and 28.22 p.c., respectively); on the other hand, the Dutch, German, and Scandinavian races comprise 26.65 p.c. of the American-born and only 8.20 p.c. of the total Canadian population; while the remaining races together make up 4.57 p.c. of the American-born and 11.73 p.c. of the total.

The "preference" for rural or urban life of each race in the American-born is shown by comparison with the similar preference in the total Canadian population, i.e., where the rural or urban percentage in the American-born for any reason exceeds the rural or urban percentage of the same race in the whole Dominion, a United States preference is predicted. It will be seen from Table XXXIX that the percentage rural in the American-born in 1931 exceeded that in the total population in the case of every race except the following: French, Dutch, Ukrainian, Orientals, Aborigines, and Negroes; thus the American-born in Canada may be said to be more rural than other Canadians irrespective of race, the exceptions being small

*The term "racial origin" in the Canadian Census has a combined biological, cultural and geographical meaning. It signifies primarily the country of original family habitat and the implied biological and cultural background. [See Administrative Report on the Seventh Census of Canada, 1931, pp. 19-20, also in *Seventh Census of Canada, 1931*, I (Ottawa, 1936), p. 45.]

numerically if the French and the Dutch are omitted. (The Dutch have an exceptionally strong rural tendency in Canada as a whole, while the French Canadian also, omitting the cities of Montreal and Quebec, is essentially a rural race.)

Reverting to Table XXXVIII, the racial distribution (not the preference) is given. The number of each race is expressed as a percentage of all races severally for rural and urban in both the American-born and the total population of Canada. The American-born have markedly increased the percentage rural in Canada in the Dutch, German, and Scandinavian races, but as the percentage urban has been increased by the same American-born races in even greater degree, preference and contribution clearly do not go hand in hand. The fact is that these three races have come to Canada in larger numbers than the others (except, of course, the English, Irish, and Scottish).

Table XL shows that in 1931 in the four eastern provinces, origins other than British and French constituted only a small percentage in rural parts, and only a slightly larger percentage in urban. In Ontario and British Columbia the proportions of British and French were very nearly the same in both rural and urban. Only in the rural sections of the Prairie Provinces did the "other origins" approach the percentages of the British and French; rural Saskatchewan actually exceeded in "other origins." In prairie urban localities also, "other origins," although still below British and French, had a much larger representation than elsewhere.

TABLE XXXVIII

Percentage Distribution of American-Born and of Total Population,
Rural and Urban, Classified by Racial Origin: 1931

Racial Origin	American-Born			Total Population		
	Total	Rural	Urban	Total	Rural	Urban
ALL RACES	100.00	100.00	100.00	100.00	100.00	100.00
British—						
English	24.93	21.88	28.22	26.42	23.23	29.17
Irish	13.70	13.02	14.42	11.86	11.62	12.07
Scottish	10.93	10.27	11.64	12.97	12.17	13.67
Other British	1.07	1.09	1.04	0.60	0.55	0.65
French	16.15	12.86	19.69	28.22	28.07	28.35
Other European—						
Austrian, *n.o.s.*	0.33	0.44	0.21	0.47	0.63	0.33
Belgian	0.20	0.27	0.12	0.27	0.36	0.18
Czechoslovak	0.36	0.47	0.23	0.29	0.31	0.28
Dutch	2.82	3.21	2.41	1.44	2.05	0.91

TABLE XXXVIII—concluded

*Percentage Distribution of American-Born and of Total Population,
Rural and Urban, Classified by Racial Origin: 1931*

Racial Origin	American-Born			Total Population		
	Total	Rural	Urban	Total	Rural	Urban
Finnish	0.43	0.58	0.28	0.42	0.50	0.36
German	13.06	16.72	9.10	4.56	6.22	3.14
Hebrew	1.26	0.13	2.49	1.51	0.12	2.71
Hungarian	0.19	0.21	0.16	0.39	0.43	0.36
Italian	0.61	0.24	1.00	0.95	0.38	1.44
Polish	0.53	0.58	0.47	1.40	1.62	1.22
Roumanian	0.09	0.10	0.07	0.28	0.33	0.23
Russian	0.89	1.38	0.36	0.85	1.33	0.43
Scandinavian	10.77	15.05	6.13	2.20	3.21	1.32
Ukrainian	0.21	0.27	0.14	2.17	3.30	1.19
Other European	0.27	0.21	0.32	0.40	0.28	0.49
Asiatic—						
Chinese and Japanese	0.02	0.01	0.02	0.67	0.42	0.89
Other Asiatic	0.08	0.03	0.13	0.14	0.06	0.21
Indian and Eskimo	0.27	0.45	0.07	1.24	2.58	0.09
Negro	0.64	0.35	0.96	0.19	0.16	0.21
Unspecified and other	0.24	0.19	0.30	0.10	0.08	0.10

TABLE XXXIX

*Percentage Rural and Urban Distribution of Each Race for American-
Born and for Total Population: 1931*

Racial Origin	American-Born		Total Population	
	Rural	Urban	Rural	Urban
British—				
English	45.61	54.39	40.70	59.30
Irish	49.41	50.59	45.35	54.65
Scottish	48.82	51.18	43.41	56.59
Other British	53.01	46.99	42.24	57.76
French	41.39	58.61	46.04	53.96
Other European—				
Austrian, *n.o.s.*	69.83	30.17	62.18	37.82
Belgian	71.60	28.40	62.92	37.08
Czechoslovak	68.72	31.28	48.37	51.63
Dutch	59.02	40.98	66.05	33.95
Finnish	69.03	30.97	54.20	45.80

TABLE XXXIX—concluded

Percentage Rural and Urban Distribution of Each Race for American-Born and for Total Population: 1931

Racial Origin	American-Born		Total Population	
	Rural	Urban	Rural	Urban
German	66.52	33.48	63.06	36.94
Hebrew	5.20	94.80	3.55	96.45
Hungarian	57.63	42.37	50.53	49.47
Italian	20.73	79.27	18.45	81.55
Polish	57.21	42.79	53.43	46.57
Roumanian	60.60	39.40	55.37	44.63
Russian	80.59	19.41	72.66	27.34
Scandinavian	72.64	27.36	67.70	32.30
Ukrainian	67.56	32.44	70.47	29.53
Other European	41.12	58.88	32.90	67.10
Asiatic—				
Chinese and Japanese	27.45	72.55	29.18	70.82
Other Asiatic	18.08	81.92	20.60	79.40
Indian and Eskimo	87.99	12.01	96.08	3.92
Negro	28.22	71.78	39.18	60.82
Unspecified and other	40.28	59.72	39.08	60.92

TABLE XL

Percentage in Each Province of American-Born of British and French Origin, and of American-Born of Other than British and French Origin, Rural and Urban: 1931

Province	British and French		Other than British and French	
	Rural	Urban	Rural	Urban
Prince Edward Island	96.00	95.27	4.00	4.73
Nova Scotia	91.59	89.83	8.41	10.17
New Brunswick	96.25	93.23	3.75	6.77
Quebec	96.84	90.76	3.16	9.24
Ontario	74.85	75.50	25.15	24.50
Manitoba	54.72	64.96	45.28	35.04
Saskatchewan	40.07	54.08	59.93	45.92
Alberta	53.76	64.43	46.24	35.57
British Columbia	71.37	75.82	28.63	24.18

TABLE XLI

American-Born Classified by Racial Origin: Canada, 1921, and Canada and Provinces, 1931

Racial Origin	CANADA 1921	CANADA 1931	Prince Edward Island	Nova Scotia	New Brunswick	Quebec
	No.	No.	No.	No.	No.	No.
ALL RACES	374,024	344,574	1,380	7,222	8,794	49,406
British—						
English	108,008	85,894	405	2,978	3,239	8,885
Irish	51,642	47,195	285	973	1,219	2,910
Scottish	41,948	37,652	487	1,823	1,026	1,880
Other British	3,591	3,675	2	41	31	92
French	50,630	55,630	143	740	2,853	31,780
Other European—						
Austrian, *n.o.s.*	1,402	1,127	....	1	2	21
Belgian	734	676	....	11	....	36
Bulgarian	11	17	....	....	....	1
Czechoslovak	1,044	1,231	1	2	1	29
Danish	4,122	3,880	1	23	51	58
Dutch	10,176	9,731	12	93	75	197
Finnish	1,427	1,492	1	....	5	24
German	40,009	44,998	28	242	101	787
Greek	122	176	....	6	4	42
Hebrew	4,851	4,346	1	78	48	1,408
Hungarian	575	642	....	7	1	44
Icelandic	1,008	1,011	....	....	....	2
Italian	1,912	2,084	2	32	17	364
Lithuanian	44	91	....	1	....	23
Norwegian	22,186	21,451	2	17	10	89
Polish	1,507	1,825	....	6	5	71
Roumanian	144	302	....	....	....	16
Russian	6,158	3,065	....	6	4	39
Swedish	11,625	10,750	4	38	34	115
Ukrainian	297	712	....	....	....	7
Yugoslavic	234	240	....	....	....	9
Other European	2,039	388	....	8	5	52
Asiatic—						
Chinese	35	23	....	1	....	2
Japanese	16	28	....	1	....	1
Other Asiatic	270	271	1	11	14	30
Indian and Eskimo	663	916	1	10	25	167
Negro	3,099	2,211	....	62	19	190
Other	23	44	....	....	....	13
Unspecified	2,472	800	4	11	5	22

TABLE XLI—concluded

American-Born Classified by Racial Origin: Canada, 1921, and Canada and Provinces, 1931

Racial Origin	Ontario	Manitoba	Saskatchewan	Alberta	British Columbia	Yukon	Northwest Territories
	No.	No.	No.	No.	No.	No.	No.
ALL RACES	72,525	17,903	73,008	78,959	34,706	526	145
British—							
English	24,775	3,599	11,202	18,413	12,205	150	43
Irish	12,701	2,643	9,462	11,577	5,327	85	13
Scottish	9,157	2,162	6,200	9,160	5,665	81	11
Other British	695	175	658	1,259	715	6	1
French	7,293	2,080	4,542	4,505	1,656	29	9
Other European—							
Austrian, n.o.s.	139	249	350	242	121	2	....
Belgian	210	89	158	112	59	1	....
Bulgarian	13	....	....	....	3	....	....
Czechoslovak	121	95	458	388	136	....	....
Danish	265	152	1,087	1,850	386	5	2
Dutch	2,315	517	2,597	2,845	1,062	18	....
Finnish	479	71	298	390	224	....	....
German	7,137	2,316	16,866	14,387	3,072	42	20
Greek	60	9	6	26	23	....	....
Hebrew	1,945	355	119	152	240	....	....
Hungarian	220	25	232	76	37	....	....
Icelandic	12	419	436	89	53	....	....
Italian	1,133	97	62	138	239	....	....
Lithuanian	36	3	5	14	8	1	....
Norwegian	651	984	11,251	7,016	1,413	16	2
Polish	530	275	473	381	81	3	....
Roumanian	67	4	149	55	11	....	....
Russian	133	157	1,263	1,280	182	1	....
Swedish	753	723	4,354	3,597	1,120	10	2
Ukrainian	103	198	207	183	14	....	....
Yugoslavic	94	4	71	21	41	....	....
Other European	107	26	52	78	57	3	....
Asiatic—							
Chinese	1	1	1	6	10	1	....
Japanese	1	....	3	....	22	....	....
Other Asiatic	141	7	31	17	19	....	....
Indian and Eskimo	222	92	135	73	85	64	42
Negro	740	302	175	480	235	8	....
Other	13	5	1	5	7	....	....
Unspecified	263	69	104	144	178	....	....

TABLE XLII

Percentage Distribution of Total Population and of American-Born for Canada and Each Province, Classified by Racial Origin: 1931

Racial Origin	CANADA		Prince Edward Island		Nova Scotia		New Brunswick	
	Total Population	American-Born	Total Population	American-Born	Total Population	American-Born	Total Population	American-Born
ALL RACES	100.00	100.00	100.00	100.00	100.00	100.00	100.00	100.00
British—								
English	26.42	24.93	26.58	29.35	37.67	41.24	31.82	36.83
Irish	11.86	13.70	20.10	20.65	11.01	13.47	16.38	13.86
Scottish	12.97	10.93	36.90	35.29	27.30	25.24	13.86	11.67
Other British	0.60	1.07	0.20	0.14	0.44	0.57	0.54	0.35
French	28.22	16.15	14.72	10.36	11.04	10.25	33.56	32.44
Other European—								
Austrian, *n.o.s.*	0.47	0.33	0.01	....	0.07	0.01	0.02	0.02
Belgian	0.27	0.20	....	....	0.12	0.15	0.05	....
Bulgarian	0.03	0.01	....	....	0.02	....	0.01	....
Czechoslovak	0.29	0.36	....	0.07	0.09	0.03	....	0.01
Danish	0.33	1.13	0.14	0.07	0.15	0.32	0.37	0.58
Dutch	1.44	2.82	0.34	0.87	2.62	1.29	0.88	0.85
Finnish	0.42	0.43	....	0.07	0.02	....	0.03	0.06
German	4.56	13.06	0.32	2.03	5.28	3.35	0.65	1.15
Greek	0.09	0.05	....	....	0.06	0.08	0.02	0.05
Hebrew	1.51	1.26	0.02	0.07	0.40	1.08	0.31	0.55
Hungarian	0.39	0.19	....	....	0.11	0.10	0.01	0.01
Icelandic	0.19	0.29	....	....	....	....	....	....
Italian	0.95	0.61	0.03	0.14	0.37	0.44	0.10	0.19
Lithuanian	0.06	0.03	....	....	0.04	0.01	....	....
Norwegian	0.90	6.23	0.02	0.14	0.10	0.24	0.15	0.11
Polish	1.40	0.53	....	....	0.29	0.08	0.03	0.06
Roumanian	0.28	0.09	....	....	0.04	....	0.01	....
Russian	0.85	0.89	....	....	0.11	0.08	0.04	0.05
Swedish	0.78	3.12	0.02	0.29	0.11	0.53	0.13	0.39
Ukrainian	2.17	0.21	....	....	0.17	....	....	....
Yugoslavic	0.16	0.07	....	....	0.05	....	....	....
Other European	0.06	0.11	....	....	0.09	0.11	0.03	0.06
Asiatic—								
Chinese	0.45	0.01	0.04	....	0.07	0.01	0.06	....
Japanese	0.22	0.01	....	....	....	0.01	....	....
Other Asiatic	0.14	0.08	0.15	0.07	0.24	0.15	0.16	0.16
Indian and Eskimo	1.24	0.27	0.26	0.07	0.43	0.14	0.41	0.28
Negro	0.19	0.64	0.08	....	1.44	0.86	0.28	0.22
Other	0.01	0.01	....	....	....	....	....	....
Unspecified	0.09	0.23	0.04	0.29	0.07	0.15	0.08	0.06

TABLE XLII—continued

Percentage Distribution of Total Population and of American-Born
for Canada and Each Province, Classified by Racial Origin: 1931

Racial Origin	Quebec		Ontario		Manitoba		Saskatchewan	
	Total Population	American-Born	Total Population	American-Born	Total Population	American-Born	Total Population	American-Born
ALL RACES	100.00	100.00	100.00	100.00	100.00	100.00	100.00	100.00
British—								
English	8.17	17.98	38.45	34.16	24.71	20.10	22.30	15.34
Irish	3.77	5.89	18.88	17.51	11.08	14.76	11.29	12.96
Scottish	3.04	3.81	16.02	12.63	16.04	12.08	13.18	8.49
Other British	0.08	0.19	0.66	0.96	0.73	0.98	0.73	0.90
French	78.98	64.32	8.73	10.06	6.72	11.62	5.50	6.22
Other European—								
Austrian, *n.o.s.*	0.07	0.04	0.28	0.19	1.27	1.39	1.85	0.48
Belgian	0.15	0.07	0.21	0.29	0.90	0.50	0.48	0.22
Bulgarian	0.01	....	0.07	0.02	0.01	....	0.01	....
Czechoslovak	0.15	0.06	0.26	0.17	0.34	0.53	0.55	0.63
Danish	0.06	0.12	0.14	0.37	0.46	0.85	0.72	1.49
Dutch	0.06	0.40	1.76	3.19	3.56	2.89	2.68	3.56
Finnish	0.10	0.05	0.79	0.66	0.14	0.40	0.25	0.41
German	0.37	1.59	5.07	9.84	5.44	12.94	14.02	23.10
Greek	0.09	0.09	0.12	0.08	0.04	0.05	0.06	0.01
Hebrew	2.09	2.85	1.82	2.68	2.76	1.98	0.56	0.16
Hungarian	0.14	0.09	0.40	0.30	0.28	0.14	1.45	0.32
Icelandic	....	....	0.01	0.02	1.92	2.34	0.42	0.60
Italian	0.86	0.74	1.47	1.56	0.34	0.54	0.11	0.08
Lithuanian	0.08	0.05	0.04	0.05	0.05	0.02	0.06	0.01
Norwegian	0.05	0.18	0.15	0.90	0.75	5.50	4.31	15.41
Polish	0.33	0.14	1.24	0.73	5.75	1.54	2.82	0.65
Roumanian	0.11	0.03	0.24	0.09	0.30	0.02	1.03	0.20
Russian	0.12	0.08	0.29	0.18	1.65	0.88	3.84	1.73
Swedish	0.06	0.23	0.31	1.04	1.35	4.04	2.44	5.96
Ukrainian	0.15	0.01	0.71	0.14	10.51	1.11	6.88	0.28
Yugoslavic	0.05	0.02	0.24	0.13	0.04	0.02	0.18	0.10
Other European	0.03	0.11	0.05	0.15	0.15	0.15	0.04	0.07
Asiatic—								
Chinese	0.10	....	0.20	....	0.25	0.01	0.38	....
Japanese	....	....	0.01	....	0.01	....	0.01	....
Other Asiatic	0.15	0.06	0.15	0.19	0.07	0.04	0.09	0.04
Indian and Eskimo	0.47	0.34	0.88	0.31	2.21	0.51	1.66	0.18
Negro	0.06	0.38	0.20	1.02	0.07	1.69	0.04	0.24
Other	0.01	0.03	0.01	0.02	0.01	0.03	....	...
Unspecified	0.04	0.04	0.13	0.36	0.08	0.39	0.06	0.14

TABLE XLII—concluded

Percentage Distribution of Total Population and of American-Born for Canada and each Province, Classified by Racial Origin: 1931

Racial Origin	Alberta		British Columbia		Yukon		Northwest Territories	
	Total Population	American-Born	Total Population	American-Born	Total Population	American-Born	Total Population	American-Born
ALL RACES	100.00	100.00	100.00	100.00	100.00	100.00	100.00	100.00
British—								
English	25.76	23.32	39.25	35.17	19.50	28.52	3.04	29.66
Irish	10.93	14.66	10.31	15.35	7.04	16.16	1.01	8.97
Scottish	15.13	11.60	19.45	16.32	13.62	15.40	2.21	7.59
Other British	1.38	1.59	1.55	2.06	0.99	1.14	0.14	0.69
French	5.25	5.71	2.16	4.77	5.91	5.51	2.21	6.21
Other European—								
Austrian, *n.o.s.*	0.92	0.31	0.56	0.35	0.33	0.38	0.02	....
Belgian	0.37	0.14	0.23	0.17	0.38	0.19	0.03	....
Bulgarian	0.02	....	0.01	0.01	0.05	....	....	....
Czechoslovak	0.88	0.49	0.40	0.39	0.21	....	0.04	....
Danish	1.56	2.34	0.57	1.11	0.80	0.95	0.20	1.38
Dutch	1.87	3.60	0.90	3.06	0.61	3.42	0.06	....
Finnish	0.45	0.49	0.99	0.65	0.80	....	0.04	....
German	10.18	18.22	2.45	8.85	2.32	7.98	0.40	13.79
Greek	0.08	0.03	0.14	0.07	0.07	....	....	....
Hebrew	0.51	0.19	0.40	0.69	0.09	....	0.02	....
Hungarian	0.75	0.10	0.19	0.11	0.19	....	....	....
Icelandic	0.12	0.11	0.12	0.15	....	....	0.01	....
Italian	0.65	0.17	1.77	0.69	0.52	....	0.01	....
Lithuanian	0.09	0.02	0.04	0.02	0.02	0.19	0.01	....
Norwegian	3.74	8.89	1.86	4.07	2.55	3.04	0.20	1.38
Polish	2.89	0.48	0.66	0.23	0.28	0.57	0.04	....
Roumanian	0.64	0.07	0.17	0.03	....	....	....	....
Russian	2.24	1.62	1.50	0.52	0.33	0.19	0.14	....
Swedish	2.71	4.56	2.32	3.23	2.65	1.90	0.29	1.38
Ukrainian	7.64	0.23	0.37	0.04	0.05	....	0.01	....
Yugoslavic	0.18	0.03	0.42	0.12	0.47	....	0.05	....
Other European	0.09	0.10	0.11	0.16	0.21	0.57	0.01	....
Asiatic—								
Chinese	0.53	0.01	3.91	0.03	0.02	0.19	....	....
Japanese	0.09	....	3.20	0.06	1.23	....	0.01	....
Other Asiatic	0.05	0.02	0.23	0.05	0.02	....	0.10	....
Indian and Eskimo	2.08	0.09	3.54	0.24	38.49	12.17	89.64	28.97
Negro	0.13	0.61	0.08	0.68	0.19	1.52	....	....
Other	0.01	0.01	0.01	0.02	....	....	0.04	....
Unspecified	0.08	0.18	0.13	0.51	0.02	....	....	....

TABLE XLIII

Percentage Distribution of American-Born for Each Province, Rural and Urban, Classified by Racial Origin: 1931

Racial Origin	Prince Edward Island		Nova Scotia		New Brunswick	
	Rural	Urban	Rural	Urban	Rural	Urban
ALL RACES	100.00	100.00	100.00	100.00	100.00	100.00
British—						
English	27.53	34.12	41.04	41.46	34.80	40.42
Irish	21.12	19.42	11.96	15.21	12.84	15.67
Scottish	35.64	34.38	24.42	26.19	10.67	13.43
Other British	0.20	....	0.65	0.48	0.27	0.50
French	11.51	7.35	13.52	6.49	37.67	23.21
Other European—						
Austrian, n.o.s	....	....	....	0.03	0.02	0.03
Belgian	....	....	0.08	0.24	....	....
Czechoslovak	0.10	....	0.03	0.03	0.02	....
Dutch	1.20	....	1.63	0.89	0.78	0.98
Finnish	0.10	....	....	....	0.02	0.13
German	1.60	3.15	3.63	3.04	0.87	1.64
Hebrew	....	0.26	0.05	2.26	0.12	1.29
Hungarian	....	....	0.05	0.15	....	0.03
Italian	....	0.52	0.31	0.60	0.20	0.19
Polish	....	....	0.08	0.09	0.04	0.09
Roumanian	....	....	....	....	....	....
Russian	....	....	0.08	0.09	0.04	0.06
Scandinavian	0.40	0.79	1.11	1.04	1.14	0.98
Ukrainian	....	....	....	....	....	....
Other European	....	....	0.16	0.27	0.02	0.25
Asiatic—						
Chinese and Japanese	....	....	0.03	0.03	....	....
Other Asiatic	0.10	....	....	0.33	0.02	0.41
Indian and Eskimo	0.10	....	0.26	....	0.39	0.09
Negro	....	....	0.78	0.95	0.04	0.53
Unspecified and other	0.40	....	0.16	0.15	0.05	0.06

Racial Origin	Quebec		Ontario		Manitoba	
ALL RACES	100.00	100.00	100.00	100.00	100.00	100.00
British—						
English	10.36	20.32	32.92	34.68	17.08	23.50
Irish	3.69	6.56	17.35	17.58	12.73	17.05
Scottish	2.49	4.21	11.80	12.97	10.56	13.79
Other British	0.04	0.23	0.76	1.04	0.84	1.13
French	80.26	59.44	12.02	9.23	13.51	9.49
Other European—						
Austrian, n.o.s	0.03	0.05	0.21	0.19	2.47	0.18
Belgian	0.03	0.08	0.75	0.10	0.66	0.31
Czechoslovak	0.02	0.07	0.18	0.16	0.69	0.36
Dutch	0.34	0.42	3.83	2.93	3.22	2.52

TABLE XLIII—continued

Percentage Distribution of American-Born for Each Province, Rural and Urban, Classified by Racial Origin: 1931

Racial Origin	Quebec		Ontario		Manitoba	
	Rural	Urban	Rural	Urban	Rural	Urban
Finnish	0.01	0.06	1.06	0.49	0.51	0.27
German	0.51	1.93	10.77	9.45	15.65	9.88
Hebrew	0.12	3.69	0.65	3.53	0.18	4.01
Hungarian	0.01	0.11	0.35	0.28	0.21	0.06
Italian	0.22	0.90	0.82	1.87	0.05	1.09
Polish	0.13	0.15	0.68	0.75	1.87	1.16
Roumanian	....	0.04	0.05	0.11	0.03	0.01
Russian	0.07	0.08	0.23	0.16	1.17	0.55
Scandinavian	0.18	0.64	3.02	2.02	15.27	9.86
Ukrainian	0.01	0.02	0.15	0.14	1.58	0.57
Other European	0.04	0.32	0.42	0.43	0.26	0.20
Asiatic—						
Chinese and Japanese	....	0.01	....	[1]	....	0.01
Other Asiatic	0.02	0.07	0.06	0.25	0.03	0.05
Indian and Eskimo	1.37	0.02	0.78	0.11	0.95	0.02
Negro	0.02	0.50	0.80	1.11	0.22	3.34
Unspecified and other	0.04	0.08	0.35	0.39	0.26	0.58

Racial Origin	Saskatchewan		Alberta		British Columbia	
ALL RACES	100.00	100.00	100.00	100.00	100.00	100.00
British—						
English	13.93	19.08	21.91	26.73	34.28	36.00
Irish	11.76	16.13	13.95	16.37	14.84	15.82
Scottish	7.60	10.85	10.81	13.52	15.15	17.42
Other British	0.83	1.09	1.53	1.75	2.14	1.98
French	5.95	6.93	5.56	6.06	4.96	4.60
Other European—						
Austrian, *n.o.s.*	0.51	0.39	0.32	0.26	0.30	0.40
Belgian	0.25	0.12	0.17	0.08	0.17	0.17
Czechoslovak	0.73	0.36	0.49	0.50	0.47	0.32
Dutch	3.47	3.80	3.65	3.50	3.44	2.70
Finnish	0.54	0.07	0.57	0.31	0.89	0.41
German	24.38	19.73	20.04	13.84	10.28	7.51
Hebrew	0.02	0.53	0.03	0.58	0.10	1.25
Hungarian	0.35	0.22	0.11	0.06	0.14	0.07
Italian	0.09	0.08	0.15	0.24	0.44	0.92
Polish	0.71	0.48	0.52	0.40	0.22	0.25
Roumanian	0.23	0.13	0.07	0.07	0.05	0.02
Russian	2.06	0.85	1.98	0.77	0.60	0.45
Scandinavian	25.49	18.09	17.09	13.02	9.84	7.36
Ukrainian	0.31	0.22	0.23	0.24	0.04	0.04
Other European	0.20	0.15	0.14	0.27	0.38	0.38

[1] Less than 0.01 p.c.

TABLE XLIII—concluded

Percentage Distribution of American-Born for Each Province, Rural and Urban, Classified by Racial Origin: 1931

Racial Origin	Saskatchewan		Alberta		British Columbia	
	Rural	Urban	Rural	Urban	Rural	Urban
Asiatic—						
Chinese and Japanese	0.01	1	1	0.02	0.05	0.13
Other Asiatic	0.03	0.06	0.01	0.06	0.04	0.07
Indian and Eskimo	0.23	0.05	0.11	0.05	0.45	0.05
Negro	0.19	0.38	0.44	1.02	0.32	1.02
Unspecified and other	0.13	0.19	0.15	0.28	0.42	0.64

1 Less than 0.01 p.c.

TABLE XLIV

American-Born, Rural and Urban, by Sex, Classified by Racial Origin, Canada: 1931

Racial Origin	Rural			Urban		
	Both Sexes	Male	Female	Both Sexes	Male	Female
	No.	No.	No.	No.	No.	No.
ALL RACES	179,036	98,991	80,045	165,538	76,149	89,389
British—						
English	39,177	21,163	18,014	46,717	21,375	25,342
Irish	23,319	13,148	10,171	23,876	11,050	12,826
Scottish	18,383	10,145	8,238	19,269	9,038	10,231
Other British	1,948	1,201	747	1,727	887	840
French	23,028	12,039	10,989	32,602	14,655	17,947
Other European—						
Austrian, n.o.s.	787	435	352	340	132	208
Belgian	484	258	226	192	89	103
Czechoslovak	846	499	347	385	160	225
Dutch	5,743	3,237	2,506	3,988	1,899	2,089
Finnish	1,030	598	432	462	205	257
German	29,932	16,856	13,076	15,066	6,921	8,145
Hebrew	226	108	118	4,120	1,926	2,194
Hungarian	370	193	177	272	119	153
Italian	432	230	202	1,652	799	853
Polish	1,044	577	467	781	348	433
Roumanian	183	95	88	119	48	71
Russian	2,470	1,302	1,168	595	267	328
Scandinavian	26,945	15,487	11,458	10,147	4,554	5,593
Ukrainian	481	257	224	231	102	129
Other European	375	213	162	537	252	285
Asiatic—						
Chinese and Japanese	14	8	6	37	17	20
Other Asiatic	49	22	27	222	96	126
Indian and Eskimo	806	415	391	110	58	52
Negro	624	342	282	1,587	939	648
Unspecified and other	340	163	177	504	213	291

CHAPTER VI

LANGUAGE—MOTHER TONGUE

Ability to speak the language of the country as a test of assimilation is overlaid in Canada by the fact that there are two official languages. The Canadian Census accordingly has two rubrics on language: (1) official language spoken, i.e., English or French or both; (2) language spoken as "mother tongue." By the latter is meant the first language learned in childhood and still understood.

Mother tongue, of course, does not necessarily coincide with racial origin; the longer the stay of an immigrant family of non-British race and tongue, the greater the probability that the descendants will speak the language of the country as mother tongue. The majority of the American-born in Canada would therefore be expected to speak English as mother tongue. At the same time the exchange in French-speaking population under the circumstances previously described should also imply a considerable proportion of French mother tongue.

This is borne out in Table XLV. Of the 344,574 American-born in Canada in 1931, 83.28 p.c. reported that of the two official languages, they could speak English only, while 3.85 could speak French only. Another 12.60 p.c., however, could speak both English and French, so that only 0.27 p.c. were unable to speak either of the official languages of the country. At the same time only 68.72 p.c. of them gave English as their mother tongue, and only 13.72 gave French; thus a residue of 17.56 p.c. had learned some other language at their mother's knee and had retained their knowledge of it. (Table XLVII.)

The materials for detailed study of mother tongue appear in Table XLVI. The analyses immediately following set out: (1) a comparison of the distribution of American-born by mother tongue with that of the total population of Canada 10 years of age or over; (2) the percentage distribution of American-born and total foreign-born immigrants according to mother tongue and sex; and (3) a rural and urban segregation by provinces and sex of the American-born speaking English, French, or some other mother tongue. As stated above, only 68.72 p.c. of the American-born in 1931 spoke English as mother tongue and 13.72 spoke French, while 17.56 p.c. spoke other than English or French. This would indicate that the American-born not only contained a considerable element of non-English and non-

French races, but that the element in question had not been long in the United States when the children who had since emigrated to Canada were born.

Of the American-born, 13.42 p.c. reported German or Scandinavian as mother tongue, as compared with 5.03 p.c. of the total Canadian population. On the other hand, French and other than Scandinavian and German languages bulked larger among the total Canadian population than among the American-born. English stood relatively higher in the latter. In rural Manitoba and Saskatchewan, however, 31.25 p.c. and 39.10 p.c., respectively, of the American-born gave mother tongues other than English or French.

Among the total foreign-born in Canada in 1931, the chief languages spoken as mother tongue were, in order: (1) English, (2) German, (3) Ukrainian, (4) Yiddish, (5) French, (6) Polish, (7) Norwegian, and (8) Italian. The mother tongues of the American-born ranked as follows: (1) English, (2) French, (3) German, (4) Norwegian, (5) Swedish, (6) Yiddish, (7) Italian, and (8) Danish and Polish. Reasons have already been given why French stands higher among the American-born than among the foreign-born in general.

TABLE XLV

American-Born, by Sex, Classified by Official Language Spoken: 1931

Official Language	Numbers			Percentages		
	Both Sexes	Male	Female	Both Sexes	Male	Female
TOTAL...............................	344,574	175,140	169,434	100.00	100.00	100.00
English only..........................	286,953	147,353	139,600	83.28	84.13	82.39
French only..........................	13,273	5,574	7,699	3.85	3.18	4.54
English and French..............	43,430	21,826	21,604	12.60	12.46	12.75
Neither English nor French..	918	387	531	0.27	0.23	0.31

TABLE XLVI

American-Born, Rural and Urban, Classified by Mother Tongue,
Canada and Provinces: 1931

Mother Tongue	CANADA			Prince Edward Island			Nova Scotia		
	Total	Rural	Urban	Total	Rural	Urban	Total	Rural	Urban
	No.	No.	No.	No.	No.	No.	No.	No.	No.
TOTAL....................	344,574	179,036	165,538	1,380	999	381	7,222	3,862	3,360
English.................	236,779	118,310	118,469	1,263	904	359	6,392	3,312	3,080
Germanic Group—									
Dutch.................	882	670	212	....	....	....	3	3	....
Flemish.............	297	252	45	....	....	....	3	1	2
German.............	23,765	17,802	5,963	3	1	2	24	9	15
Latin and Greek Group—									
French.............	47,267	18,930	28,337	106	88	18	475	376	99
Greek.................	100	10	90	....	....	....	4	....	4
Italian................	1,609	263	1,346	1	....	1	21	4	17
Roumanian........	136	77	59	....	....	....	....	....	....
Spanish..............	123	42	81	....	....	....	1	....	1
Magyar..................	490	267	223	....	....	....	8	2	6
Scandinavian Group—									
Swedish.............	5,867	4,455	1,412	1	1	....	6	5	1
Norwegian..........	14,432	11,758	2,674	....	....	....	4	1	3
Danish................	1,361	974	387	....	....	....	5	3	2
Icelandic............	840	554	286	....	....	....	....	....	....
Slavic Group—									
Austrian.............	77	41	36	....	....	....	....	....	....
Bohemian..........	447	351	96	....	....	....	1	1	....
Bulgarian..........	14	1	13	....	....	....	....	....	....
Lithuanian........	75	22	53	....	....	....	....	....	....
Polish.................	1,344	764	580	....	....	....	5	3	2
Russian..............	661	458	203	....	....	....	2	1	1
Servo-Croatian..	142	80	62	....	....	....	....	....	....
Slovak..............	481	312	169	....	....	....	1	1	....
Ukrainian[1]........	705	511	194	....	....	....	....	....	....
Syrian and Arabic	178	28	150	....	....	....	6	....	6
Yiddish.................	3,989	190	3,799	1	....	1	65	1	64
Chinese.................	18	2	16	....	....	....	....	....	....
Finnish.................	1,258	896	362	1	1	....	....	....	....
Various[2]................	1,237	1,016	221	4	4	....	196	139	57

[1] Includes Galician and Ruthenian mother tongues.   [2] Includes Gaelic and Japanese mother tongues.

Table XLVI—continued

American-Born, Rural and Urban, Classified by Mother Tongue, Canada and Provinces: 1931

Mother Tongue	New Brunswick			Quebec			Ontario		
	Total	Rural	Urban	Total	Rural	Urban	Total	Rural	Urban
	No.	No.	No.	No.	No.	No.	No.	No.	No.
TOTAL	8,794	5,615	3,179	49,406	11,588	37,818	72,525	21,462	51,063
English	5,945	3,491	2,454	15,085	2,028	13,057	60,552	17,380	43,172
Germanic Group—									
Dutch	2	1	1	7	1	6	80	30	50
Flemish	....	....	....	....	....	....	145	130	15
German	15	5	10	274	30	244	1,975	735	1,240
Latin and Greek Group—									
French	2,708	2,054	654	31,746	9,290	22,456	4,562	1,855	2,707
Greek	....	....	....	33	1	32	41	2	39
Italian	8	6	2	314	14	300	924	138	786
Roumanian	....	....	....	7	....	7	45	5	40
Spanish	....	....	....	28	....	28	38	14	24
Magyar	1	....	1	27	1	26	205	65	140
Scandinavian Group—									
Swedish	11	7	4	43	6	37	321	151	170
Norwegian	1	1	....	36	6	30	331	209	122
Danish	24	22	2	24	....	24	72	25	47
Icelandic	....	....	....	1	....	1	3	....	3
Slavic Group—									
Austrian	....	....	....	....	....	....	18	5	13
Bohemian	1	1	....	6	....	6	18	6	12
Bulgarian	....	....	....	1	....	1	13	1	12
Lithuanian	....	....	....	24	2	22	31	6	25
Polish	2	2	....	60	8	52	438	115	323
Russian	4	1	3	25	6	19	91	23	68
Servo-Croatian	....	....	....	3	....	3	58	27	31
Slovak	....	....	....	25	3	22	65	21	44
Ukrainian[1]	....	....	....	7	3	4	89	31	58
Syrian and Arabic	10	....	10	24	2	22	102	9	93
Yiddish	36	4	32	1,386	12	1,374	1,672	121	1,551
Chinese	....	....	....	2	....	2	....	....	....
Finnish	3	1	2	20	....	20	445	207	238
Various[2]	23	19	4	198	175	23	191	151	40

[1] Includes Galician and Ruthenian mother tongues. [2] Includes Gaelic and Japanese mother tongues.

TABLE XLVI—continued

American-Born, Rural and Urban, Classified by Mother Tongue,
Canada and Provinces: 1931

Mother Tongue	Manitoba			Saskatchewan			Alberta		
	Total	Rural	Urban	Total	Rural	Urban	Total	Rural	Urban
	No.	No.	No.	No.	No.	No.	No.	No.	No.
TOTAL	17,903	9,483	8,420	73,008	52,965	20,043	78,959	55,824	23,135
English	11,784	5,398	6,386	44,568	30,131	14,437	59,950	40,756	19,194
Germanic Group—									
Dutch	82	64	18	439	369	70	208	168	40
Flemish	50	36	14	66	62	4	26	18	8
German	1,661	1,286	375	11,322	8,969	2,353	7,586	6,223	1,363
Latin and Greek Group—									
French	1,708	1,122	586	2,983	2,123	860	2,409	1,721	688
Greek	4	....	4	5	1	4	3	2	1
Italian	84	3	81	27	15	12	65	37	28
Roumanian	1	....	1	77	69	8	6	3	3
Spanish	6	2	4	3	1	2	18	13	5
Magyar	24	20	4	155	126	29	45	36	9
Scandinavian Group—									
Swedish	398	265	133	2,664	2,201	463	1,871	1,489	382
Norwegian	629	491	138	8,169	6,893	1,276	4,489	3,678	811
Danish	51	28	23	387	313	74	673	507	166
Icelandic	369	232	137	381	267	114	61	44	17
Slavic Group—									
Austrian	5	5	....	11	7	4	17	13	4
Bohemian	42	33	9	201	178	23	150	112	38
Bulgarian	....	....	....	....	....	....	....	....	....
Lithuanian	4	3	1	4	2	2	5	4	1
Polish	224	146	78	312	265	47	260	205	55
Russian	28	17	11	268	215	53	183	162	21
Servo-Croatian	2	1	1	35	27	8	12	11	1
Slovak	24	14	10	149	135	14	151	98	53
Ukrainian[1]	221	166	55	217	178	39	161	125	36
Syrian and Arabic	2	2	....	17	11	6	10	2	8
Yiddish	347	17	330	120	14	106	141	8	133
Chinese	1	....	1	1	....	1	3	....	3
Finnish	57	42	15	255	243	12	324	281	43
Various[2]	95	90	5	172	150	22	132	108	24

[1] Includes Galician and Ruthenian mother tongues. [2] Includes Gaelic and Japanese mother tongues.

TABLE XLVI—concluded

American-Born, Rural and Urban, Classified by Mother Tongue, Canada and Provinces: 1931

Mother Tongue	British Columbia			Yukon			Northwest Territories		
	Total	Rural	Urban	Total	Rural	Urban	Total	Rural	Urban
	No.	No.	No.	No.	No.	No.	No.	No.	No.
TOTAL	34,706	16,809	17,897	526	284	242	145	145	....
English	30,745	14,620	16,125	400	195	205	95	95	....
Germanic Group—									
Dutch	57	30	27	4	4	....	....	....	....
Flemish	7	5	2	....	....	....	....	....	....
German	886	533	353	18	10	8	1	1	....
Latin and Greek Group—									
French	546	283	263	17	11	6	7	7	....
Greek	10	4	6	....	....	....	....	....	....
Italian	165	46	119	....	....	....	....	....	....
Roumanian	....	....	....	....	....	....	....	....	....
Spanish	25	12	13	4	....	4	....	....	....
Magyar	25	17	8	....	....	....	....	....	....
Scandinavian Group—									
Swedish	549	328	221	3	2	1	....	....	....
Norwegian	762	473	289	11	6	5	....	....	....
Danish	123	74	49	1	1	....	1	1	....
Icelandic	25	11	14	....	....	....	....	....	....
Slavic Group—									
Austrian	25	10	15	1	1	....	....	....	....
Bohemian	28	20	8	....	....	....	....	....	....
Bulgarian	....	....	....	....	....	....	....	....	....
Lithuanian	7	5	2	....	....	....	....	....	....
Polish	43	20	23	....	....	....	....	....	....
Russian	60	33	27	....	....	....	....	....	....
Servo-Croatian	32	14	18	....	....	....	....	....	....
Slovak	66	40	26	....	....	....	....	....	....
Ukrainian [1]	10	8	2	....	....	....	....	....	....
Syrian and Arabic	7	2	5	....	....	....	....	....	....
Yiddish	221	13	208	....	....	....	....	....	....
Chinese	10	2	8	1	....	1	....	....	....
Finnish	153	121	32	....	....	....	....	....	....
Various [2]	119	85	34	66	54	12	41	41	....

[1] Includes Galician and Ruthenian mother tongues.　　[2] Includes Gaelic and Japanese mother tongues.

TABLE XLVII

Percentage Distribution of the American-Born Compared with that of the Total Population of Canada 10 Years of Age or Over, by Chief Mother Tongue: 1931

Mother Tongue	American-Born	Population of Canada 10 Years of Age or Over [1]
TOTAL	100.00	100.00
English	68.72	58.50
French	13.72	25.57
German	6.90	3.47
Scandinavian	6.52	1.71
Other	4.14	10.75

[1] Age "not stated" omitted.

TABLE XLVIII

Percentage Distribution of American-Born and of Total Foreign-Born, by Sex, Classified by Mother Tongue: 1931

Mother Tongue	American-Born			Total Foreign-Born		
	Both Sexes	Male	Female	Both Sexes	Male	Female
TOTAL	100.00	100.00	100.00	100.00	100.00	100.00
English	68.72	68.38	69.06	22.30	19.10	26.97
French	13.72	12.94	14.52	6.09	5.11	7.52
German	6.90	7.34	6.44	13.83	13.28	14.68
Norwegian	4.19	4.66	3.70	4.07	4.41	3.58
Swedish	1.70	1.93	1.47	3.74	4.27	2.96
Yiddish	1.16	1.05	1.27	7.20	6.11	8.80
Italian	0.47	0.45	0.49	3.96	4.23	3.56
Danish	0.39	0.42	0.36	1.59	1.85	1.20
Polish	0.39	0.39	0.39	6.07	6.41	5.56
Finnish	0.37	0.39	0.34	2.60	2.63	2.56
Various	0.28	0.29	0.29	0.34	0.33	0.32
Dutch	0.26	0.27	0.24	1.19	1.21	1.17
Icelandic	0.24	0.25	0.24	0.56	0.48	0.69
Ukrainian	0.20	0.21	0.20	9.85	10.00	9.64
Russian	0.19	0.20	0.18	2.56	2.71	2.34
Magyar	0.14	0.14	0.14	2.52	2.84	2.05
Slovak	0.14	0.14	0.14	1.79	2.30	1.04
Bohemian	0.13	0.14	0.12	0.37	0.37	0.37
Flemish	0.09	0.08	00.9	11.6	1.13	1.21

TABLE XLVIII—concluded

Percentage Distribution of American-Born and of Total Foreign-Born, by Sex, Classified by Mother Tongue: 1931

Mother Tongue	American-Born			Total Foreign-Born		
	Both Sexes	Male	Female	Both Sexes	Male	Female
Gaelic	0.07	0.07	0.07	0.02	0.02	0.03
Syrian and Arabic	0.05	0.05	0.06	0.40	0.39	0.42
Roumanian	0.04	0.04	0.04	0.86	0.96	0.71
Servo-Croatian	0.04	0.04	0.04	0.77	1.03	0.40
Spanish	0.04	0.04	0.03	0.08	0.09	0.07
Greek	0.03	0.03	0.03	0.46	0.56	0.30
Austrian	0.02	0.02	0.02	0.36	0.39	0.32
Lithuanian	0.02	0.03	0.02	0.35	0.39	0.28
Chinese	0.01	0.01	0.01	4.72	7.16	1.15
Bulgarian	[1]	[1]	[1]	0.19	0.25	0.10

[1] Less than 0.01 p.c.

TABLE XLIX

Percentage Distribution of American-Born, Rural and Urban, by Sex, for Canada and Each Province, Classified by English, French, or Other Mother Tongue: 1931

Province and Mother Tongue	Total	Rural		Urban	
		Male	Female	Male	Female
CANADA—					
English	68.72	65.89	66.32	71.63	71.51
French	13.72	9.96	11.33	16.81	17.38
Other	17.56	24.15	22.35	11.56	11.11
Prince Edward Island—					
English	91.52	90.76	90.22	93.41	94.97
French	7.68	8.63	8.98	4.95	4.52
Other	0.80	0.61	0.80	1.64	0.51
Nova Scotia—					
English	88.51	84.72	86.72	91.18	92.06
French	6.58	10.33	9.19	2.94	2.95
Other	4.91	4.95	4.09	5.88	4.99
New Brunswick—					
English	67.60	60.54	63.62	77.42	77.01
French	30.79	38.06	35.28	20.37	20.73
Other	1.61	1.40	1.10	2.21	2.26

TABLE XLIX—concluded

Percentage Distribution of American-Born, Rural and Urban, by Sex, for Canada and Each Province, Classified by English, French, or Other Mother Tongue: 1931

Province and Mother Tongue	Total	Rural		Urban	
		Male	Female	Male	Female
Quebec—					
English	30.53	16.63	18.40	35.16	33.99
French	64.26	81.06	79.25	58.52	60.11
Other	5.21	2.31	2.35	6.32	5.90
Ontario—					
English	83.49	80.04	81.92	84.08	84.94
French	6.29	9.05	8.23	5.67	4.99
Other	10.22	10.91	9.85	10.25	10.07
Manitoba—					
English	65.82	57.54	56.19	77.03	74.83
French	9.54	11.09	12.71	6.01	7.77
Other	24.64	31.37	31.10	16.96	17.40
Saskatchewan—					
English	61.05	56.61	57.26	72.70	71.43
French	4.09	3.87	4.20	3.70	4.82
Other	34.86	39.52	38.54	23.60	23.75
Alberta—					
English	75.93	72.93	73.12	83.08	82.86
French	3.05	3.03	3.16	2.59	3.31
Other	21.02	24.04	23.72	14.33	13.83
British Columbia—					
English	88.59	86.82	87.18	89.63	90.48
French	1.57	1.68	1.68	1.37	1.55
Other	9.84	11.50	11.14	9.00	7.97
Yukon—					
English	76.05	71.92	60.49	83.95	86.25
French	3.23	3.45	4.94	2.47	2.50
Other	20.72	24.63	34.57	13.58	11.25
Northwest Territories—					
English	65.52	74.07	40.54	....	....
French	4.83	1.85	1.35	....	....
Other	29.65	24.08	58.11	....	....

CHAPTER VII

CITIZENSHIP

IN approaching the subject of citizenship, a point on naturalization should be premised: an alien must have resided in Canada for not less than one year immediately preceding his application for naturalization, and must have resided either in Canada or in some other part of His Majesty's Dominions for a period of four years within the last eight years before the application. The child of a British subject born in a foreign country does not require to be naturalized on becoming a resident unless he has acquired foreign citizenship. Children of persons naturalized under the Dominion Naturalization Act, in force before 1915, are British subjects within Canada if they were minors and in Canada with the parents on the latters' naturalization, or later but before Jan. 1, 1915. Children of persons naturalized under the Naturalization Acts, based on the Imperial Act, in force since 1915 are deemed to be British subjects only if their names are endorsed on the parents' certificates. Before 1932 the wife of an alien became naturalized automatically on the same date as her husband.

Table L gives the numbers and percentages naturalized and alien among the American-born for the census years 1901 to 1931. The percentage of naturalized reached 72.44 in 1931.

TABLE L

*Numbers and Percentages of American-Born Naturalized and Alien,
Canada: Census Years 1901-31*

Year	Total	Naturalized		Alien	
	No.	No.	p.c.	No.	p.c.
1901	127,899	87,049	68.06	40,850	31.94
1911	303,680	152,308	50.15	151,372	49.85
1921	374,022	237,993	63.63	136,029	36.37
1931	344,574	249,595	72.44	94,979	27.56

In 1931, of the 344,574 American-born in Canada, 249,595 were naturalized and 94,979 were alien. In addition, there were 18,306 persons owing allegiance to the United States but not born there. Table LI gives an *aperçu* of the naturalized and alien American-born by provinces, while the chart at p. 39 compares the American-born with the other foreign-born.

129

TABLE LI

American-Born, Classified as Naturalized and Alien, by Sex, for All
Ages and for 21 Years or Over, Canada and Provinces: 1931

Province	Males		Females	
	All Ages	21 Years or Over	All Ages	21 Years or Over
	NATURALIZED			
	No.	No.	No.	No.
CANADA	118,104	94,527	131,491	108,332
Prince Edward Island	514	225	605	317
Nova Scotia	2,603	1,346	3,303	2,106
New Brunswick	2,898	1,463	4,111	2,756
Quebec	16,507	11,693	21,420	16,675
Ontario	19,894	13,387	28,884	22,532
Manitoba	5,550	4,584	6,592	5,588
Saskatchewan	29,799	26,507	26,867	23,620
Alberta	29,214	26,391	26,358	23,547
British Columbia	10,970	8,789	13,233	11,086
Yukon	131	121	104	93
Northwest Territories	24	21	14	12
	ALIEN			
	No.	No.	No.	No.
CANADA	57,036	44,294	37,943	26,024
Prince Edward Island	166	93	95	31
Nova Scotia	752	519	564	318
New Brunswick	1,139	875	646	399
Quebec	6,740	5,355	4,739	3,315
Ontario	14,123	10,755	9,624	6,448
Manitoba	3,477	2,667	2,284	1,607
Saskatchewan	9,865	7,536	6,477	4,390
Alberta	13,952	10,823	9,435	6,530
British Columbia	6,504	5,381	3,999	2,921
Yukon	234	213	57	47
Northwest Territories	84	77	23	18

In the table immediately following, the naturalized American-born
21 years of age or over are compared, on a percentage basis, by sex, with
those of all ages.

TABLE LII

Percentages of Total American-Born Naturalized, by Sex, for All Ages and for 21 Years or Over, Canada and Provinces: 1931

Province	Both Sexes		Males		Females	
	All Ages	21 Years or Over	All Ages	21 Years or Over	All Ages	21 Years or Over
CANADA	72.44	74.26	67.43	68.09	77.61	80.63
Prince Edward Island	81.09	81.38	75.59	70.75	86.43	91.09
Nova Scotia	81.78	80.48	77.59	72.17	85.42	86.88
New Brunswick	79.70	76.81	71.79	62.57	86.42	87.35
Quebec	76.77	76.59	71.01	68.59	81.88	83.42
Ontario	67.26	67.62	58.48	55.45	75.01	77.75
Manitoba	67.82	70.41	61.48	63.22	74.27	77.67
Saskatchewan	77.62	80.78	75.13	77.86	80.58	84.33
Alberta	70.38	74.21	67.68	70.92	73.64	78.29
British Columbia	69.74	70.54	62.78	62.03	76.79	79.15
Yukon	44.68	45.15	35.89	36.23	64.60	66.43
Northwest Territories	26.21	25.78	22.22	21.43	37.84	40.00

Age and sex have a notable bearing on naturalization, as will be seen from Tables LI to LIV. The age distribution of naturalized and alien American-born is shown in the Census Reports for the group "over 21" or "under 21" only. However, quinquennial age distributions are available for all persons owing allegiance to the United States, as well as for the total American-born; it is also known that in 1931 nearly all non-American-born owing allegiance to that country were over the age of 20. Consequently, the age distribution of those under 20 is come-at-able. By making certain assumptions for persons over 20 as to comparability of distribution between the American-born and those owing allegiance to the United States, also the total American-born, a worthwhile estimate of the quinquennial age distribution of the total naturalized and alien American-born can be obtained as in Table LI.* Tables LIII and LIV give further basic data.

*For age groups up to 20 it is assumed that the distribution of American-born aliens is *numerically* the same as the distribution of those owing allegiance to the United States. The naturalized are calculated by the subtraction of aliens from the total American-born in Canada at each age group. From this point on, the same percentage distribution is taken for the naturalized as that of the total American-born in Canada for each age group above 20 years. The result is 202,422 over 20, naturalized (estimated), compared with 202,859 naturalized over 21 years of age as given by the Census (Vol. IV). This is short 437 besides the number 20 years of age, to make up for which an additional 1 p.c. is added to age group 20-24 and 0.18 p.c. to age group 25-29. The aliens are calculated by subtraction of naturalized from the total American-born in Canada.

TABLE LIII

Estimated Distribution of Naturalized and Alien American-Born,
Classified by Quinquennial Age Groups: 1931

Age Group	Total[1]	Naturalized		Alien	
	No.	No.	p.c.	No.	p.c.
ALL AGES	344,480	249,590	100.0	94,890	100.0
0- 4	11,030	8,210	3.3	2,820	3.0
5- 9	15,780	10,960	4.4	4,820	5.1
10-14	16,000	10,120	4.1	5,880	6.2
15-19	22,500	14,810	5.9	7,690	8.1
20-24	34,340	27,460	11.0	6,880	7.3
25-29	37,240	27,530	11.0	9,710	10.2
30-34	38,230	27,700	11.1	10,530	11.1
35-39	40,880	29,700	11.9	11,180	11.8
40-44	35,520	25,710	10.3	9,810	10.3
45-49	29,200	21,220	8.5	7,980	8.4
50-54	20,710	14,980	6.0	5,730	6.0
55-59	15,300	10,980	4.4	4,320	4.6
60-64	10,900	7,990	3.2	2,910	3.1
65-69	7,110	5,240	2.1	1,870	2.0
70-74	5,220	3,740	1.5	1,480	1.5
75 or over	4,520	3,240	1.3	1,280	1.3

[1] Age "not stated" omitted.

TABLE LIV

Percentage Distribution of Total Foreign-Born Aliens and of Total
Naturalized, by Sex, Classified by Quinquennial Age Groups: 1931

Age Group	Foreign-Born Aliens			Naturalized		
	Both Sexes	Male	Female	Both Sexes	Male	Female
ALL AGES	100.00	100.00	100.00	100.00	100.00	100.00
0- 4	1.72	1.34	2.44	1.36	1.34	1.39
5- 9	5.18	4.09	7.21	2.21	2.15	2.28
10-14	3.74	2.98	5.15	2.18	2.13	2.24
15-19	4.82	3.65	7.02	3.72	3.46	4.01
20-24	11.16	9.40	14.47	7.46	6.45	8.59
25-29	16.87	17.33	16.02	9.17	7.69	10.82
30-34	15.26	16.54	12.86	10.59	9.38	11.93
35-39	12.07	13.10	10.15	13.08	12.63	13.58
40-44	9.31	10.41	7.23	12.89	13.59	12.11

TABLE LIV—concluded

Percentage Distribution of Total Foreign-Born Aliens and of Total Naturalized, by Sex, Classified by Quinquennial Age Groups: 1931

Age Group	Foreign-Born Aliens			Naturalized		
	Both Sexes	Male	Female	Both Sexes	Male	Female
45-49	7.07	7.92	5.49	11.44	12.57	10.17
50-54	4.81	5.36	3.77	8.41	9.33	7.38
55-59	3.05	3.29	2.60	6.01	6.67	5.28
60-64	2.04	2.09	1.94	4.29	4.73	3.81
65-69	1.31	1.19	1.52	3.17	3.50	2.80
70-74	0.81	0.69	1.03	2.19	2.42	1.93
75-79	0.44	0.35	0.61	}		
80-84	0.20	0.14	0.29			
85-89	0.08	0.06	0.13	} 1.80	1.94	1.64
90-94	0.02	0.01	0.04			
95 and over	0.01	[1]	0.02	}		
Not stated	0.05	0.07	0.02	0.03	0.04	0.02

[1] Less than 0.01 p.c.

TABLE LV

Numerical and Percentage Distributions of United States Citizens, by Sex, Classified by Quinquennial Age Groups: 1931

Age Group	Numbers			Percentages		
	Both Sexes	Male	Female	Both Sexes	Male	Female
ALL AGES	108,375	59,239	49,136	100.00	100.00	100.00
0- 4	2,822	1,423	1,399	2.60	2.40	2.85
5- 9	4,813	2,507	2,306	4.44	4.23	4.69
10-14	5,879	3,038	2,841	5.42	5.13	5.78
15-19	7,691	3,849	3,842	7.10	6.50	7.82
20-24	10,503	5,107	5,396	9.69	8.62	10.98
25-29	12,027	6,207	5,820	11.10	10.48	11.84
30-34	11,972	6,482	5,490	11.05	10.94	11.17
35-39	12,085	6,587	5,498	11.15	11.12	11.19
40-44	10,726	6,203	4,523	9.90	10.47	9.21
45-49	8,991	5,326	3,665	8.30	8.99	7.46
50-54	6,861	4,173	2,688	6.33	7.04	5.47
55-59	4,815	2,937	1,878	4.44	4.96	3.82
60-64	3,544	2,151	1,393	3.27	3.63	2.83
65-69	2,516	1,532	984	2.32	2.59	2.00
70-74	1,600	913	687	1.48	1.54	1.40

TABLE LV—concluded

*Numerical and Percentage Distributions of United States Citizens,
by Sex, Classified by Quinquennial Age Groups: 1931*

Age Group	Numbers			Percentages		
	Both Sexes	Male	Female	Both Sexes	Male	Female
75-79	899	479	420	0.83	0.81	0.85
80-84	406	211	195	0.37	0.36	0.40
85-89	143	71	72	0.13	0.12	0.15
90-94	38	16	22	0.04	0.03	0.04
95-99	6	2	4	0.01	[1]	0.01
100 or over	2	....	2	[1]	....	[1]
Not stated	36	25	11	0.03	0.04	0.02

[1] Less than 0.01 p.c.

Comparing the percentage of American-born naturalized with the total naturalized Canadian population, it will be seen from Tables LIII, LIV, and LV that 17.7 p.c. of the former and 9.5 p.c. of the latter are under 20 years of age. This is explained by the large number of American-born children of Canadian parents who automatically become naturalized when coming to Canada, whereas children of foreign-born parents must await the required residence of their parents. Between the ages of 20 and 45, the percentage naturalized among the American-born is 55.3 compared with 53.2 for naturalized of total foreign-born in the same age group—a negligible difference. For ages over 45, the percentages are 27.0 for American-born and 37.3 for naturalized of total foreign-born in the same age group. In the light of data as to the period of immigration, the higher percentages for total naturalized at the later years may be attributed to the heavy foreign immigration between 1901 and 1913.

The percentages under 20 years of age of the American-born aliens and of all aliens in Canada under 20 are 22.4 and 15.5 respectively, i.e., there are relatively more alien children among the American-born than among immigrant-born in other countries. This would seem to indicate delay on the part of American-born parents in becoming naturalized, with the result that their children retain United States citizenship. But year of immigration must also be taken into account. In Table LVI the proportion of American-born immigrants who are naturalized is compared with the corresponding proportion of foreign-born immigrants by period of immigration. Of the total foreign-born immigrants who arrived between 1926 and 1930 only 11.88 p.c. were naturalized in 1931, many of the later arrivals, of course, not having then acquired residence. For the same years the percentage of American-born who were naturalized is much higher.

TABLE LVI

Numerical and Percentage Distributions of American-Born and Foreign-Born Immigrants Naturalized in 1931, Classified by Period of Immigration

Period of Immigration	American-Born			Foreign-Born		
	Total	Naturalized		Total	Naturalized	
	No.	No.	p.c.	No.	No.	p.c.
TOTAL............	344 574	249,595	72.44	1,122,695	614,971	54.78
1931........................	5,115	1,747	34.15	7,735	2,010	25.99
1926-30..................	52,704	22,200	42.12	291,075	34,592	11.88
1921-25..................	28,787	16,881	58.64	126,951	55,957	44.08
1916-20..................	42,634	25,923	60.80	78,918	44,048	55.81
1911-15..................	64,294	49,356	76.77	206,670	139,661	67.58
1901-10..................	102,825	90,100	87.62	292,843	240,268	82.05
Before 1901............	46,347	42,202	91.06	114,323	96,465	84.38
Not stated............	1,868	1,186	63.49	4,180	1,970	47.13

A section of the American-born in Canada to whom attention has not yet been directed are the 4,910 who owe allegiance to other countries than Canada or the United States. The data distributed by provinces are given in Table LIX, p. 138. The chief countries rank as follows: (1) Norway, (2) Russia, (3) Germany, (4) Poland, (5) Sweden, (6) Italy, (7) Denmark, and (8) Finland. The 4,910 doubtless include some who left the United States, became naturalized in another country and immigrated to Canada later, but there are other possible explanations, e.g., American-born females marrying citizens of some other country, and American-born children of foreign-born aliens retaining in Canada the citizenship of their parents.

Tables LVII, LVIII, and LIX will enable the subject to be pursued into details beyond the compass of brief review. Table LVII is particularly interesting as showing the increased tendency to seek naturalization which a term of sojourn in the United States bestows upon a racial type. The Icelandic, Hebrew, Italian, Japanese, and "Other Asiatic" races are the only exceptions to this rule.

TABLE LVII

American-Born and Other Foreign-Born Compared as to Percentage Naturalized, Classified by Racial Origin: 1931

Racial Origin	American-Born		Born Elsewhere	
	Number	Percentage Naturalized	Number	Percentage Naturalized
ALL RACES	344,574	72.4	802,863	45.9
British—				
English	85,894	71.1	10,064	35.6
Irish	47,195	71.6	3,244	23.2
Scottish	37,652	75.8	4,128	30.6
Other British	3,675	70.6	397	57.2
French	55,630	83.8	22,373	54.8
Other European—				
Austrian, *n.o.s.*	1,127	54.3	21,600	50.0
Belgian	676	62.9	15,664	48.7
Bulgarian	17	70.6	2,082	51.4
Czechoslovak	1,231	63.0	20,785	21.2
Danish	3,880	65.0	17,214	31.0
Dutch	9,731	66.7	20,149	39.7
Finnish	1,492	65.6	30,138	29.0
German	44,998	65.2	99,667	50.1
Greek	176	69.9	5,179	62.0
Hebrew	4,346	66.0	80,305	67.8
Hungarian	642	52.5	28,720	21.0
Icelandic	1,011	84.0	5,730	90.5
Italian	2,084	61.9	43,600	62.0
Lithuanian	91	40.7	3,943	19.9
Norwegian	21,451	74.4	32,521	56.2
Polish	1,825	59.9	75,692	36.6
Roumanian	302	58.9	14,094	44.5
Russian	3,065	64.9	37,662	42.3
Swedish	10,750	71.4	35,828	58.6
Ukrainian	712	67.3	97,217	56.0
Yugoslavic	240	56.3	12,708	18.6
Other European	388	58.0	2,539	46.4
Asiatic—				
Chinese	23	39.1	41,188	5.3
Japanese	28	32.1	12,079	36.0
Other Asiatic	271	69.0	5,677	73.3
Indian and Eskimo	916	72.3	134	......
Negro	2,211	52.0	201	36.8
Various	44	47.7	210	53.8
Unspecified	800	59.0	131	61.1

TABLE LVIII

Naturalized American-Born under 21 Years of Age and over 21 Years of Age, by Sex, Rural and Urban, Classified by Period of Immigration, Canada: 1931

Period of Immigration	Under 21 Years			Over 21 Years		
	Both Sexes	Male	Female	Both Sexes	Male	Female
	TOTAL					
	No.	No.	No.	No.	No.	No.
ALL YEARS	46,736	23,577	23,159	202,859	94,527	108,332
1931	1,433	718	715	314	......	314
1926-1930	17,040	8,704	8,336	5,160	449	4,711
1921-1925	9,055	4,481	4,574	7,826	2,384	5,442
1916-1920	10,379	5,222	5,157	15,544	5,526	10,018
1911-1915	8,097	4,107	3,990	41,259	19,315	21,944
1901-1910	326	159	167	89,774	46,709	43,065
Before 1901	......	......	......	42,202	19,885	22,317
Not stated	406	186	220	780	259	521
	RURAL					
	No.	No.	No.	No.	No.	No.
ALL YEARS	23,280	12,189	11,091	108,835	57,542	51,293
1931	760	397	363	133	......	133
1926-1930	7,911	4,100	3,811	2,107	202	1,905
1921-1925	4,389	2,267	2,122	3,502	1,211	2,291
1916-1920	5,534	2,882	2,652	8,397	3,324	5,073
1911-1915	4,366	2,386	1,980	24,011	12,670	11,341
1901-1910	172	95	77	53,118	30,845	22,273
Before 1901	......	......	......	17,256	9,182	8,074
Not stated	148	62	86	311	108	203
	URBAN					
	No.	No.	No.	No.	No.	No.
ALL YEARS	23,456	11,388	12,068	94,024	36,985	57,039
1931	673	321	352	181	......	181
1926-1930	9,129	4,604	4,525	3,053	247	2,806
1921-1925	4,666	2,214	2,452	4,324	1,173	3,151
1916-1920	4,845	2,340	2,505	7,147	2,202	4,945
1911-1915	3,731	1,721	2,010	17,248	6,645	10,603
1901-1910	154	64	90	36,656	15,864	20,792
Before 1901	......	......	......	24,946	10,703	14,243
Not stated	258	124	134	469	151	318

TABLE LIX

American-Born Aliens, by Sex, Classified by Country of Allegiance, Canada: 1931

Country of Allegiance	Both Sexes	Male	Female
	No.	*No.*	*No.*
ALL COUNTRIES	94,979	57,036	37,943
European—			
Austria	121	41	80
Belgium	114	48	66
Czechoslovakia	142	65	77
Denmark	238	89	149
Finland	234	109	125
France	110	42	68
Germany	545	237	308
Greece	31	16	15
Holland	104	43	61
Hungary	187	75	112
Iceland	22	9	13
Italy	297	118	179
Lithuania	47	25	22
Norway	716	317	399
Poland	514	233	281
Roumania	144	50	94
Russia	620	230	390
Sweden	442	159	283
Switzerland	62	23	39
Ukraine	34	16	18
Yugoslavia	72	37	35
Other European	26	9	17
Asiatic—			
China	15	6	9
Japan	22	9	13
Other Asiatic	27	12	15
United States	90,069	55,009	35,060
Other	24	9	15

CHAPTER VIII

SCHOOL ATTENDANCE AND ILLITERACY

SCHOOL ATTENDANCE

AMONG the American-born in Canada in 1931, 23,047, or 6.69 p.c., were children attending school. This compares with 4.02 p.c. for the British-born and 15.75 p.c. for the Canadian population as a whole. Obviously there are relatively fewer children of school age among the immigrants from overseas than from the United States. In Chapter III, Rural and Urban—Age—Sex, this is clearly brought out: immigration from the United States and from British sources differs in that the former is more largely composed of families.

Table LX gives the percentage distribution by provinces of American-born children, 7-14 years of age, attending school in 1931. The high percentage shown for Ontario (28.50 p.c.) is remarkable in view of the fact that, compared with Saskatchewan and Alberta, Ontario's total American-born population was less. It is equally remarkable that Quebec and the Maritimes combined had only 24.92 p.c., while the Prairie Provinces had 36.03 p.c., though the number under 14 years of age in the former totalled 13,282, and in the latter 12,726. Evidently many of the children in Quebec and the Maritimes were still under school age in 1931.

TABLE LX

Percentage Distribution of the American-Born, 7-14 Years of Age at School, Rural and Urban, by Provinces: 1931

Province	Total	Rural	Urban
CANADA	100.00	100.00	100.00
Prince Edward Island	0.99	1.48	0.51
Nova Scotia	3.28	4.26	2.30
New Brunswick	4.35	6.02	2.69
Quebec	16.30	9.20	23.39
Ontario	28.50	16.90	40.10
Manitoba	4.89	5.77	4.01
Saskatchewan	14.90	22.03	7.78
Alberta	16.24	23.96	8.53
British Columbia	10.54	10.38	10.70

139

TABLE LXI

*American-born, 7-14 Years of Age at School, Rural and
Urban, by Sex, Canada and Provinces: 1931*

Province	Total			Rural			Urban		
	Both Sexes	Male	Female	Both Sexes	Male	Female	Both Sexes	Male	Female
	No.	No.	No.	No.	No.	No.	No.	No.	No.
CANADA	23,047	11,836	11,211	11,517	6,003	5,514	11,530	5,833	5,697
Prince Edward Island	229	122	107	170	93	77	59	29	30
Nova Scotia	756	396	360	491	276	215	265	120	145
New Brunswick	1,003	512	491	693	355	338	310	157	153
Quebec	3,757	1,935	1,822	1,060	558	502	2,697	1,377	1,320
Ontario	6,569	3,380	3,189	1,946	1,026	920	4,623	2,354	2,269
Manitoba	1,126	598	528	664	361	303	462	237	225
Saskatchewan	3,434	1,760	1,674	2,537	1,321	1,216	897	439	458
Alberta	3,743	1,896	1,847	2,760	1,419	1,341	983	477	506
British Columbia	2,430	1,237	1,193	1,196	594	602	1,234	643	591

An urban and rural analysis of the American-born, 7-14 years of age, such as is given in the summary Table LXI, brings out several significant facts. The number attending school is almost identical in rural and in urban Canada. It must not, however, be concluded that there is an even spread over the whole of Canada: in individual provinces circumstances alter cases. In the Maritimes and in the Prairie Provinces there is a preponderance in rural school attendance, while in Ontario and Quebec urban attendance is much higher than rural. Attendance in British Columbia is almost the same in rural as in urban. This indicates that families from the United States settled in rural rather than in urban localities in the Maritimes and the Prairie Provinces, while in Ontario and Quebec they did the opposite.

Differences in the number attending rural and urban schools might be expected to influence the regularity of school attendance. Although there are no data to prove this as regards the American-born, there is no reason why they should not conform to the general Canadian pattern. In the 1931 Census Monograph *Illiteracy and School Attendance,** the writer says ". . . we would expect that physical environment, especially climatic conditions, would affect *regularity* of attendance rather than any attendance." However, he continues, "the differences in average months at school

*M. C. MacLean, *Illiteracy and School Attendance* (Ottawa, 1937), pp. 102-3.

during the year associated with geographical conditions are surprisingly small. The average months at school vary only from a little below 7 to a little below 8 (out of the 9) in the 222 divisions, i.e., there is a variation of a little more than one month from the division showing the poorest attendance to that showing the best attendance, excluding the District of Patricia." The attendance becomes poorer as we approach the extreme north, but it is apparent that only very exceptional physical environment produces differences worth mentioning.

Detailed statistics of school attendance for the total population and particularly for the American-born immigrants, 7-14, as compared with British-born immigrants of the same age group are given in Table LXII.

TABLE LXII

Population 7-14 Years of Age Compared with Total Population, American-Born and British-Born 7-14 Years of Age at School, by Sex, Rural, and by Urban Size Groups, Canada: 1931

Item	Population 7-14 Years of Age	Population 7-14 Years of Age at School	American-Born, 7-14 Years of Age at School	British-Born, 7-14 Years of Age at School
	No.	No.	No.	No.
TOTAL	1,755,348	1,634,069	23,047	47,678
Males	886,614	826,152	11,836	24,278
Females	868,734	807,917	11,211	23,400
Rural	888,685	807,264	11,517	17,025
Males	452,691	410,373	6,003	8,845
Females	435,994	396,891	5,514	8,180
Urban	866,663	826,805	11,530	30,653
Localities 30,000 or over	438,804	420,229	5,575	19,474
Localities 1,000-30,000	356,110	337,863	4,824	10,112
Localities under 1,000	71,749	68,713	1,131	1,067
Males	433,923	415,779	5,833	15,433
Localities 30,000 or over	220,308	211,802	2,848	9,765
Localities 1,000-30,000	178,146	169,874	2,463	5,119
Localities under 1,000	35,469	34,103	522	549
Females	432,740	411,026	5,697	15,220
Localities 30,000 or over	218,496	208,427	2,727	9,709
Localities 1,000-30,000	177,964	167,989	2,361	4,993
Localities under 1,000	36,280	34,610	609	518

Illiteracy

Table LXIII shows that the percentage of American-born illiterate is higher than that of the British-born, but lower than that of any other European stock. Poland, Italy, and Greece have been sending to Canada— as to the United States—the largest proportions of illiterates. These are the sources of the illiterates among the American-born in Canada; most of them are over 50 years of age and have been in the country for some time. In both countries a heterogeneous racial composition ensures that the high illiteracy of some is offset by the low illiteracy of others. Since there is a tendency on the part of illiterates to intermarry, a high percentage of their children, especially before education was made compulsory, were probably kept illiterate.

Table LXIII

Foreign-Born Illiterate 10 Years of Age or Over, by Selected Countries: 1931

Country	Total	Illiterate	
	No.	*No.*	*p.c.*
United States	317,119	4,164	1.31
England	711,006	2,786	0.39
Scotland	271,915	780	0.29
Ireland	104,345	812	0.78
Norway	31,719	615	1.94
Sweden	33,793	609	1.80
Denmark	16,370	253	1.55
Germany	37,314	1,499	4.02
Poland	161,736	27,300	16.88
Italy	41,528	6,174	14.87
Greece	5,527	539	9.75

Table LXIV shows, by sex, for those 10 years of age or over, the distribution by provinces of the American-born illiterate in relation to total American-born population.

TABLE LXIV

American-Born Illiterate 10 Years of Age or Over, by Sex, Rural and Urban, Canada and Provinces: 1931

Province	Both Sexes		Male		Female	
	Total	Illiterate	Total	Illiterate	Total	Illiterate
	No.	No.	No.	No.	No.	No.
CANADA—						
Totals	317,119	4,164	160,831	2,503	156,288	1,661
Rural	165,550	2,793	91,893	1,757	73,657	1,036
Urban	151,569	1,371	68,938	746	82,631	625
Prince Edward Island—						
Totals	1,031	13	505	6	526	7
Rural	736	8	365	3	371	5
Urban	295	5	140	3	155	2
Nova Scotia—						
Totals	5,556	61	2,493	47	3,063	14
Rural	2,849	34	1,316	29	1,533	5
Urban	2,707	27	1,177	18	1,530	9
New Brunswick—						
Totals	7,079	464	3,115	298	3,964	166
Rural	4,361	413	1,967	264	2,394	149
Urban	2,718	51	1,148	34	1,570	17
Quebec—						
Totals	43,551	1,287	20,206	811	23,345	476
Rural	9,479	648	4,768	445	4,711	203
Urban	34,072	639	15,438	366	18,634	273
Ontario—						
Totals	64,171	723	29,710	416	34,461	307
Rural	18,666	430	9,284	259	9,382	171
Urban	45,505	293	20,426	157	25,079	136
Manitoba—						
Totals	16,832	267	8,451	156	8,381	111
Rural	8,895	209	4,827	128	4,068	81
Urban	7,937	58	3,624	28	4,313	30
Saskatchewan—						
Totals	70,434	682	38,322	386	32,112	296
Rural	51,106	535	29,211	315	21,895	220
Urban	19,328	147	9,111	71	10,217	76
Alberta—						
Totals	76,083	499	41,745	286	34,338	213
Rural	53,759	403	31,266	243	22,493	160
Urban	22,324	96	10,479	43	11,845	53
British Columbia—						
Totals	32,382	168	16,284	97	16,098	71
Rural	15,699	113	8,889	71	6,810	42
Urban	16,683	55	7,395	26	9,288	29

Table LXV displays the illiteracy of the American-born population of Canada in comparison with that of the Canadian-born (exclusive of Indians, since very few Indians are found among American-born immigrants). The difference in the actual degree of illiteracy (the American-born show less illiteracy) is readily explainable: their racial composition is the more favourable. More meaningful than this difference, however, is the fact that the percentages of illiteracy (rural and urban as well as provincial) follow the same trend for the American-born as for the Canadian-born, e.g., the highest percentage illiterate among both is in rural New Brunswick and the lowest rural and the lowest urban for both are found in British Columbia. Rank differences for rural and urban are also given. That the correlations are very high will be seen at a glance. But the interesting point of these columns is their illustration of the fact that a means of measurement, which cannot be obtained directly, is often found through indirect channels. This behaviour of illiteracy demonstrates more conclusively than anything yet encountered that the American-born in Canada are made up of the same classes of people as those into whose midst they come; they arrange themselves by provinces accordingly. This has been already indicated in the data on nativity of parents, but the illiteracy distribution shows it more clearly.

TABLE LXV

Percentage Illiterate, American-Born and Canadian-Born 10 Years of Age or Over (Exclusive of Indians), Canada and Provinces: 1931

Province	Total		Rural				Urban			
					Rank				Rank	
	American-Born	Canadian-Born	American-Born	Canadian-Born	American-Born	Canadian-Born	American-Born	Canadian-Born	American-Born	Canadian-Born
CANADA[1]	1.31	2.99	1.69	4.30	....	....	0.90	1.87	....	....
P.E.I.	1.26	2.55	1.09	2.65	4	6	1.69	2.27	7	8
N.S.	1.10	4.03	1.19	5.40	5	7	1.00	2.19	6	6
N.B.	6.55	7.07	9.47	9.39	9	9	1.88	2.24	9	7
Que.	2.96	4.76	6.84	7.35	8	8	1.88	3.18	8	9
Ont.	1.13	1.67	2.30	2.51	6	5	0.64	1.07	3	5
Man.	1.59	1.43	2.35	2.01	7	4	0.73	0.71	4	4
Sask.	0.97	1.16	1.05	1.40	3	2	0.76	0.71	5	3
Alta.	0.66	1.00	0.75	1.42	2	3	0.43	0.44	2	2
B.C.	0.52	0.74	0.72	1.37	1	1	0.33	0.35	1	1

[1] Exclusive of the Northwest Territories and Yukon.

CHAPTER IX

RELIGION

THE present chapter considers the question, to what religious denominations have the American-born in Canada chiefly contributed. Comparisons with previous censuses would be informative, but unfortunately no classification of religions by birthplace was made prior to 1931.

From the simple comparison of percentage distributions given in Columns 1 and 4 of Table LXVI we note that the American-born have increased the proportions of the following denominations: Adventists, Baptists, Brethren and United Brethren, Church of Christ, Christian Science, Evangelical Association, International Bible Students, Lutherans, Mennonites, Mormons, Pentecostals, Presbyterians, United Church, "other sects," and "no religion." Eleven smaller sects, when combined, comprise 5.46 p.c. of the American-born and 3.66 of the total Canadian population. The Presbyterians are proportionally about the same in each, but membership in the United Church is much heavier among the American-born, while Roman Catholics and Anglicans constitute much smaller elements. From the same table, which compares the percentage of the American-born as to religion with those of the total foreign-born population (i.e., those born outside the British Empire), and the total population born outside Canada, several interesting features emerge. First, the American-born contribute in smaller measure to the Anglicans, Greek Orthodox, Jews, Presbyterians (to mention only the major religions) than do the total born outside of Canada. Secondly, the American-born contribute more than do the total born outside of Canada to the Baptists, Lutherans, and Roman Catholics, all of whom have large representations in the United States. (The Baptists, tracing back to Roger Williams in 1639, are linked with early immigration from the British Isles, while the Lutherans reflect the large German element in the United States.) The large contribution of the American-born to the United Church represents a combination of the various denominations in the United States that now make up that Church in Canada. Of the four religions just mentioned, the American-born influence the proportions of the Lutherans and Roman Catholics less than do the total foreign-born in Canada. The total foreign-born relatively increase the number of Anglicans, Baptists, Presbyterians and United Church less than do the total born outside of Canada. It is evident that countries contributing the largest number of immigrants likewise contribute most to the religion prevailing in the country of origin, e.g., immigrants from England and Scotland

145

increase the proportion of the Anglicans and Presbyterians, respectively. That the United States should add less to some religions and more to others reflects the fact that, as in Canada, no religion is peculiar to the country. Among the chief religious bodies whose proportion is increased more by the total foreign-born than by the American-born, besides Lutherans and Roman Catholics, are Jews, Mennonites, Confucians and Buddhists, Greek Orthodox, being religions peculiar to Continental Europe and Asia.

TABLE LXVI

Percentage Distribution of American-Born Compared with those of Foreign-Born, Population Born Outside of Canada, and of Total Population, Classified by Religion: 1931

Religion	American-Born	Foreign-Born	Born Outside of Canada	Total Population
ALL RELIGIONS	100.00	100.00	100.00	100.00
Adventists	0.66	0.36	0.22	0.15
Anglicans	9.72	4.13	26.21	15.76
Baptists	5.90	2.90	3.15	4.27
Brethren and United Brethren	0.23	0.09	0.18	0.15
Christians	0.46	0.21	0.14	0.11
Christian Science	0.62	0.22	0.28	0.18
Church of Christ, Disciples	0.36	0.13	0.11	0.15
Confucians and Buddhists	0.01	2.77	1 35	0.38
Evangelical Association	0.23	0.29	0.19	0.21
Greek Orthodox	0.17	4.32	2.11	0.99
International Bible Students	0.23	0.16	0.17	0.13
Jews	1.24	7.45	3.80	1.50
Lutherans	10.54	17.84	8.73	3.80
Mennonites	1.25	2.44	1.20	0.86
Mormons	1.20	0.42	0.26	0.21
Pentecostal	0.50	0.33	0.29	0.25
Presbyterians	8.49	3.91	11.08	8.39
Protestants	0.45	0.38	0.41	0.22
Roman Catholics	27.99	37.73	22.00	41.30
Salvation Army	0.23	0.11	0.48	0.30
United Church	27.70	10.94	15.48	19.44
Other sects	1.15	1.42	1.25	0.88
No religion	0.61	0.69	0.48	0.20
Not stated	0.08	0.77	0.42	0.15

Table LXVII indicates the distribution of the sexes in rural and urban Canada by religion, while Table LXVIII gives the ratio of urban to rural religions by rank. Examining the latter from the top down to the point where the ratio is less than 1, we have a group of the religions whose representation in urban is greater than in rural Canada: we can say, e.g., that for every American-born adherent to the Jewish faith in rural Canada there are 20 in urban Canada, whereas for the population as a whole there are 29; for every American-born Anglican in rural Canada there are 1.7 American-born Anglicans in urban Canada; and so on. Reading from the bottom up we obtain a presentation in order of the religions with heavier representation in rural than in urban Canada. From a comparison of the two columns the change in rank of the various religions may be noted, and the similarity in order of the last four religions.

TABLE LXVII

Percentage Distribution of American-Born, Rural and Urban, by Sex, Classified by Religion: 1931

Religion	Rural		Urban	
	Male	Female	Male	Female
ALL RELIGIONS	100.00	100.00	100.00	100.00
Adventists	0.87	1.17	0.25	0.33
Anglicans	6.33	7.41	12.56	13.10
Baptists	5.96	6.28	5.70	5.66
Brethren and United Brethren	0.29	0.28	0.17	0.18
Christians	0.66	0.68	0.25	0.23
Christian Science	0.24	0.39	0.81	1.07
Church of Christ, Disciples	0.39	0.48	0.28	0.31
Confucians and Buddhists	[1]	[1]	0.01	0.01
Evangelical Association	0.26	0.28	0.20	0.17
Greek Orthodox	0.15	0.18	0.18	0.16
International Bible Students	0.30	0.30	0.15	0.16
Jews	0.10	0.13	2.49	2.43
Lutherans	17.10	14.14	5.37	4.47
Mennonites	1.99	2.37	0.28	0.24
Mormons	1.34	1.35	1.10	0.99
Pentecostal	0.50	0.64	0.40	0.49
Presbyterians	7.49	7.36	9.74	9.54
Protestants	0.50	0.37	0.54	0.38
Roman Catholics	23.28	24.12	32.40	32.93
Salvation Army	0.14	0.14	0.28	0.35
United Church	29.88	30.28	24.85	25.39
Other sects	1.11	1.22	1.13	1.12
No religion	1.02	0.38	0.69	0.29
Not stated	0.09	0.04	0.17	0.03

[1] Less than 0.01 p.c.

TABLE LXVIII

Ratio of Urban to Rural American-Born, Classified by Religion According to Rank, Compared with Ratio of Urban to Rural Total Population: 1931

Rank	Religion	Ratio Urban to Rural
	AMERICAN-BORN	
1	Jews	20.35
2	Confucians and Buddhists	3.00
3	Christian Science	2.82
4	Salvation Army	2.03
5	Anglicans	1.74
6	Roman Catholics	1.28
7	Presbyterians	1.20
8	Protestants	0.95
9	Greek Orthodox	0.94
10	Other sects	0.90
11	Baptists	0.86
12	United Church	0.77
13	Pentecostal	0.74
14	Mormons	0.71
15	Church of Christ, Disciples	0.63
16	Evangelical Association	0.63
17	No religion	0.59
18	Brethren and United Brethren	0.57
19	International Bible Students	0.48
20	Christians	0.33
21	Lutherans	0.29
22	Adventists	0.27
23	Mennonites	0.11
	TOTAL POPULATION	
1	Jews	28.75
2	Christian Science	3.94
3	Salvation Army	3.77
4	Protestants	2.02
5	Confucians and Buddhists	1.88
6	Anglicans	1.62
7	Presbyterians	1.51
8	No religion	1.25
9	Pentecostal	1.18
10	Roman Catholics	1.16
11	United Church	0.97
12	Brethren and United Brethren	0.93
13	Baptists	0.91
14	International Bible Students	0.90
15	Evangelical Association	0.82
16	Mormons	0.81
17	Other sects	0.72
18	Church of Christ, Disciples	0.66
19	Greek Orthodox	0.58
20	Christians	0.49
21	Lutherans	0.49
22	Adventists	0.39
23	Mennonites	0.15

The last two tables of this chapter present detailed numerical distributions of the American-born by religions. Table LXIX gives the religious denominations of the American-born in Canada by provinces, while Table LXX effects a further segregation for the Dominion by rural and urban and by sex.

TABLE LXIX

American-Born, Classified by Religion, Canada and Provinces: 1931

Religion	CANADA	Prince Edward Island	Nova Scotia	New Brunswick	Quebec	Ontario
	No.	No.	No.	No.	No.	No.
ALL RELIGIONS	344,574	1,380	7,222	8,794	49,406	72,525
Adventists	2,285	......	33	39	104	196
Anglicans	33,476	57	943	888	3,744	12,366
Baptists	20,326	77	1,324	1,985	696	5,279
Brethren and United Brethren	800	......	2	10	9	197
Christians	1,584	10	12	20	12	171
Christian Science	2,126	1	11	13	112	582
Church of Christ, Disciples	1,257	9	13	60	7	270
Confucians and Buddhists	24	......	......	......	2	1
Evangelical Association	776	......	......	1	1	264
Greek Orthodox	570	......	......	......	79	147
International Bible Students	791	......	9	3	5	74
Jews	4,270	1	76	45	1,402	1,909
Lutherans	36,328	2	62	28	250	2,585
Mennonites	4,292	......	......	......	......	233
Mormons	4,139	......	3	4	8	197
Pentecostal	1,738	......	18	54	28	195
Presbyterians	29,248	259	733	287	1,803	8,513
Protestants	1,538	2	6	9	389	147
Roman Catholics	96,461	597	2,182	3,850	36,723	17,691
Salvation Army	783	2	19	20	12	241
United Church	95,437	346	1,704	1,440	3,645	19,915
Other sects	3,949	14	47	33	225	1,115
No religion	2,097	3	15	4	127	168
Not stated	279	......	10	1	23	69

TABLE LXIX—concluded

American-Born, Classified by Religion, Canada and Provinces: 1931

Religion	Mani-toba	Sask-atch-ewan	Alberta	British Col-umbia	Yukon	North-west Terri-tories
	No.	No.	No.	No.	No.	No.
ALL RELIGIONS	17,903	73,008	78,959	34,706	526	145
Adventists	51	443	1,070	349	......	......
Anglicans	1,758	3,122	4,386	6,010	143	59
Baptists	774	2,645	5,377	2,151	15	3
Brethren and United Brethren	25	161	338	58	......	......
Christians	26	329	880	122	2	......
Christian Science	152	162	426	657	8	2
Church of Christ, Disciples	60	427	353	58	......	......
Confucians and Buddhists	......	......	3	18	......	......
Evangelical Association	14	212	279	5	......	......
Greek Orthodox	62	153	93	36	......	......
International Bible Students	69	288	197	146	......	......
Jews	350	122	139	226	......	......
Lutherans	1,996	17,381	11,727	2,259	29	9
Mennonites	842	1,619	1,569	29	......	......
Mormons	35	333	3,448	107	3	1
Pentecostal	124	578	569	172	......	......
Presbyterians	1,345	4,857	6,965	4,409	64	13
Protestants	69	214	404	285	9	4
Roman Catholics	4,054	14,715	11,402	5,110	107	30
Salvation Army	51	170	170	98	......	......
United Church	5,725	23,726	27,673	11,127	118	18
Other sects	220	868	931	492	2	2
No religion	94	427	500	730	25	4
Not stated	7	56	60	52	1	......

TABLE LXX

American-Born, Rural and Urban, by Sex, Classified by Religion,
Canada and Provinces: 1931

Religion	Rural			Urban		
	Both Sexes	Male	Female	Both Sexes	Male	Female
			CANADA			
	No.	No.	No.	No.	No.	No.
ALL RELIGIONS	179,036	98,991	80,045	165,538	76,149	89,389
Adventists	1,801	866	935	484	191	293
Anglicans	12,202	6,269	5,933	21,274	9,566	11,708
Baptists	10,930	5,901	5,029	9,396	4,341	5,055
Brethren and United Brethren	509	288	221	291	128	163
Christians	1,193	652	541	391	187	204
Christian Science	557	242	315	1,569	617	952

TABLE LXX—continued

American-Born, Rural and Urban, By Sex, Classified by Religion, Canada and Provinces: 1931

Religion	Rural			Urban		
	Both Sexes	Male	Female	Both Sexes	Male	Female
			CANADA			
	No.	No.	No.	No.	No.	No.
Church of Christ, Disciples..............	772	384	388	485	211	274
Confucians and Buddhists...............	6	4	2	18	7	11
Evangelical Association....................	476	253	223	300	150	150
Greek Orthodox..............................	294	153	141	276	136	140
International Bible Students...........	536	296	240	255	112	143
Jews.........	200	95	105	4,070	1,898	2,172
Lutherans..	28,243	16,925	11,318	8,085	4,093	3,992
Mennonites......................................	3,867	1,968	1,899	425	210	215
Mormons.........................′..............	2,414	1,330	1,084	1,725	841	884
Pentecostal......................................	1,000	491	509	738	303	435
Presbyterians..................................	13,301	7,412	5,889	15,947	7,418	8,529
Protestants......................................	790	495	295	748	411	337
Roman Catholics..............................	42,353	23,050	19,303	54,108	24,674	29,434
Salvation Army................................	258	142	116	525	212	313
United Church.................................	53,816	29,575	24,241	41,621	18,925	22,696
Other sects......................................	2,081	1,101	980	1,868	863	1,005
No religion......................................	1,316	1,013	303	781	525	256
Not stated.......................................	121	86	35	158	130	28

	PRINCE EDWARD ISLAND					
	No.	No.	No.	No.	No.	No.
ALL RELIGIONS....................................	999	498	501	381	182	199
Adventists..	......	......		......		
Anglicans...	37	17	20	20	9	11
Baptists..	54	24	30	23	10	13
Brethren and United Brethren........	......	......	......	......	......	......
Christians..	9	6	3	1	......	1
Christian Science............................	......	......	......	1	......	1
Church of Christ, Disciples..............	3	1	2	6	1	5
Confucians and Buddhists...............	......	......	......	......	......	......
Evangelical Association....................	......	......	......	......	......	......
Greek Orthodox..............................	......	......	......	......	......	......
International Bible Students...........	......	......	......	......	......	......
Jews.........	......	......	......	1	......	1
Lutherans..	1	......	1	1	1	......
Mennonites......................................	......	......	......	......	......	......
Mormons..	......	......	......	......	......	......
Pentecostal......................................	......	......	......	......	......	......

TABLE LXX—continued

American-Born, Rural and Urban, by Sex, Classified by Religion,
Canada and Provinces: 1931

Religion	Rural			Urban		
	Both Sexes	Male	Female	Both Sexes	Male	Female

PRINCE EDWARD ISLAND—concluded

	No.	No.	No.	No.	No.	No.
Presbyterians	179	93	86	80	39	41
Protestants	1	1	......	1	1	......
Roman Catholics	440	218	222	157	73	84
Salvation Army	......	......	......	2	1	1
United Church	263	132	131	83	45	38
Other sects	9	3	6	5	2	3
No religion	3	3	......	......	......	......
Not stated	......	......	......	......	......	......

NOVA SCOTIA

	No.	No.	No.	No.	No.	No.
ALL RELIGIONS	3,862	1,859	2,003	3,360	1,496	1,864
Adventists	21	9	12	12	2	10
Anglicans	414	188	226	529	250	279
Baptists	875	408	467	449	206	243
Brethren and United Brethren	......	......	......	2	......	2
Christians	12	4	8	......	......	......
Christian Science	7	3	4	4	1	3
Church of Christ, Disciples	8	4	4	5	3	2
Confucians and Buddhists	......	......	......	......	......	......
Evangelical Association	......	......	......	......	......	......
Greek Orthodox	......	......	......	......	......	......
International Bible Students	7	2	5	2	1	1
Jews	1	1	......	75	41	34
Lutherans	41	19	22	21	11	10
Mennonites	......	......	......	3	3	......
Mormons	......	......	......	5	1	4
Pentecostal	13	5	8	5	1	4
Presbyterians	403	206	197	330	145	185
Protestants	4	2	2	2	2	......
Roman Catholics	1,112	543	569	1,070	468	602
Salvation Army	4	2	2	15	6	9
United Church	908	445	463	796	335	461
Other sects	23	13	10	24	11	13
No religion	7	4	3	8	6	2
Not stated	2	1	1	8	4	4

TABLE LXX—continued

American-Born, Rural and Urban, by Sex, Classified by Religion,
Canada and Provinces: 1931

Religion	Rural			Urban		
	Both Sexes	Male	Female	Both Sexes	Male	Female

NEW BRUNSWICK

	No.	No.	No.	No.	No.	No.
ALL RELIGIONS	5,615	2,633	2,982	3,179	1,404	1,775
Adventists	30	12	18	9	2	7
Anglicans	470	218	252	418	184	234
Baptists	1,434	643	791	551	232	319
Brethren and United Brethren	9	4	5	1	......	1
Christians	11	3	8	9	5	4
Christian Science	7	......	7	6	3	3
Church of Christ, Disciples	56	25	31	4	2	2
Confucians and Buddhists	......	......	......	......	......	......
Evangelical Association	1	......	1	......	......	......
Greek Orthodox	......	......	......	......	......	......
International Bible Students	3	1	2	......	......	......
Jews	4	2	2	41	14	27
Lutherans	17	12	5	11	7	4
Mennonites	......	......	......	......	......	......
Mormons	1	......	1	3	3	......
Pentecostal	48	18	30	6	3	3
Presbyterians	150	76	74	137	67	70
Protestants	4	3	1	5	3	2
Roman Catholics	2,584	1,261	1,323	1,266	570	696
Salvation Army	4	2	2	16	8	8
United Church	766	342	424	674	290	384
Other sects	13	9	4	20	10	10
No religion	2	2	......	2	1	1
Not stated	1	......	1	......	......	......

QUEBEC

	No.	No.	No.	No.	No.	No.
ALL RELIGIONS	11,588	5,881	5,707	37,818	17,366	20,452
Adventists	61	29	32	43	17	26
Anglicans	501	252	249	3,243	1,498	1,745
Baptists	145	75	70	551	264	287
Brethren and United Brethren	1	......	1	8	3	5
Christians	3	2	1	9	5	4
Christian Science	1	1	......	111	48	63
Church of Christ, Disciples	1	1	......	6	3	3
Confucians and Buddhists	......	......	......	2	1	1
Evangelical Association	1	......	1	......	......	......
Greek Orthodox	5	3	2	74	31	43
International Bible Students	1	......	1	4	2	2

TABLE LXX—continued
American-Born, Rural and Urban, by Sex, Classified by Religion, Canada and Provinces: 1931

Religion	Rural			Urban		
	Both Sexes	Male	Female	Both Sexes	Male	Female
	QUEBEC—concluded					
	No.	No.	No.	No.	No.	No.
Jews	14	11	3	1,388	638	750
Lutherans	14	9	5	236	133	103
Mennonites	......	......	......	......	......	......
Mormons	......	......	......	8	5	3
Pentecostal	2	1	1	26	9	17
Presbyterians	169	86	83	1,634	776	858
Protestants	47	28	19	342	178	164
Roman Catholics	9,933	5,086	4,847	26,790	12,189	14,601
Salvation Army	......	......	......	12	3	9
United Church	636	272	364	3,009	1,390	1,619
Other sects	36	12	24	189	88	101
No religion	16	12	4	111	64	47
Not stated	1	1	......	22	21	1

Religion	*ONTARIO*					
	No.	No.	No.	No.	No.	No.
ALL RELIGIONS	21,462	10,749	10,713	51,063	23,268	27,795
Adventists	113	47	66	83	29	54
Anglicans	2,962	1,452	1,510	9,404	4,229	5,175
Baptists	1,802	959	843	3,477	1,584	1,893
Brethren and United Brethren	78	33	45	119	52	67
Christians	92	46	46	79	32	47
Christian Science	69	28	41	513	214	299
Church of Christ, Disciples	105	45	60	165	71	94
Confucians and Buddhists	......	......	......	1	1	......
Evangelical Association	78	34	44	186	84	102
Greek Orthodox	39	25	14	108	61	47
International Bible Students	31	14	17	43	21	22
Jews	131	54	77	1,778	826	952
Lutherans	1,018	584	434	1,567	759	808
Mennonites	177	80	97	56	26	30
Mormons	83	44	39	114	47	67
Pentecostal	77	36	41	118	46	72
Presbyterians	2,203	1,078	1,125	6,310	2,879	3,431
Protestants	35	21	14	112	66	46
Roman Catholics	5,077	2,626	2,451	12,614	5,810	6,804
Salvation Army	48	25	23	193	71	122
United Church	6,793	3,301	3,492	13,122	5,890	7,232
Other sects	384	169	215	731	346	385
No religion	49	38	11	119	76	43
Not stated	18	10	8	51	48	3

TABLE LXX—continued

American-Born, Rural and Urban, by Sex, Classified by Religion,
Canada and Provinces: 1931

Religion	Rural			Urban		
	Both Sexes	Male	Female	Both Sexes	Male	Female
	MANITOBA					
	No.	No.	No.	No.	No.	No.
ALL RELIGIONS	9,483	5,148	4,335	8,420	3,879	4,541
Adventists	24	14	10	27	13	14
Anglicans	668	311	357	1,090	484	606
Baptists	320	171	149	454	234	220
Brethren and United Brethren	15	8	7	10	2	8
Christians	19	11	8	7	2	5
Christian Science	37	20	17	115	47	68
Church of Christ, Disciples	37	20	17	23	6	17
Confucians and Buddhists	......	......	......	......	......	......
Evangelical Association	8	6	2	6	6	......
Greek Orthodox	39	19	20	23	12	11
International Bible Students	43	19	24	26	12	14
Jews	17	9	8	333	149	184
Lutherans	1,369	803	566	627	315	312
Mennonites	812	392	420	30	13	17
Mormons	22	12	10	13	8	5
Pentecostal	57	26	31	67	24	43
Presbyterians	553	320	233	792	397	395
Protestants	28	22	6	41	24	17
Roman Catholics	2,184	1,195	989	1,870	812	1,058
Salvation Army	15	8	7	36	13	23
United Church	3,072	1,676	1,396	2,653	1,210	1,443
Other sects	111	57	54	109	48	61
No religion	32	28	4	62	42	20
Not stated	1	1	......	6	6	......
	SASKATCHEWAN					
	No.	No.	No.	No.	No.	No.
ALL RELIGIONS	52,965	30,178	22,787	20,043	9,486	10,557
Adventists	367	174	193	76	28	48
Anglicans	1,764	928	836	1,358	579	779
Baptists	1,809	1,054	755	836	388	448
Brethren and United Brethren	138	87	51	23	11	12
Christians	286	152	134	43	23	20
Christian Science	58	31	27	104	40	64
Church of Christ, Disciples	290	154	136	137	61	76
Confucians and Buddhists	......	......	......	......	......	......
Evangelical Association	164	87	77	48	28	20
Greek Orthodox	123	53	70	30	13	17
International Bible Students	204	122	82	84	39	45

TABLE LXX—continued

American-Born, Rural and Urban, by Sex, Classified by Religion, Canada and Provinces: 1931

Religion	Rural			Urban		
	Both Sexes	Male	Female	Both Sexes	Male	Female

SASKATCHEWAN—concluded

Religion	No.	No.	No.	No.	No.	No.
Jews	14	7	7	108	51	57
Lutherans	14,624	8,689	5,935	2,757	1,418	1,339
Mennonites	1,325	719	606	294	146	148
Mormons	240	126	114	93	40	53
Pentecostal	369	182	187	209	102	107
Presbyterians	3,206	1,821	1,385	1,651	806	845
Protestants	141	93	48	73	42	31
Roman Catholics	10,662	6,085	4,577	4,053	1,886	2,167
Salvation Army	81	41	40	89	38	51
United Church	16,089	8,968	7,121	7,637	3,556	4,081
Other sects	643	348	295	225	105	120
No religion	338	238	100	89	64	25
Not stated	30	19	11	26	22	4

ALBERTA

Religion	No.	No.	No.	No.	No.	No.
ALL RELIGIONS	55,824	32,286	23,538	23,135	10,880	12,255
Adventists	925	456	469	145	62	83
Anglicans	2,568	1,412	1,156	1,818	827	991
Baptists	3,567	2,048	1,519	1,810	867	943
Brethren and United Brethren	241	140	101	97	49	48
Christians	672	382	290	208	103	105
Christian Science	187	82	105	239	93	146
Church of Christ, Disciples	228	116	112	125	58	67
Confucians and Buddhists	1	1	......	2	2	......
Evangelical Association	220	124	96	59	31	28
Greek Orthodox	76	49	27	17	8	9
International Bible Students	156	91	65	41	15	26
Jews	7	5	2	132	68	64
Lutherans	9,713	5,903	3,810	2,014	1,017	997
Mennonites	1,530	771	759	39	23	16
Mormons	1,992	1,108	884	1,456	715	741
Pentecostal	370	196	174	199	76	123
Presbyterians	4,379	2,523	1,856	2,586	1,215	1,371
Protestants	339	212	127	65	40	25
Roman Catholics	7,854	4,596	3,258	3,548	1,602	1,946
Salvation Army	68	40	28	102	45	57
United Church	19,613	11,298	8,315	8,060	3,755	4,305
Other sects	668	382	286	263	123	140
No religion	414	322	92	86	68	18
Not stated	36	29	7	24	18	6

Table LXX—continued

American-Born, Rural and Urban, by Sex, Classified by Religion, Canada and Provinces: 1931

Religion	Rural			Urban		
	Both Sexes	Male	Female	Both Sexes	Male	Female

BRITISH COLUMBIA

	No.	No.	No.	No.	No.	No.
ALL RELIGIONS	16,809	9,448	7,361	17,897	8,026	9,871
Adventists	260	125	135	89	38	51
Anglicans	2,664	1,387	1,277	3,346	1,476	1,870
Baptists	916	514	402	1,235	549	686
Brethren and United Brethren	27	16	11	31	11	20
Christians	88	46	42	34	16	18
Christian Science	187	76	111	470	169	301
Church of Christ, Disciples	44	18	26	14	6	8
Confucians and Buddhists	5	3	2	13	3	10
Evangelical Association	4	2	2	1	1	......
Greek Orthodox	12	4	8	24	11	13
International Bible Students	91	47	44	55	22	33
Jews	12	6	6	214	111	103
Lutherans	1,422	882	540	837	422	415
Mennonites	23	6	17	6	2	4
Mormons	72	37	35	35	20	15
Pentecostal	64	27	37	108	42	66
Presbyterians	2,002	1,167	835	2,407	1,084	1,323
Protestants	186	110	76	99	49	50
Roman Catholics	2,419	1,377	1,042	2,691	1,235	1,456
Salvation Army	38	24	14	60	27	33
United Church	5,608	3,088	2,520	5,519	2,403	3,116
Other sects	191	106	85	301	129	172
No religion	443	356	87	287	189	98
Not stated	31	24	7	21	11	10

YUKON

	No.	No.	No.	No.	No.	No.
ALL RELIGIONS	284	203	81	242	162	80
Adventists	......	......	......	......	......	......
Anglicans	95	64	31	48	30	18
Baptists	5	2	3	10	7	3
Brethren and United Brethren	......	......	......	......	......	......
Christians	1	......	1	1	1	......
Christian Science	2	......	2	6	2	4
Church of Christ, Disciples	......	......	......	......	......	......
Confucians and Buddhists	......	......	......	......	......	......
Evangelical Association	......	......	......	......	......	......
Greek Orthodox	......	......	......	......	......	......

TABLE LXX—concluded

American-Born, Rural and Urban, by Sex, Classified by Religion, Canada and Provinces: 1931

Religion	Rural			Urban		
	Both Sexes	Male	Female	Both Sexes	Male	Female
	YUKON—concluded					
	No.	No.	No.	No.	No.	No.
International Bible Students............	......	......	......	......	......	......
Jews..........	......	......	......	......	......	......
Lutherans..........	15	15	......	14	10	4
Mennonites..........	......	......	......	......	......	......
Mormons..........	3	2	1	......	......	......
Pentecostal..........	......	......	......	......	......	......
Presbyterians..........	44	30	14	20	10	10
Protestants..........	1	1	......	8	6	2
Roman Catholics..........	58	42	16	49	29	20
Salvation Army..........	......	......	......	......	......	......
United Church..........	50	39	11	68	51	17
Other sects..........	1	......	1	1	1	......
No religion..........	8	7	1	17	15	2
Not stated..........	1	1	......	......	......	......

	NORTHWEST TERRITORIES					
	No.	No.	No.	No.	No.	No.
ALL RELIGIONS..........	145	108	37	......	......	......
Adventists..........	......	......	......	......	......	......
Anglicans..........	59	40	19	......	......	......
Baptists..........	3	3	......	......	......	......
Brethren and United Brethren........	......	......	......	......	......	......
Christians..........	......	......	......	......	......	......
Christian Science..........	2	1	1	......	......	......
Church of Christ, Disciples..........	......	......	......	......	......	......
Confucians and Buddhists..........	......	......	......	......	......	......
Evangelical Association..........	......	......	......	......	......	......
Greek Orthodox..........	......	......	......	......	......	......
International Bible Students..........	......	......	......	......	......	......
Jews..........	......	......	......	......	......	......
Lutherans..........	9	9	......	......	......	......
Mennonites..........	......	......	......	......	......	......
Mormons..........	1	1	......	......	......	......
Pentecostal..........	......	......	......	......	......	......
Presbyterians..........	13	12	1	......	......	......
Protestants..........	4	2	2	......	......	......
Roman Catholics..........	30	21	9	......	......	......
Salvation Army..........	......	......	......	......	......	......
United Church..........	18	14	4	......	......	......
Other sects..........	2	2	......	......	......	......
No religion..........	4	3	1	......	......	......
Not stated..........	......	......	......	......	......	......

CHAPTER X

OCCUPATION AND UNEMPLOYMENT

ALTHOUGH other social features (notably family composition) might profitably engage attention, this final chapter is given over to an economic aspect, viz., the occupational structure of the American-born and the crucial incident of unemployment.

OCCUPATION

Table LXXI gives the percentage distribution of the American-born compared with that of the total population of Canada in the main classes of the gainfully employed. Taking the males first, the American-born show higher percentages than the total population under the following headings: agriculture, metal products, non-metallic mineral products, chemicals and allied products, electric light and power, railway transportation, trade, finance and insurance, and professional and recreational services. In all but agriculture, railway transportation, and the professional and recreational services, the percentages are quite close. But over 50 p.c. of the American-born males as against less than 39 p.c. of all males are in agriculture, fishing and trapping, logging and mining. The female American-born show higher percentages in agriculture, "other" transportation, finance and insurance, and professional and recreational services, the differences being marked in agriculture and the two service classes. In the case of both American-born and total population, nearly the same percentage (52.93 and 52.10, respectively) are in four occupational classes, viz., the manufacture of textile products, trade, professional services, and clerical.

The next following tables present basic data summarized for certain groupings: Table LXXII gives the numbers and percentages of the gainfully occupied American-born, by sex, grouped as "owners and managers," "foremen and overseers," and "other," under the heading of each industry; while Table LXXIII sets out the main occupations in descending order, the object being to emphasize the craft rather than the industrial and status aspect. On the wide and even distribution of the American-born among the industries and trades which these tables disclose, a previous page has dilated (see Part I, pp. 10-12).

A feature of the occupational structure already adverted to (see Part I, p. 11) as illustrated in these tables, calls for special inquiry. While the American-born in Canada may be similar to the Canadian-born in that they are found in the same industries and services, they might conceivably be of different occupational status, e.g., an American-born and a Canadian-

159

born might be found side by side in food manufacturing, but the one as manager and the other as labourer. It is difficult to develop this aspect fully, but an attempt is made in Table LXXIV wherein American-born and Canadian-born workers are shown in their respective numbers and proportions in positions entailing responsibility. Superficially, the census segregation of owners, managers, foremen, and overseers might be considered as sufficing for this distinction—and this probably holds for the primary industries and manufactures. In the case of construction, transportation, etc., however, others than these enter into the picture, and *ad hoc* methods must be used for their determination. Thus in railway transportation we may include agents, railway conductors and engineers, and street railway motormen and conductors; in trade, all but hawkers, pedlars, and newsboys; in finance and insurance, public administration, and professional service, everybody (the clerical positions being classified separately and not by industrial and similar groups); in recreational services all but stage-hands and ushers; and in personal services, only hotel owners and managers. The basis of distinction throughout is not skill but managerial responsibility: a highly skilled carpenter under supervision would have little of the latter, while a less skilled carpenter running an establishment without help would have much. It would have been desirable to include "personal" occupations such as barbers, undertakers, etc., but the data do not permit: all, therefore, are excluded.

Admittedly subject to many defects, Table LXXIV in which these distinctions are worked out is of definite interest. The totals of 814,200 and 75,905 which it gives for Canadian-born and American-born, respectively, are too large to justify describing the positions as *highly* responsible, but it must be remembered that more than half are in agriculture while trade is probably over-weighted. Omitting these two occupational groups, we have 227,971 Canadian-born and 17,374 American-born in responsible positions out of 1,182,291 and 61,412, respectively, in all other occupations i.e., 1 in 5.2 Canadian-born and 1 in 3.5 American-born. If bookkeepers and cashiers are also omitted the proportions are 1 in 5.6 and 1 in 3.7, respectively.

The last column of Table LXXIV shows that while in the total figures there was 1 American-born for every 15.3 Canadian-born, the proportion rose to 1 for every 10.7 in responsible positions. The implication is that the status of the American-born was 43 p.c. higher than that of the Canadian-born. The groups wherein the chances of the Canadian-born for responsibility stood higher than or the same as those of the American-born are indicated by an asterisk; they include water transportation, miscellaneous transportation and communication, trade, public administration, and the one class of clerical occupation included, viz., bookkeepers and cashiers. (Cashiers could not be separated from bookkeepers, which is a skilled rather than a responsible occupation.) Of these five, trade and communications show the same ratings for both American-born and Canadian-born. The occupations in which the opportunities of the American-born for the higher positions are overwhelmingly greater than those of the Canadian-born are: "other" mining (about 3 to 1), warehousing and storage (3 to 1), recreational, and road transportation (cartage, taxicabs, etc.). Admitting the defects in the figures, it would seem safe to say that the American-born are of definitely higher status than the Canadian-born. No doubt other considerations, such as age, enter into the situation, but not to the extent of total explanation. The figures, however, should not be regarded as confirming a popular conception of the immigrant as a specially enterprising figure: popular conceptions rest on individual observations that unconsciously single out the prominent and successful. But the prominent and successful at best form only a small percentage of the whole, and the higher and lower positions are distinct as types. The 17,374 American-born who hold positions of responsibility in Canada are comparatively few in number and are drawn from a reservoir of 120,000,000: the 227,971 Canadian-born are drawn from but 11,000,000. Many of the former came from identical positions in the United States, so that it is important not to overlook the size of the parent population. If the 17,000 highest Canadian-born positions and the 17,000 highest American-born positions could be brought into comparison the results might be quite different. The point is, that the figures of the table do not assess comparative qualities or qualifications—they indicate merely some of the causes and effects of immigration and emigration.

TABLE LXXI

Percentage Distribution of Total and American-Born Gainfully Occupied 10 Years of Age or Over, by Sex: 1931

Industry or Service	Total			American-Born		
	Both Sexes	Male	Female	Both Sexes	Male	Female
TOTAL	100.00	100.00	100.00	100.00	100.00	100.00
Agriculture	28.82	33.97	3.62	41.98	47.68	6.52
Fishing, hunting and trapping	1.22	1.45	0.07	0.49	0.57	0.01
Logging	1.12	1.35	......	0.91	1.06	......
Mining, quarrying, oil and salt wells	1.49	1.80	......	1.30	1.51	0.01
Manufacturing—						
Vegetable products	0.92	0.91	1.00	0.66	0.66	0.65
Animal products	1.29	1.31	1.18	0.70	0.74	0.44
Textile products	2.42	1.14	8.72	1.48	0.81	5.59
Wood products, pulp and paper, printing and publishing	1.83	2.00	1.00	1.57	1.73	0.60
Metal products	4.30	5.06	0.55	4.47	5.14	0.29

Table LXXI—concluded

Percentage Distribution of Total and American-Born Gainfully Occupied
10 Years of Age or Over, by Sex: 1931

Industry or Service	Total			American-Born		
	Both Sexes	Male	Female	Both Sexes	Male	Female
Manufacturing—concluded						
Non-metallic mineral products..........	0.24	0.28	0.05	0.28	0.32	0.04
Chemicals and allied products............	0.12	0.13	0.07	0.17	0.19	0.04
Miscellaneous...	0.14	0.14	0.15	0.12	0.13	0.10
Electric light and power..........................	0.83	1.00	......	0.92	1.07	......
Building and construction.......................	5.17	6.22	0.01	3.84	4.46	0.01
Transportation and Communication—						
Railway................	2.13	2.57	......	2.70	3.13	......
Water....................	0.75	0.90	0.03	0.39	0.45	0.01
Road......................	2.45	2.95	0.01	2.25	2.61	0.02
Other transportation and						
communication...........................	1.43	1.20	2.55	1.16	0.89	2.79
Warehousing and storage....................	0.90	0.83	1.23	0.55	0.52	0.69
Trade...	7.99	7.97	8.13	8.16	8.20	7.90
Finance and insurance............................	0.94	1.11	0.09	1.08	1.22	0.18
Service—						
Public administration and defence....	0.80	0.96	0.03	0.53	0.61	0.01
Professional............................	6.07	3.70	17.69	6.69	4.13	22.59
Recreational..................................	0.21	0.23	0.09	0.43	0.45	0.28
Personal............................	8.51	3.51	33.02	6.66	2.54	32.30
Laundering; cleaning, dyeing and						
pressing...........................	0.58	0.42	1.35	0.27	0.14	1.12
Clerical................................	6.14	3.81	17.56	4.33	2.32	16.85
Other...........................	11.13	13.04	1.76	5.89	6.69	0.92
Unspecified............................	0.04	0.04	0.04	0.03	0.03	0.02

Table LXXII

American-Born Gainfully Occupied and Percentages of Total, by Sex,
Classified by Certain Occupations: 1931

Occupation Class	Males		Females	
	Number	Percentage of Total	Number	Percentage of Total
All Occupations..	139,197	4.27	22,379	3.36
Agriculture—				
Owners and managers.................	46,904	7.49	1,268	6.61
Foremen and overseers............................	261	8.64	5	17.24
Farm labourers...	19,196	4.01	185	3.81
Others...	3	1.36	......	......

TABLE LXXII—continued

American-Born Gainfully Occupied and Percentages of Total, by Sex,
Classified by Certain Occupations: 1931

Occupation Class	Males		Females	
	Number	Percentage of Total	Number	Percentage of Total
Fishing, Hunting and Trapping..................	797	1.68	2	0.40
Logging—				
Owners and managers..............................	199	8.08	......	......
Foremen and overseers............................	52	5.70	......	......
Foresters and timber cruisers.................	131	4.12	......	......
Lumbermen...	1,091	2.91	......	......
Coal Mining—				
Owners and managers..............................	21	5.75	......	......
Foremen and overseers............................	24	2.53	......	......
Others...	517	1.96	......	......
Other Mining—				
Owners and managers..............................	158	17.87	2	40.00
Foremen and overseers............................	58	5.52	......	......
Others...	1,327	4.59	......	......
Vegetable Products (mfg.)—				
Owners and managers..............................	314	6.30	6	7.89
Foremen and overseers............................	82	4.32	16	4.02
Others...	523	2.30	124	2.00
Animal Products (mfg.)—				
Owners and managers..............................	210	5.80	1	3.57
Foremen and overseers............................	63	5.29	9	5.17
Others...	751	1.98	89	1.16
Textile Products (mfg.)—				
Owners and managers..............................	257	6.82	11	5.56
Foremen and overseers............................	132	7.88	30	2.87
Others...	743	2.34	1,211	2.13
Wood and Paper Products (mfg.)—				
Owners and managers..............................	562	6.85	5	5.62
Foremen and overseers............................	178	5.19	7	3.48
Others...	1,670	3.12	122	1.91
Metal Products (mfg.)—				
Owners and managers..............................	815	10.79	3	8.33
Foremen and overseers............................	360	5.92	4	2.26
Others...	5,974	3.94	59	1.71
Non-Metallic Mineral Products (mfg.)—				
Owners and managers..............................	171	8.98	1	4.55
Foremen and overseers............................	70	6.57	2	6.45
Others...	209	3.32	5	1.87

TABLE LXXII—continued

American-Born Gainfully Occupied and Percentages of Total, by Sex, Classified by Certain Occupations: 1931

Occupation Class	Males		Females	
	Number	Percentage of Total	Number	Percentage of Total
Chemical and Allied Products (mfg.)—				
Owners and managers	156	13.60	2	11.11
Foremen and overseers	31	5.67	3	5.26
Others	75	2.85	4	1.06
Miscellaneous Products (mfg.)—				
Owners and managers	87	8.85	1	7.14
Foremen and overseers	15	4.82	2	2.60
Others	76	2.31	20	2.25
Electric Light and Power—				
Owners and managers	52	7.98	......	......
Foremen and overseers	22	4.52	......	......
Others	1,410	4.50	......	......
Building and Construction—				
Owners and managers	561	4.31	3	33.33
Foremen and overseers	242	4.50	......	......
Others	5,406	2.93	......	......
Transportation and Communication—				
Officials and managers	937	6.70	49	4.71
Foremen and agents	692	5.12	19	4.42
Others	8,237	3.73	565	3.58
Warehousing and Storage—				
Owners and managers	135	14.11	......	......
Foremen and overseers	13	3.35	......	......
Others	579	2.26	154	1.88
Finance and Insurance—				
Officials	319	3.73	3	7.89
Agents	1,051	4.66	35	7.06
Others	326	6.36	3	8.11
Trade—				
Owners and managers	4,822	4.49	273	4.01
Foremen and overseers	50	3.24	8	2.73
Others	6,549	4.34	1,487	3.16
Public Administration and Defence—				
Officials and officers	405	3.80	......	......
Others	448	2.18	2	2.15
Professional Service	5,747	4.76	5,056	4.29

TABLE LXXII—concluded

*American-Born Gainfully Occupied and Percentages of Total, by Sex,
Classified by Certain Occupations: 1931*

Occupation Class	Males		Females	
	Number	Percentage of Total	Number	Percentage of Total
Recreational Service—				
Owners and managers	323	10.50	4	5.88
Others	306	6.99	59	10.57
Personal Service	3,533	3.08	7,228	3.29
Laundering; Cleaning, etc.—				
Owners and managers	55	2.99	6	10.17
Foremen and overseers	10	6.21	5	4.24
Others	129	1.11	239	2.71
Clerical	3,223	2.60	3,770	3.22
Unskilled Workers (not in agriculture, mining or logging)	9,312	2.19	207	1.77
Unspecified—				
Owners and managers	9	8.74	......	......
Foremen and overseers	3	3.23	......	......
Others	28	2.41	5	1.77

TABLE LXXIII

*Total and American-Born Gainfully Occupied Males in Occupations
Employing 200 or more American-Born, and Percentages American-
Born of Total, in Order of Magnitude of Percentages, Classified
by Occupation: 1931*

Occupation	Total	American-Born	Percentage American-Born of Total
ALL OCCUPATIONS (with 200 or more American-born)	No. 2,745,382	No. 123,380	4.49
Oil drillers (other than coal mining)	551	205	37.21
Porters—railway (railway transportation)	1,654	421	25.45
Purchasing agents and buyers (trade)	6,298	959	15.23
Mining engineers (professional service)	1,498	219	14.62
Paper makers (wood and paper products, mfg.)	2,949	327	11.09
Owners and managers (metal products, mfg.)	7,552	815	10.79
Owners and managers—other entertainment (recreational service)	2,061	201	9.75

TABLE LXXIII—continued

Total and American-Born Gainfully Occupied Males in Occupations Employing 200 or more American-Born, and Percentages American-Born of Total, in Order of Magnitude of Percentages, Classified by Occupation: 1931

Occupation	Total	American-Born	Percentage American-Born of Total
	No.	*No.*	
Owners and managers—garage (road transportation)	4,114	383	9.31
Mechanical engineers (professional service)	2,859	248	8.67
Foremen and overseers (agriculture)	3,022	261	8.64
Brokers and agents, *n.e.s.* (trade)	6,073	492	8.10
Electrical engineers (professional service)	3,937	307	7.80
Railway conductors—steam railway (railway transportation)	4,673	361	7.73
Switchmen, signalmen, flagmen (railway transportation)	4,349	331	7.61
Farmers and stock-raisers (agriculture)	614,299	46,639	7.59
Locomotive engineers (railway transportation)	7,920	580	7.32
Locomotive firemen (railway transportation)	5,948	432	7.26
Owners and managers—wholesale (trade)	13,336	965	7.24
Agents—ticket and station (railway transportation)	5,323	381	7.16
Chemists, assayers (professional service)	3,200	222	6.94
Owners and managers (wood and paper products, mfg.)	8,207	562	6.85
Owners and managers (textile products, mfg.)	3,768	257	6.82
Hotel managers and keepers (personal service)	5,399	368	6.82
Telegraph operators (other than road, railway or water transportation)	6,035	401	6.64
Brakemen (railway transportation)	8,495	562	6.62
Sales agents, canvassers, demonstrators (trade)	6,441	418	6.49
Real estate agents and dealers (finance, insurance)	5,518	350	6.34
Owners and managers (vegetable products, mfg.)	4,987	314	6.30
Stock and bond brokers (finance, insurance)	4,873	303	6.22
Musicians and music teachers (professional service)	4,145	258	6.22
Civil engineers and surveyors (professional service)	7,524	459	6.10
Mechanics (metal products, mfg.)	43,775	2,607	5.96
Foremen and overseers (metal products, mfg.)	6,079	360	5.92
Owners and managers (animal products, mfg.)	3,621	210	5.80
Stationary enginemen, *n.e.s.* (electric light and power)	16,538	857	5.18
Barbers, hairdressers, manicurists (personal service)	15,906	806	5.07
Clergymen and priests (professional service)	12,662	602	4.75
Foremen and overseers (building and construction)	5,381	242	4.50
Teachers (school) (professional service)	18,274	801	4.38
Owners, managers, builders, contractors (building and construction)	13,012	561	4.31
Insurance agents (finance, insurance)	17,049	701	4.11
Owners, managers and dealers—retail stores (trade)	94,162	3,857	4.10
Commercial travellers (trade)	16,495	671	4.07
Linemen and cablemen (other transportation)	6,784	274	4.04

TABLE LXXIII—concluded

Total and American-Born Gainfully Occupied Males in Occupations Employing 200 or more American-Born, and Percentages American-Born of Total, in Order of Magnitude of Percentages, Classified by Occupation: 1931

Occupation	Total	American-Born	Percentage American-Born of Total
	No.	No.	
Electricians and wiremen (building and construction)	20,231	814	4.02
Farm labourers (agriculture)	478,632	19,196	4.01
Public service officials (public administration and defence)	9,970	387	3.88
Teamsters, draymen, carriage drivers (road transportation)	22,286	858	3.85
Accountants and auditors (professional service)	17,052	623	3.65
Truck drivers (road transportation)	43,698	1,525	3.49
Salesmen (trade)	100,537	3,510	3.49
Miners (other than coal mining)	12,883	437	3.39
Blacksmiths, hammermen, forgemen (metal products, mfg.)	15,902	537	3.38
Machinists (metal products, mfg.)	30,739	1,026	3.34
Chauffeurs and bus drivers (road transportation)	15,388	502	3.26
Restaurant, cafe and tavern keepers (personal service)	9,765	316	3.24
Physicians and surgeons (professional service)	9,817	307	3.13
Carpenters (building and construction)	79,764	2,384	2.99
Boiler firemen (electric light and power)	6,817	203	2.98
Bookkeepers and cashiers (clerical)	29,553	879	2.97
Compositors and printers, n.e.s. (wood and paper products, mfg.)	10,869	219	2.93
Lumbermen (logging)	37,438	1,091	2.91
Painters, decorators, glaziers (building and construction)	33,687	971	2.88
Plumbers, steamfitters, gasfitters (building and construction)	15,593	413	2.65
Hunters, trappers and guides (fishing, hunting and trapping)	13,788	345	2.50
Cooks (personal service)	17,832	440	2.47
Office clerks (clerical)	90,816	2,236	2.46
Waiters and waitresses (personal service)	11,203	270	2.41
Watchmen and caretakers, n.e.s. (personal service)	13,411	320	2.39
Janitors and sextons (personal service)	14,691	335	2.28
Gardeners, florists, nurserymen (agriculture)	10,714	239	2.23
Police and detectives (public administration and defence)	10,900	241	2.21
Labourers (not agricultural, mining or logging)	425,408	9,312	2.19
Shippers (warehousing and storage)	15,045	324	2.15
Butchers and slaughterers (animal products, mfg.)	9,485	203	2.14
Miners (coal mining)	17,515	357	2.04
Section foremen, sectionmen: trackmen (railway transportation)	23,587	458	1.94
Fishermen (fishing, hunting and trapping)	33,620	452	1.34

TABLE LXXIV

American-Born and Canadian-Born Males in Positions of Responsibility,
and Proportion of Canadian-Born to Each American-Born,
Classified by Occupation: 1931

Occupation	American-Born (1)	Canadian-Born (2)	Proportion of Canadian-Born to Each American-Born (2) ÷ (1)
	No.	No.	
ALL GAINFULLY OCCUPIED..	139,197	2,130,009	15.3
TOTALS IN RESPONSIBLE POSITIONS............................	75,905	814,200	10.7
Primary Industries..	47,680	419,285	8.8
Agriculture (except farm labourers).......................	47,168	415,041	8.8
Logging (owners, managers and overseers)............	251	2,504	10.0
Coal mining (owners, managers and overseers)....	45	564	12.5
Other mining (owners, managers and overseers)..	216	1,176	5.4
Other Occupational Groups...................................	28,225	394,915	14.0
Manufacturing...	3,503	30,978	8.8
Building and construction.....................................	803	12,021	15.0
Transportation and Communication—			
Railway..	1,915	22,345	11.7
Water*..	225	5,669	25.2
Road..	617	5,834	9.5
Other transportation and communication*............	227	3,465	15.3
Warehousing and storage......................................	148	754	5.1
Trade (except hawkers, pedlars and newsboys)*......	11,363	171,188	15.1
Finance (except insurance agents)............................	995	13,528	13.6
Service—			
Public Administration*...	853	19,171	22.5
Professional..	5,747	82,217	14.3
Recreational (except stage-hands and ushers)......	508	3,286	6.5
Laundering, cleaning, etc. (owners, managers and foremen)...	65	584	9.0
Bookkeepers and cashiers*....................................	879	20,270	23.1
Hotel owners and managers..................................	368	3,536	9.6
Unspecified...	9	69	7.7

UNEMPLOYMENT

In Table LXXV the unemployment of the American-born 10 years of age or over is compared with that of the total immigrant population of the same age groups. To increase homogeneity, both are broken up by races. For the males of all the races except the French and the Chinese the American-born lost less time. In the case of the females, in all but the Polish, Hebrew, and Italian groups the American-born lost more time—a situation for which it is difficult to find an explanation. An enlargement of the purview by years of immigration shows that new-comers tend to suffer more unemployment. Thus 15.35 weeks of unemployment is indicated for all immigrants of 1926-29, against 10.65 weeks for immigrants of 1911-20. Individual races, however, show marked deviation from this tendency of the aggregate. Thus the British show little connection between year of arrival and unemployment, while the French show some tendency to reverse the general rule.

The reverse generalization applies to the American-born in Canada. Among them, taking males only, we find a steady rise in the weeks lost per wage-earner as we go back from arrivals of 1930-31 to those of 1901-10. Analysing the American-born by racial origin it seems that the higher unemployment for earlier arrivals applies to all the groups separately. The reason the gradients for particular races reverse for the American-born is an interesting field for conjecture; possibly the same causes enter here that make the American-born suffer on the whole less unemployment than Canadians while all immigrants have higher unemployment than Canadians.

That male wage-earners of United States birthplace reported less unemployment than Canadians as a whole is due to their occupational distribution. Table LXXI in the previous section of this chapter shows that in so far as the American-born vary occupationally from the remainder of the Canadian population they tend to be in highly specialized work or in farming. Thus, as has been pointed out before, they contribute somewhat more than a due proportion of engineers, owners and managers, etc., which classes suffered least from unemployment in 1931, and they are relatively poorly represented among the unskilled workers, whose unemployment has been most severe. Male agricultural wage-earners of all birthplaces lost 8.22 weeks in 1930-31, against 10.68 weeks for all occupations, while labourers and unskilled workers (exclusive of those in agriculture, mining and logging) lost 18.98 weeks.

TABLE LXXV

Average Number of Weeks Lost during the Year by American-Born and by Immigrant Wage-Earners 10 Years of Age or Over, by Sex, Classified by Racial Origin: 1931

	Average Weeks Lost by—			
Racial Origin	American-Born Wage-Earners		Immigrant Wage-Earners	
	Male	Female	Male	Female
	No.	No.	No.	No.
ALL RACES	9.45	5.72	11.85	5.34
British	8.63	5.22	9.09	4.85
French	10.80	6.01	10.59	5.69
Central European	9.43	6.36	17.47	5.72
German and Austrian	9.06	6.30	13.39	5.39
Other Central European	16.46	7.75	22.26	7.00
Dutch	9.55	5.79	10.37	5.65
Eastern European	14.65	6.43	19.63	5.47
Polish	14.27	6.10	19.68	6.36
Russian	11.26	6.11	17.16	5.54
Ukrainian	17.09	7.57	20.12	6.76
Other Eastern European	17.60	6.74	20.14	4.09
Hebrew	6.84	8.75	11.01	10.46
Italian	12.89	7.10	15.45	10.78
Scandinavian	10.65	6.02	14.21	5.06
Chinese	15.80	......	14.17	5.14
Japanese	10.00	......	10.02	5.13
Indian	14.77	6.67	15.11	5.88
Other	9.89	6.29	12.72	5.29

THE AMERICAN-BORN IN THE PROFESSIONS IN CANADA

Of the 139,000 male and 22,000 female American-born in the Canadian population gainfully occupied in 1931, nearly 11,000, almost equally divided by sex, were in the professional class. It seemed worth while comparing not only the proportion of American-born in professions with the rest of the Canadian population but also their distribution among the professions. More than 4 p.c. of the American-born males gainfully occupied in Canada, and more than 22.5 p.c. of American-born females, were in professions, these proportions exceeding those of Canadian-born of both sexes and far exceeding the proportion of British-born females though slightly less than that of British-born males.

The types of professions attracting the American-born as compared with the Canadian and British-born in Canada would seem to be measured by the percentage of the total gainfully occupied represented by each profession. If we regard all the thirty-two male professions of the Census of 1931 as 100 p.c. and arrange the American-born males in order of preference, we find a decided bias in favour of three, viz., school teachers, accountants and auditors, and clergymen (altogether 35 p.c.). This bias, however, is shared with the Canadian-born and British-born. Taking the next seven, however, we find a decided American bias (35 p.c. as compared with 27 p.c. in the case of both Canadian-born and British-born). Five of the seven (that is, excepting physicians and surgeons and musicians and music teachers) are in the engineering class: more than 25.32 p.c. of the United States professionals are engineers, chemists and metallurgists, as compared with less than 14 p.c. Canadian and 20 p.c. British. Further, the list of professions in which the American-born exceed both the Canadian and British are: engineers, religious brothers, osteopaths, agricultural professionals, health professionals, and mission workers. They fall below in accountants and auditors, designers, opticians, officials of industrial organizations, magistrates, librarians, and religious workers. They exceed the Canadian but not the British in clergymen, musicians and music teachers, miscellaneous professions, authors, artists, photographers, architects, dancing teachers, and social welfare workers. They exceed the British but not the Canadian in school teachers, medical doctors, notaries, dentists, veterinary surgeons, and professors. Arranging the professions in seven classes we obtain:—

	American-Born	Canadian-Born	British-Born
ALL PROFESSIONS	100.00	100.00	100.00
Religion	13.54	12.01	12.69
Health	10.78	16.29	4.00
Education	16.43	20.04	9.42
Art	12.56	9.39	19.58
Law	3.44	8.97	2.88
Technical and commercial	36.80	27.13	43.71
All others	6.45	6.17	7.72

From this point of view religion is the one class in which the American-born exceed both the others, although they surpass the Canadian-born also in art and technical, and the British-born in health, education and law.

(The persistence of religion is partly due to the large representation of American-born children of parents who went to the United States from Quebec.) Two combinations of two classes constitute more than half the American-born professionals, viz., technical and education, and technical and religion. No two classes constitute half the Canadian-born professionals, but four combinations of two classes constitute half the British-born.

So much for the American-born males. Of the American-born females a higher percentage is found in the professions than of either Canadian or British-born. Almost 58 p.c. are school teachers, a higher proportion than for Canadians and a much higher one than for British (35 p.c.). Arranging the twenty-six professional occupations into classes, as above for males, we have:—

	American-Born	Canadian-Born	British-Born
ALL PROFESSIONS	100.00	100.00	100.00
Religion	11.22	7.91	5.71
Health	21.27	27.52	42.86
Education	57.93	56.93	35.56
Art	5.71	4.77	10.36
Law	0.04	0.05	0.02
Technical and commercial	0.75	0.54	1.01
All others	3.08	2.28	4.48

Again religion is prominent; under both religion and education the American-born surpass the other two; in health workers alone do they fall below the Canadians.

All in all, the American-born do not spread so evenly among the professions as among other occupations, though the males spread much more evenly than the females. However, the American-born, whether male or female, spread decidedly more evenly than either the Canadian-born or the British-born.* This is the more remarkable when it is considered that in absolute numbers they fall far below either.

*An index below shows the comparative spread of the American-born, Canadian-born, and British-born in Canada among the professions (32 male and 26 female professions). The index is derived by summing up the excesses over the average of the professions exceeding the average, dividing by the average, and taking the result as a multiple of the number of professions that exceed the average. A high index indicates a poor spread.

	Male	Female
American-born	1.14	3.76
Canadian-born	2.12	4.86
British-born	1.77	4.33

TABLE LXXVI

*Numbers of Males per 10,000 of All Professionally Employed American-
Born, Canadian-Born, and British-Born, Classified by Profession,
Ranked by American-Born: 1931*

Profession	American Born	Canadian Born	British Born	Profession	American Born	Canadian Born	British Born
	No.	No.	No.		No.	No.	No.
School teachers	1,394	1,722	818	Artists, art teachers, sculptors and painters	197	121	228
Accountants and auditors	1,084	1,225	2,312	Photographers	190	155	241
Clergymen	1,048	965	1,082	Brothers, n.e.s	172	112	8
Civil engineers and surveyors	799	598	699	Osteopaths and chiropractors	129	35	30
Electrical engineers	534	269	477	Architects	94	86	176
Physicians and surgeons	534	1,058	195	Agricultural professionals	78	74	63
Musicians and music teachers	449	254	494	Health professionals	70	24	54
Mechanical engineers	432	178	382	Religious workers, n.e.s	68	103	145
Chemists, assayers and metallurgists	386	242	295	Mission workers	66	21	34
Mining engineers	381	98	150	Veterinary surgeons	64	103	56
Notaries and lawyers	332	841	263	Opticians	61	75	64
Dentists	284	437	57	Dancing teachers and physical instructors	42	36	136
Designers and draughtsmen	284	287	683	Social welfare workers, n.e.s	28	22	60
Others	280	260	305	Officials of industrial associations	17	19	35
Professors and college principals	249	282	124	Magistrates and justices	12	56	25
Authors, editors and journalists	238	226	286	Librarians	5	16	23

Table LXXVII

Numbers of Females per 10,000 of all Professionally Employed American-Born, Canadian-Born, and British-Born, Classified by Profession, Ranked by American-Born: 1931

Profession	American-Born	Canadian-Born	British-Born	Profession	American-Born	Canadian-Born	British-Born
	No.	No.	No.		No.	No.	No.
School teachers	5,767	5,672	3,528	Mission workers	32	13	66
Graduate nurses	1,335	1,637	3,139	Osteopaths and chiropractors	28	7	7
Nuns	989	709	210				
Nurses in training	643	1,004	879	Professors and college principals	26	21	28
Musicians and music teachers	435	367	661	Physicians and surgeons	22	16	22
Others	107	82	171				
Religious workers	93	68	293	Dancing teachers and physical instructors	14	17	66
Social welfare workers	89	57	158	Chemists, assayers and metallurgists	14	10	9
Health professionals	81	68	171				
Authors, editors and journalists	67	36	71	Clergy	8	1	2
Artists, art teachers, sculptors, painters	65	52	139	Designers and draughters	6	7	35
Accountants and auditors	61	44	92	Agricultural professionals	4	4	6
Librarians	55	66	105	Dentists	4	3	2
Photographers	51	34	135	Magistrates	2	......	......
				Notaries and lawyers	2	5	2

INDEX

The tabular matter is not indexed. The reader is referred to the Table of Contents for list and description of the tables.

Abitibi, 5
Adventists, 145
Age, 44, 77-95, 96, 130-7, 140-4, 161-2
Agriculturists, *see* Distribution by occupations, Occupations
Alberta, 63, 80, 139
Alien, *see* Citizenship
American stock, 2 (footnote), 61
Analysis, method of, 2, 12
Anglicans, 145-7
Areas, *see* Distribution by
Artists, 171
Asiatics, 62, 108

Baptists, 145
Belgium, 4
Birthplace, 49, 52, 63
Births, *see* Vital statistics
Border crossings, 42-52
Brebner, J. B., 1 (footnote)
Brethren, 145
British, 2, 12, 19, 28, 63, 108
British stock, 63
British Columbia, 19, 63, 69, 109, 140, 144
British subject, *see* Citizenship
Buddhists, 146
Bulgarians, 4, 67

Canadian-born, 2, 7, 22, 61
Canadian stock, 27, 29, 61, 63
Capacity of distribution, 4
Causal factors, 12
Census, 1, 2, 10, 14, 18, 23, 25, 61
Chinese, 9, 13
Christian Scientists, 145
Church of Christ, 145
Citizenship, 129-38; *see also* Naturalization
Climate, 10
Confucians, 146
Conjugal condition, 36, 96-9
Criminality, 37
Czechoslovak, 108

Deaths, *see* Vital statistics
Denmark, 7
Densities, population, 22, 70
Deux Montagnes, 5
Distribution, 2-5
  by areas, 5-7, 25, 67-78
  by population groups, 7-10, 25
  by occupations, 10-12, 26, 28
  factors in, 12, 28

Distribution—*Continued*
  influences affecting, 34-7
  significance of, 37-8, 41
  by age, 79-80
Divorce, 96
Doctors, 171
Dutch, *see* Holland

East Windsor, 22
Economic aspect, 3
Education, 171-2; *see also* School attendance
Emigration, 23-4, 27
England, 2, 68
English, 108-9
Evangelical Association, 145
"Exodus," the, 22, 29

Family composition, 99-100
Farming, *see* Occupations
Finnish, 108
Ford City, 22
Foreign-born, 2, 3, 4, 15, 20, 60, 62, 120
France, 7
French, *see* Language
French-Canadian, 4, 5, 19, 20, 108-19

Gaspe, 69
Geography, 3, 5, 67-78
German stocks, 7, 8, 9, 19, 28, 40, 75-6, 108-9
Germany, 12
Greece, 142

Hansen, M. L., 1 (footnote), 27 (footnote)
Health services, 174
Hebrews, 9, 13, 19, 40, 169
History, 1
Holland, 7, 19, 108-9
House of Commons, 43

Icelandic-born, 4, 40, 67
Illiteracy, 37, 139-44
Immigration, Immigrant population, 1-2, 14, 15-18, 20, 24, 27, 36, 41, 46-52, 57-61, 70-6, 77, 83, 96-9
Indexes of distribution, 7, 9
Indians, 144
Intermarriage, 38, 40-1, 44-5, 49, 62, 101-2
International Bible Students, 145
Irish-born, 20, 68, 108-9
Italian, 19, 40, 142, 169

175